Anthony Rogers grew up in Malta where he later served in the Royal Marines Commandos. As a freelance photojournalist in the 1980s and 1990s he covered wars on three continents. More recently, his enduring interest in the Second World War has led to the publication of *Battle over Malta* (2000) and the writing of *Churchill's Folly*.

Churchill's Folly

LEROS AND THE AEGEAN

THE LAST GREAT BRITISH DEFEAT OF WORLD WAR TWO

ANTHONY ROGERS

FOREWORD BY
THE RT. HON. THE EARL JELLICOE KBE, DSO, MC, FRS

CASSELL

Cassell Military Paperbacks

Cassell
Wellington House, 125 Strand
London WC2R 0BB

First published in 2003
by Cassell
This Cassell Military Paperbacks edition 2004

British Library Cataloguing-in-Publication Data.
A catalogue record for this book is available from the British Library.

ISBN 0 304 36655 2

Printed and bound in Great Britain by
Cox and Wyman Ltd., Reading, Berks.

For Sonja

Contents

APPENDICES

Foreword

by The Rt. Hon. The Earl Jellicoe KBE, DSO, MC, FRS

THIS IS A WORK WHICH HAS CLEARLY demanded, and which in preparation has certainly received, a great deal of research.

Since those far-off days in late 1943 I have read many accounts of the war in the Aegean and of the Battle of Leros. The author of this deeply interesting book has wisely, unlike most others, examined German as well as British sources. He has also obtained useful information from Italian, Greek and, not least, American sources. It is also good and a tribute to the author's industry and enterprise that he has managed to obtain much useful information from those who played their part in those often most gruelling days nearly sixty years ago, be it in Leros, be it in Kos or be it in other of the Dodecanese Islands.

Anthony Rogers has also brought back to life for me many dormant memories. I now recall well being summoned down from the Lebanon to Egypt and to learn, to my surprise on my arrival in Cairo, of the armistice with Italy which was to become effective that evening and, moreover, that the armistice had come as an almost equal surprise to our C-in-C, Middle East.

I remember so vividly my subsequent parachute arrival in Rhodes for discussions with Admiral Campioni, the Italian C-in-C in the Aegean, his friendly reception and his disappointment that my most able aide, the Polish Count Dobrski (whom I had only met two days before under his SOE alias as Major Dolbey) and I were not able to guarantee the admiral the much-needed speedy military support which he most certainly required if he were to cope with his German ex-allies in Rhodes and evict them from the vital airfields on that island. Equally, I recall the very warm and helpful reception which I received two days later from the Italians in Kos and from Admiral Mascherpa in Leros. I am of course aware of the criticism which the Italians have received for their apparent lack of support for us in this Aegean campaign. Personally, I feel this criticism to be somewhat unfair. It is not easy in war to swop sides overnight. We were not able to offer instant and much-needed support to them. And, the dangers for would-be Italian supporters were considerable, as demonstrated by the number of Italian officers shot by the Germans after the fall of Kos, and the subsequent execution of both Campioni and Mascherpa.

I also of course remember the active role which our military Special Forces – the LRDG and the SBS – played in this campaign: the early and essential occupation of Kastellorizo by David Sutherland's SBS Squadron; the eviction of the Germans from Lipsos by an SBS detachment under the command of Jock Lapraik, together with that memorable young Danish officer, Anders Lassen; the quick arrival of David Lloyd Owen and the LRDG in Leros; the part which the LRDG played in the Leros battle and, also, the part which those two units played in a number of smaller islands, including Levitha, where the LRDG found themselves saddled with a pretty impossible task. Moreover, when I remind myself of the role played by our Special Forces I recall how much we owed to brave and gallant naval officers like Frank Ramseyer and Adrian Seligman, who organised our transport by launch and caique.

It is of course the two major battles in this campaign – that in Kos and later that in Leros – with which our author is mainly concerned. I was in the nearby island of Kalymnos on the day of the German attack on Kos and I have only too clear a memory of my concern even at that early stage as to its outcome. However, our forces and the German forces in Leros were not unevenly balanced and for the first days of the battle it seemed as if it might be won. I, to this day, recall the first parachute attack as the Germans landed close to where I, with a small detachment, was based and I was all too struck by their courage and professionalism. However, as our author rightly points out, it was total German air superiority that above all won the day for the Germans.

Our casualties were indeed heavy and whenever I visit the fine War Graves Commission cemetery in Leros I have much in mind two very special

Commanding Officers, Lieutenant Colonel Jake Easonsmith of the LRDG and Lieutenant Colonel Maurice French of the Royal Irish Fusiliers, of whom Brigadier Tilney, our overall commander, later wrote: 'When we lost Maurice we lost the battle.'

I also think of a young naval officer called Alan Phipps, who had been a special friend of mine in Leros and who was killed on the last day of the battle. However, when we consider our quite heavy losses it is also right to bear in mind, as indeed the author reminds us, the considerable losses in ships and men in this whole campaign incurred by the Navy and the RAF. It is also good to remember how many of our forces escaped capture and managed to make their way back to Egypt, often with the help extended to them by friendly Greeks at considerable risk to themselves and their families.

I happened to be among the lucky ones who managed to escape and found myself, a few days after our defeat in Leros, at the British Embassy in Ankara. I had barely arrived there when I was told that I was urgently required in Cairo. I took the train to Adana and from there flew to Cairo. There a car was awaiting me in which I was whisked off towards the Pyramids. We stopped at a stately house where I was informed the Prime Minister was staying following the Teheran Conference. It was then early afternoon and I was promptly ushered into the room where I found Winston Churchill in bed, taking his customary post-prandial rest. Without further ado Winston asked me for my impression of the Aegean campaign and why things had gone so wrong. I must have been by his side for at least half an hour; unfortunately, I cannot recall the exact words I used in reply to the Great Man. I cannot believe, however, that I did not make it clear that I felt it had been a folly to embark on the Aegean campaign, for which there was much to be said, if we were not in a pretty sure position to capture Rhodes and its essential airfields at the start and that this had not proved to be the case.

It was typical of Winston Churchill to ask the view of those, however young or junior, who had been on the spot and it was typical of him, too, despite my implied critique, to invite me and a number of other young officers to dinner at our Embassy in Cairo a few days later.

That said, I happen to share our author's opinion that the Leros campaign, given the circumstances, was a sad mistake.

Introduction and Acknowledgements

DURING THE PREPARATION OF THIS book I was often asked: why write about the battles for Kos and Leros? In a way, the decision came about as a consequence of my connection with another Mediterranean island. My mother was from Malta, where I lived as a child and later served in the Royal Marines Commandos. I have always been fascinated by Malta's history, the war years in particular, and it was while researching my last book, *Battle over Malta*, that I became interested in the fate of the many British infantrymen who had garrisoned the island during the siege of 1940–2. Afterwards, units were relocated, often as part of a brigade. 2nd Battalion The Devonshire Regiment, 1st Battalion The Hampshire Regiment and 1st Battalion The Dorsetshire Regiment had subsequently fought in Sicily and Italy as 231 Infantry Brigade before being withdrawn to take part in the Normandy landing as 231 (Malta) Independent Brigade Group. 234 Infantry Brigade, comprising 1st Battalion The Durham Light Infantry, 2nd Battalion The Royal Irish Fusiliers (Faughs) and 2nd Battalion The Queen's Own Royal West Kent Regiment had been deployed to the Dodecanese Islands in the Aegean only to be defeated while defending Kos and Leros in autumn 1943. If I was looking for a subject for another book, 231 Brigade certainly offered potential, except that the Italian campaign and the war in Western Europe have already been covered by numerous authors. The option was to look elsewhere, or to consider writing about the lesser known conflict into which 234 Brigade was flung.

When I read, in *After the Battle* magazine, Dr Peter Schenk's excellent feature about the fighting on Kos and Leros, I decided to see the islands for myself. As my partner, Sonja Stammwitz, was looking for an alternative holiday destination to Malta, the Aegean seemed an ideal choice. We visited Leros for the first time in September 2000. Many hours were spent clambering over barren, windswept hills, in exploring treacherous ravines and walking along the rocky shoreline and I could only wonder what it must have been like to fight for one's life over such rugged terrain. If it was tough for the defender, it had to be an equally daunting prospect for the attacker. I came away convinced that here was a tale waiting to be told; about the courage and tenacity displayed by ordinary soldiers, sailors and airmen of both sides, and the waste and sacrifice caused by poor planning and the ineptitude of politicians and senior staff officers who should have known better.

Back in England, I was invited to meet Ted Johnson who had fought on Leros as a young subaltern in the Faughs. His personal account, *Island Prize*, is essential reading for anyone interested in learning more about life on Leros in an infantry regiment. Ted provided me with his own documentation and material relating to the battle including correspondence with German veterans, all of which was to prove invaluable. By this time, I had been given an unofficial go-ahead for the book by Ian Drury, my friend and Publishing Director at Cassell. I began to research and write about events soon after.

Some British Army War Diaries do exist, although any information they contain was compiled by survivors at a later date. I have relied on these as well as after-action reports, both official and unofficial; patrol reports of the Long Range Desert Group, and records of the Royal Navy and Royal Air Force. The original War Diary of *Kampfgruppe* Müller was lost with the SS *Leda*, when she was bombed on 2 February 1944 while en route from Samos to Crete. However, substitute reports were prepared by *Generalleutnant* Friedrich-Wilhelm Müller, copies of which, together with other *Wehrmacht* records, were provided via the ever helpful Peter Schenk, in Berlin. Very few books cover the fighting on Kos and Leros and what is available is not always reliable. The best researched publication is without doubt *War in the Aegean* by Peter Smith and Edwin Walker. This explains the background to events in September–November 1943 and gives a good overall picture of the battles fought in the air, at sea and on the ground. A most informative account about the war in the Aegean between 1943 and 1945 has also been provided by J. S. Guard with *Improvise and Dare*. However, the full story of 234 Brigade and supporting units in the fighting for Kos and Leros has never been told.

This book could not have been written without the input of Sonja Stammwitz. In addition to interviewing German veterans, Sonja dealt with their correspondence and also translated German wartime documents. Neither did she complain when our 'holidays' in the Aegean invariably turned into fact-finding tours. Peter Schenk was a constant source of information. During our second trip to the Aegean, Sonja and I were joined by Peter and his wife, Michaela, who shared with us their acquired knowledge of the Dodecanese. I am also indebted to Ted Johnson and his wife, Ruth, for their help and generous hospitality. Equally kind hosts were William and Judy Chatterton Dickson, daughter of Lieutenant Colonel Maurice French who commanded the Faughs on Leros until his death in action on 14 November 1943. Another unexpected source of information was Mike Ramseyer, son of the late Lieutenant Commander L. F. Ramseyer of Force 133, who allowed me unrestricted access to his father's wartime notes and reports. The images in this book are from private collections, and include a selection of official German press photographs 'liberated' at the end of the war by a passing British soldier and reproduced here courtesy of Garry Symonds.

Many former members of the armed forces of both sides selflessly gave of their time to corroborate events and/or to provide their own recollections. To this end, *Churchill's Folly* is as accurate as can be expected, but if there are any errors, the responsibilty is mine. My sincere thanks and appreciation to all who helped to make this work possible, not least the following veterans (ranks are those held in autumn 1943):

ROYAL NAVY Chief Petty Officer Frank Forster (HMS *Panther*), Lieutenant Commander Geoffrey Searle (ML 355, ML 349). ROYAL MARINES Marine Cecil Wareham (HMS *Echo*). ROYAL TANK REGIMENT Captain Stanley Beckinsale (Levant Fishing Patrol/*Constantinos*). 1ST BATTALION THE DURHAM LIGHT INFANTRY Lance Corporal Bob Hawkesworth. 2ND BATTALION THE ROYAL IRISH FUSILIERS Lieutenant R. Austin Ardill, Sergeant Douglas Cone, Corporal John Harte, Lieutenant Ted Johnson, Corporal Vic 'Taffy' Kenchington, Lance Corporal Walter Pancott, the late Jimmy Silver, Lieutenant Frank Smith. 2ND BATTALION THE QUEEN'S OWN ROYAL WEST KENT

REGIMENT Lieutenant Clifford Clark, Sergeant George Hatcher, Lieutenant R. A. 'Jimmy' James. 4TH BATTALION THE ROYAL EAST KENT REGIMENT (THE BUFFS) the late Major Vincent 'Pistol' Bourne, Sergeant Bob Earle (attached 234 Brigade Headquarters), Private A. Goodman, Lieutenant Geoffrey Hart, Sergeant Albert Lukehurst, Lieutenant Eric Ransley, Private Jack Swinnock. 1ST BATTALION THE KING'S OWN ROYAL REGIMENT (LANCASTER) Lieutenant Bob King, the late Lance Corporal Bill Moss, Sergeant Reg Neep, Private Jack Ponsford. LONG RANGE DESERT GROUP the late Major David Lloyd Owen. 11TH BATTALION THE PARACHUTE REGIMENT Corporal J. S. Bourne. SPECIAL BOAT SQUADRON Major Lord Jellicoe. ROYAL ARMY MEDICAL CORPS J. Rawlinson. 3RD LIGHT ANTI-AIRCRAFT BATTERY, ROYAL ARTILLERY Major J. M. 'Pat' McSwiney. ROYAL CORPS OF SIGNALS Sergeant George Gilchrist Hall. UNITED STATES ARMY AIR FORCES Major Bill Leverette.

KRIEGSMARINE *Oberleutnant zur See* Hansjürgen Weissenborn (R *194,* R *210*). *II. BATAILLON/GRENADIERREGIMENT 16* *Oberfeldwebel* Hans-Walter Lünsmann, *Oberleutnant* Günther Steinmann. *II. BATAILLON/GRENADIER-REGIMENT 65* *Feldwebel* Gustav Wehrs. *JÄGERREGIMENT 1 BRANDENBURG* *Oberstleutnant* Uwe Wilhelm Walther. *III. BATAILLON/JÄGERREGIMENT 1 BRANDENBURG* *Oberjäger* Haat Haacke, *Sanitätsgefreiter* Rudolf Kahlert. *1. KOMPANIE/KÜSTENJÄGERABTEILUNG BRANDENBURG* *Obergefreiter* Fritz Kramer, *Hauptmann* Armin Kuhlmann, the late *Leutnant* Hans Schädlich and *Oberstabsarzt* Martin Schrägle. *I. BATAILLON/FALLSCHIRMJÄGERREGIMENT 2* *Gefreiter* Georg Goldschmidt, the late *Obergefreiter* Walter Keller, *Hauptmann* Martin Kühne, *Leutnant* Karl Franz Schweiger. *II. GRUPPE/TRANSPORT-GESCHWADER 4* *Unteroffizier* Andreas Hutter.

My thanks are extended to the Trustees of the Imperial War Museum for granting permission to reproduce extracts from archive material and to the Army Attaché at the Embassy of Italy in London and the staff at *Stato Maggiore della Marina* in Rome for providing Italian source references. I am also grateful to Sergio Andreanelli, Tim Broderick, Mrs Adrianne Browne, Major (Retired) R. S. Cross DL, Mrs S. A. Dickinson at the Air Historical Branch (RAF), Otto Dieterle (publisher of *1. Regiments Brandenburg 'Panduren'* old comrades' newsletter *Die guet Brandenburg alle Wege*), Frau Marianne Dülken, Nigel Gander, Daniele Guglielmi, Edwin Horlington (President of The Brotherhood of Veterans of The Greek Campaign 1940–1), Mrs Anne Judd (daughter of the late Brigadier Robert

Tilney), Tassos Kanaris, Dr Kostas Kogiopoulos MD, Mrs Cathy Leverette, Mrs Ursula Lloyd Owen, Frau Uschi Lohmann, Frau Alise Mandalka, Gino Mancione, Mrs Amanda Moreno (Curator of The Royal Irish Fusiliers Regimental Museum), Ioannis and Sophia Paraponiaris, Stephen Petroni, Jeremy Phipps, Frank Rixon (Overseas Secretary of the George Cross Island Association), Peter Rothwell (Honorary General Secretary of the George Cross Island Association), Frau Brigitte Schädlich, Frau Charlotte Schönau, Major John Shephard, Derek Sullivan and Dimitris Tsaloumas.

Finally, thank you to all involved with the publication of this book, not least Ian Drury and the diligent and remarkably patient Caroline Cambridge.

CHAPTER 1

Italy and the Aegean

SITUATED IN THE EASTERN Mediterranean between Greece and Turkey, the Aegean Sea provides access via the Dardanelles to the Sea of Marmara which, in turn, is linked by the Bosporus to the Black Sea. The Aegean is characterised by its many islands, with two main archipelagos forming the Cyclades, in the south, and the Dodecanese, in the south-east. The Dodecanese lie close to the coast of Turkey and consists of fourteen principal islands (not twelve as the name implies). These are: Patmos, Lipsi, Leros, Kalymnos, Kos, Astipalaea, Nisyros, Tilos, Halki, Symi, Rhodes, Karpathos, Kasos and Kastellorizo.[1]

Although populated mainly by those of Greek extraction, the Dodecanese were ruled by Turkey from the sixteenth century until the Italo-Turkish war of 1911–12, which resulted from Italian colonial expansion in North Africa. After invading Libya, then under Turkish administration, Italy moved against the Turkish Aegean islands. While the primary objective was to secure bases from which to impede supplies and reinforcements from the Ottoman Empire to Libya, the intention was also to acquire a useful bargaining tool during peace negotiations, and to have a location for possible future operations against Asia Minor. The Italians quickly occupied Astipalaea and Rhodes followed by other islands in the Dodecanese, except for Kastellorizo, which avoided coming under Italian rule until 1921.

The Turks sued for peace and on 18 October 1912, ceded Libya to Italy. An undertaking by Italy to withdraw from the Dodecanese when the Turks had fulfilled their obligations in Libya was pre-empted by the Balkan

War of 1912–13 between Turkey and the allied forces of Greece, Serbia and Bulgaria, which were separately seeking to consolidate and extend their respective territorial gains from earlier wars of independence against the Ottoman Empire. The situation was further complicated by the outbreak of World War One in August 1914. Turkey entered the war on the side of the Central Powers on 29 October. As an inducement for the Italians to come on side, a secret treaty was signed in which the Allies accorded Italy full possession of the Dodecanese. Italy joined the Allies one month later, on 23 May 1915. Greece, another potential ally, remained neutral until 1917 – the year that America also came into the war.

The rapid advance by the Ottomans into the Caucasus had so alarmed the Tsarist high command that it prompted an appeal to Britain and France for diversionary assistance, and led to one of the worst Allied defeats of the Great War. Partly in response to Russia's request, and partly in an attempt to break the impasse on the Western front, the Allies decided to force the Dardanelles as the first step to an assault on Constantinople [Istanbul]. Initially, the First Lord of the Admiralty, Winston Churchill, thought that this could be achieved by naval action. Accordingly, in mid-January 1915, an operation began with the bombardment of shore targets in the Dardanelles. The results were disappointing, with mines and determined resistance from Turkish coast defences, taking their toll on British and French warships. There followed a combined effort by British and French land forces together with troops of the Australian and New Zealand Army Corps (ANZACs) to secure the Gallipoli Peninsula, beginning with an amphibious assault on 25 April 1915. The operation was another costly failure and resulted in stalemate. In December 1915 and January 1916, the Allies withdrew. The disaster forced the resignation of Churchill as First Sea Lord, and fostered in him an obsession with the Dardanelles that would resurface in another war nearly twenty-eight years later.

After the Armistice, the future of the Dodecanese again became a subject for debate and on 29 July 1919, Italy agreed to cede the islands to Greece, with the exception of Rhodes, which was to have broad local autonomy. Italy reneged a year later only to renew a similar agreement within a month. In October 1922, the latest accord was also denounced by the Italian Government. Events were overtaken by the Greco-Turkish war in Anatolia, which ended in 1923 with the signing of the Treaty of Lausanne.

This included a clause whereby Turkey renounced in favour of Italy all rights and titles to the Dodecanese, including Kastellorizo, to enable the transfer of territory to Greece. However, this was not to be, and the islands remained under Italian rule until World War Two.

When, on 3 September 1939, Britain and France declared war on Germany, Italy remained neutral until *Il Duce*, Benito Mussolini, judged that the time was right to join what looked like being the winning side. On 10 June 1940, Italy entered the war against Britain and France. At dawn the next day, the *Regia Aeronautica* opened hostilities by bombing the Mediterranean island of Malta, an outpost of the British Empire since 1814. Initially, Britain retained the upper hand in the Mediterranean as well as in the Western Desert, but Mussolini's offensive against Malta, the campaign in North Africa and, ultimately, Italy's invasion of mainland Greece on 28 October 1940 finally led Adolf Hitler to support the efforts of *Il Duce* by transferring south the *Luftwaffe*'s Norwegian-based *X Fliegerkorps*. By mid-January 1941, the Germans had assembled in Sicily a formidable array of front-line aircraft. For Malta, the war was about to begin in earnest. The arrival of *X Fliegerkorps* also posed a far more serious threat than had the Italians for the Royal Navy's Mediterranean Fleet, and ended British hopes of seizing Pantellaria (Operation 'Workshop'), some 120 miles west of Malta. Concerns that the *Luftwaffe* would extend operations eastward were well founded, and prompted British plans for a pre-emptive take-over in the Aegean, with Rhodes as the main objective. In Britain, Special Service troops originally intended for Operation 'Workshop' were reallocated for this task. An additional force was assembled in the Middle East and had already started training when events took an unexpected turn for the worse.

On 25 February 1941, Royal Marines and troops of 50 (Middle East) Commando carried out an amphibious assault on Kastellorizo, codenamed Operation 'Abstention'. It was intended for the force to overcome the weak Italian garrison, prior to being relieved by a garrison unit in the form of 'B' Company 1st Battalion The Sherwood Foresters (Nottinghamshire and Derbyshire Regiment). When it was decided, somewhat prematurely, that the Commandos could achieve their objectives without support, the Marines were re-embarked on the gunboat, *Ladybird*. By this time, it was daylight and the appearance of Italian aircraft intent on destroying the little vessel persuaded the captain to withdraw back to Cyprus. The Sherwood Foresters were to have arrived in the early hours of the 26th, but the landing flotilla was unavoidably delayed. The operation fell further behind schedule when the destroyer HMS *Hereward* was sent ahead to prepare the way for the assault. She arrived off Kastellorizo late that night and received a signal from shore warning her that enemy surface vessels were in the vicinity. *Hereward* promptly sent an enemy report which led the operation commander, Rear Admiral E. de F. Renouf, on HMS *Gloucester*, to believe that she had actually sighted the ships. Such was the confusion resulting from this exchange that the landing had to be postponed until the following night.

By the 27th, Italian reinforcements had reached Kastellorizo. Faced by this new threat, under continuing air attacks and running short of food and ammunition, the raiders had not only lost the initiative but were having to fight for their lives. Unfortunately, the departure of *Ladybird*, who was to have provided a communications link with the assault troops, meant that the Commandos were unable to use their short-range wireless sets to report the situation.

It was not until the night of 27–28 February that the Sherwood Foresters arrived to find the Commandos hopelessly demoralised and the Italians in control of the island. The officer commanding the Sherwood Foresters, Major L. C. Cooper, thought that with the Royal Navy providing supporting fire his men might regain the initiative, but the flotilla had orders to clear the area before dawn and therefore was unable to comply. Under the circumstances, Cooper had little choice but to order his force to re-embark. For the British, it was an ignominious failure that cost the lives of at least four men; many more were wounded and 'about thirty-two' posted missing. In turn, twelve prisoners were taken (including two Greeks in Italian uniform); fourteen Italians were reported killed and forty-two wounded. The operation had failed for a variety of reasons including inadequate planning and preparation based on unreliable intelligence, lack of respect for opposing forces, a breakdown in communications and non-existent air cover. If Kastellorizo had proved such a problem, what hope was there of conducting a successful combined operation against Rhodes? In the event, the British were forced to rethink their strategy.

Initially, the Greeks had declined the offer of British troops in their struggle against the Italians, fearing that this might precipitate a German invasion of their country. But after meeting with the British Foreign Secretary, Anthony Eden, in February 1941, Greek Government ministers were persuaded that Germany intended in any event to subjugate their homeland, and readily accepted the offer of assistance. The Royal Navy had already been granted the use of port facilities at Piraeus and at Suda Bay on the island of Crete. Within days of the disaster at Kastellorizo, British forces also began to arrive in mainland Greece. The Germans invaded four weeks later and by the end of April they had overrun the country. Surviving British and Greek forces withdrew to Crete, which fell to a German airborne assault in May. For the Germans, it was an expensive victory. Consequently, the *Fallschirmjäger* (paratroopers) would never again be deployed in such a large-scale airborne operation.

British plans for the Aegean were scuppered not just by events in Greece and Crete. German troops had recently arrived in Libya and were proving themselves a very different adversary than their Italian allies. In the central Mediterranean, Malta continued to provide the Royal Air Force and the Royal Navy with an ideal base from which to disrupt Axis supply routes, but was proving expensive to maintain. Destruction of the enemy in North Africa became the main priority of Middle East Command. The outcome of the desert war remained in the balance until mid-1942, by which time the British forces had been pushed back towards Alexandria, before the line was eventually stabilised at El Alamein.

Even before America's entry into the war in December 1941, there was a conflict of interests over British strategy. There was little confidence in the United States with the existing British policy of wearing down Germany by conducting peripheral operations combined with intensive air bombardment. The United States Military Command considered that the Middle East was a liability from which the British should withdraw and that there was really only one way to defeat Hitler: by striking at Germany itself. For the British, of course, there could be no question of abandoning the Middle East. The withdrawal of hundreds of thousands of men, not to mention an untold quantity of arms and equipment, presented a logistical nightmare. Not only was such a proposition tactically unsound, but Britain had a vested interest in protecting its Persian oil supplies. When, in their plans for operations in 1942, the United States advocated an Anglo-American invasion of France (Operation 'Sledgehammer'), Britain protested that the time was not yet right and pressed for a move against French North Africa, partly to forestall any similar move by the Germans, but ultimately to open up the Mediterranean for the through passage of Allied shipping. In July 1942, the Americans were persuaded to postpone plans for a cross-Channel invasion and instead to conduct an Anglo-American landing in French North Africa, to take place no later than 30 October 1942.

On 18 October, the final Italo-German air offensive against Malta ended in victory for the defenders – though they did not yet realise it. On the night of the 23rd, the British Eighth Army also launched a major offensive – against the Axis forces in the Western Desert. It was the beginning of the end for the *Deutsches Afrikakorps*. October 1942 heralded a welcome reversal of British fortunes in the Mediterranean and the Middle East. By November, the *Afrikakorps* was retreating westward and, on the 8th, a little later than planned, the Allies landed in Algeria and Morocco.

Now that they were in a position to do so, the Commanders-in-Chief in the Middle East began to contemplate action in the Eastern Mediterranean. If they could reoccupy Crete and take possession of the Dodecanese, the British would be ideally placed to restrict Axis movements in the region, with obvious repercussions for the enemy. Such a development was bound to inspire Turkish confidence and, perhaps, finally persuade Turkey to declare openly for the Allies. This would allow the use of Turkish air bases from which to strike at Greece, Romania and Bulgaria; it would open the way through the Dardanelles and Bosporus and, controversially, could even lead to action in the Balkans (a notion suggested by the British Chiefs of Staff, but later rejected by Prime Minister Winston Churchill).[2] However, after considering the problems, it was concluded that the defences in Crete were such that any operation at the present was doomed to failure unless the island was selected as the primary objective in the Mediterranean. The possibility of capturing Rhodes and the Dodecanese with the object of opening the Aegean as far as Izmir, in Turkey, was seen as feasible, but only if the *Luftwaffe* was preoccupied elsewhere. There would also be a requirement for additional resources: two auxiliary aircraft carriers, ten aircraft squadrons and eighty-eight assorted landing craft. A proposal was referred to Winston Churchill, then in Morocco attending the Casablanca Conference with President Roosevelt. The idea appealed to the Prime Minister, who decided to seek the opinions of General Sir Harold Alexander and the Chiefs of Staff. The Casablanca Conference concluded with Britain and the United States in agreement over a number of key issues, including the decision to proceed with an Allied invasion of Sicily (Operation 'Husky'), and to create a situation in which Turkey could be persuaded to join the Allies. A few days later, on 27 January 1943, Churchill instructed the Commanders-in-Chief to plan and prepare for the capture of the Dodecanese employing the utmost 'ingenuity and resource'.[3]

CHAPTER 2

Calm before the Storm
February—September 1943

ON 16 FEBRUARY 1943, GENERAL Sir Harold Alexander was succeeded as Commander-in-Chief, Middle East, by General Sir Henry Maitland Wilson who was entrusted by Winston Churchill with four main tasks:

a) You will maintain the Eighth Army and support its operations to the utmost, until Tunisia is finally cleared of the enemy.

b) In conformity with the requirements of General Eisenhower, you will take all measures necessary for the mounting of that part of Operation 'Husky' which is launched from the area under your command.

c) You will make preparations for supporting Turkey in such measures as may be necessary to give effect to the policy of His Majesty's Government as communicated to you from time to time by the Chiefs of Staff.

d) You will prepare for amphibious operations in the Eastern Mediterranean.[1]

Accordingly, a new headquarters was established in Cairo with personnel drawn mainly from officers of III Corps Headquarters to plan and command operations in the Aegean. Number 2 Planning Staff (redesignated Force 292 in June) had an unenviable task complicated by the conflicting ambitions of Greece and Turkey regarding ownership of the Dodecanese. It was thought prudent not to discuss the future of the islands with either country and to carry out initial operations using only British forces. By 2 May a plan was produced for Operation 'Accolade',[2] which outlined a full-scale attack on Rhodes and Karpathos and the subsequent occupation of other islands, for which the minimal requirement was three infantry divisions, one armoured brigade, two independent infantry battalions, two parachute battalions and corps troops. The main problem was the provision of adequate air cover from remote bases, but it was hoped that other large-scale operations would be underway in the central Mediterranean to deter the enemy from reinforcing the Aegean. Planning was further complicated by the insistence of General Dwight D. Eisenhower, Commander-in-Chief, Mediterranean Theatre, that any redeployment of British troops from North Africa to the Middle East after the Tunisian campaign depended on the decisions of the Combined Chiefs of Staff and was subject to developments following Operation 'Husky'.

On 12 May, the British and American leaders and their advisers gathered in Washington for a conference, codenamed 'Trident'. Churchill propounded the view that an opportunity might present itself whereby Turkey would permit the Allies to use bases from which to carry out air-strikes on the Ploesti oilfields in Romania as well as for launching operations in the Aegean. The Americans were unconvinced: if the British insisted on a Mediterranean strategy that was likely to delay the defeat of Germany and Japan, the US representatives were instructed to announce the preparedness of their government to revise its basic strategy and extend its operations and commitments in the Pacific. If Churchill wanted to pursue his goals in the eastern Mediterranean, Britain would have to do so alone. The eventual outcome of 'Trident' was general agreement for a continuation of operations against Italy following the expected success of 'Husky'. All forces in the Mediterranean were to be made available for these operations, except for four American and three British divisions. These were to be held in readiness from 1 November for withdrawal to the United Kingdom from where there would be a landing on the Continent provisionally scheduled for 1 May 1944. It was also decided that in order to maintain pressure on the Japanese, a combined operation against the Arakan in Burma was to be staged later in the year, with priority of resources after the main operations against Italy. This was to have considerable repercussions on subsequent British plans in the eastern Mediterranean.

In late June 1943, raiders from the Special Boat Squadron (SBS) landed on the south coast of Crete to strike at three airfields which could be used by the *Luftwaffe* during 'Husky'. The mission was only a partial success. Explosive charges were placed against several aircraft and a fuel dump at Kastèli; another airfield, Timbáki, had been abandoned by the Germans, while that at Heraklion was no longer in use as a major air base. A fuel dump was therefore selected as an alternative target. In 1942, there had been similar operations on Crete and Rhodes. Hit-and-run raids had an undeniable nuisance value, but they had little or no effect on the bigger picture. The North African campaign had ended with the surrender of the *Afrikakorps* in May. Operation 'Husky' commenced two months later, on 10 July. The Allies made rapid headway and with the Italians facing an invasion of the mainland, Mussolini was ousted on 25 July and replaced by *Maresciallo* Pietro Badoglio.

By August, a British plan of action had been approved in anticipation of a suitably favourable development in the Aegean and the Balkans. Among the proposals were an emergency 'walk-in' in to Rhodes and other islands in the event of Italy's collapse and the withdrawal of German forces; a quick 'Accolade' against German opposition only, and a full-scale 'Accolade' (though not before 1944). On 3 August, the British Chiefs of Staff advised:

> Should the Italians in Crete and the Aegean area resist Germans and deadlock ensue, our policy should be to help the Italians against the Germans wherever possible.[3]

It was recommended that a force be made immediately available together with ships for use as troop transports. Mediterranean Air Command (formed in February under Air Chief Marshal Sir Arthur Tedder) was approached for additional transport aircraft sufficient to lift a parachute battalion group. Four squadrons of American P-38 Lightnings were also requested. The latter were essential, for apart from Bristol Beaufighters, there were no fighters in the Middle East with the range to operate over the operational area. The paratroopers and their aircraft were to be in position by 14 August; the Lightnings were required to arrive in Cyprus by the 15th, and the seaborne element was to be ready to sail at any time after 18 August. Much depended on the destruction or containment of *Luftwaffe* units in the region, but this was achievable only if available bombers were released from all other commitments.

An exasperated General Eisenhower, faced with mounting pressure by the British to reallocate resources to the eastern Mediterranean, finally relented and on 7 August, Allied Force Headquarters advised the Middle East that the required troops could be provided, though not before 14 August. Certain ships could also be released, but current requirements meant that no aircraft would be spared: no transports were available for parachute operations, and Lightning squadrons were fully employed in escorting the Strategic Bomber Force in attacks against Italian targets and were specifically required for Operation 'Avalanche' – the Allied landing at Salerno, in Italy. In Eisenhower's opinion, which was apparently shared by both the Naval and Air Commanders-in-Chief in the Mediterranean, 'Accolade' should be abandoned. Eisenhower was assured that 'Accolade' would take place only if conditions presented a reasonable prospect of success with the forces available and when the situation in Italy might allow the release of the all-important Lightnings. The target date of readiness was postponed to three days' notice from 19 August, by which time Operation 'Husky' had been concluded successfully and the Allied armies were about to push north into Italy.

In the meantime, Churchill and his top military advisers were in Quebec for another Anglo-American conference ('Quadrant'). By now, the Americans were convinced that Churchill's apparent obsession with the eastern Mediterranean was influenced more than anything else by the prospect of post-war political gains. If the Prime Minister's motives were personal, those of his Chiefs of Staff were purely professional. It was their considered opinion that Allied pressure in the Mediterranean was essential for a successful cross-Channel invasion in 1944. While the Allied offensive continued so, too, did the perceived threat to southern France, Austria and the Balkans, thereby forcing the *Wehrmacht* to draw on forces which might otherwise be utilised in northern France. Despite such reasoning, the US Chiefs of Staff were unconvinced. As they saw it, British Mediterranean strategy was overly reliant on the speculation that a political and economic collapse could be brought about in the occupied countries, especially in the Balkans. If that assessment proved to be faulty, the Allies would be drawn into a prolonged struggle of blockade and attrition in Europe. Ultimately, the

Americans had their way and Operation 'Overlord', the Allied invasion of northern France, became the primary Anglo-American ground and air effort against the Axis in Europe.

While Churchill and his advisers discussed strategy with their American counterparts in Canada, in Germany, Hitler and his staff prepared for the inevitable as Badoglio's government negotiated surrender terms with the Allies. At the same time, in the Middle East, the British stood by to move into the Aegean. With Italy on the point of collapse, 8th Indian Division was embarked to undertake the capture of Rhodes and was to have sailed on 1 September. However, as a result of 'Quadrant', on 26 August the troop transports were released to India and 8th Indian Division was ordered to Italy.[4] On 8 September, when the Italian armistice was announced, the force had been dispersed and with it went any opportunity for a rapid deployment. Furthermore, the Commander-in-Chief, Middle East, was kept in ignorance of events and only learned about the armistice just before it was made public![5] The Germans wasted no time in taking over from the Italians in Crete, but were slower in reacting to the situation elsewhere. General Wilson decided therefore to act on recommendations of the Joint Planning Staff. The task of securing Rhodes was reallocated to 234 Infantry Brigade, whose line regiments, 1st Battalion The Durham Light Infantry, 2nd Battalion The Royal Irish Fusiliers (Faughs) and 2nd Battalion The Queen's Own Royal West Kent Regiment, had recently arrived in the Middle East from Malta.[6] Italian co-operation was essential to British planning. A prerequisite to occupation was the provision of a suitable airfield, either at Maritsa, in Rhodes itself, or on the island of Kos. Moreover, an amphibious landing was considered feasible only if it was unopposed. A military mission was to pave the way for the main assault, while the SBS spearheaded the occupation of other islands including Kastellorizo, Kos and Samos. The British Prime Minister was a keen advocate of the plan which was approved by him on 9 September: 'Good. This is a time to play high. Improvise and dare.'[7]

By then, events were already well underway. On 7 September, the SBS commander, Major Lord Jellicoe, was dining with a fellow officer and his new bride at the St George's Hotel in Beirut when a military policeman arrived with orders for him to make his way to Raiding Force Headquarters, near Haifa.[8] There, Jellicoe was instructed to collect his battledress and field kit and present himself at Haifa airport where an aeroplane was standing by for a dawn take-off for Cairo. On arrival, he was taken to Middle East Headquarters, shown to a room and seated with others around a large table. To his surprise, Jellicoe learned that the Italian armistice was taking effect that day and that it had been planned to try to occupy Rhodes with the assistance of the island's Italian garrison. It was hoped that the Italians had been forewarned by an agent of the Special Operations Executive (SOE), but no one had been able to contact him due to a breakdown in communications. It was proposed therefore to send a landing party by fast craft from Alexandria. Jellicoe recalled:

> After about 20 minutes I really couldn't contain myself any longer and I said, 'I'm surprised at this. Would it not be much easier for a small party to drop in this evening, as clearly it should be done as quickly as possible.' Why all of this was being done at the last moment; why the Italian armistice had not been anticipated; why our Raiding Forces had not been alerted, God alone knows.[9]

It was decided that Jellicoe would parachute in to Rhodes, establish contact with the Italian Governor, *Ammiraglio* Inigo Campioni, and ask for his support for a British take-over. Subject to the success of Jellicoe's mission, Colonel D. J. T. Turnbull of General Headquarters was to follow up to discuss matters in detail. A Polish SOE officer (Count Julian Dobrski) with the *nom de guerre* Major Dolbey then asked if Jellicoe spoke Italian. He did not, and readily agreed to the multi-lingual Dolbey joining him as an interpreter. A wireless operator, Sergeant Kesterton, completed the ad hoc team. They took off in a Halifax that evening, but adverse weather conditions combined with an inadequate briefing prevented the crew from locating Rhodes.

The following night, Lieutenant Commander L. F. (Frank) Ramseyer and a landing party, composed mainly of SBS under Major David Sutherland, arrived off Kastellorizo in two motor launches (*349* and *357*) to secure the island as a staging post for Aegean operations; a two-man team was parachuted into Kos to prepare the Italians there for the arrival of British troops, and a further effort was made to infiltrate Rhodes which had become a battleground between pro-Badoglio Italians and the Germans of *Generalleutnant* Ulrich Kleeman's *Sturmdivision Rhodos*. Major Jellicoe:

The next night [9th] we took off again. By that time they [the aircrew] had brushed up their geography and we were dropped at Rhodes. Just before we dropped, Major Dolbey said to me, 'I think I must make a confession to you. I said that I was parachute trained. I'm not. I've never actually dropped by parachute, so give me a push if necessary'... He dropped on to the main coast road near Lemnos, on the east of the island and broke his leg, his thigh, extremely badly. I was dropped, as was the wireless operator, Sgt Kesterton, on to the hills above [a few hundred yards away] and shot at quite fiercely. The shooting continued – we were behind rocks by then. We didn't know who was shooting at us. I had a letter from General 'Jumbo' Wilson, C-in-C in Cairo, for the Italian commander, Admiral Campioni. I was told that in danger of capture by the Germans, this should be got rid of. I had no idea whether they were Germans or Italians firing at us and there was nowhere to get rid of this letter – it was very rocky, hard ground. Of course, they were getting closer so I decided the only thing to do was to eat it which was not the most appetising meal I've ever had. And then I heard them approaching and I heard that they were shouting to each other in Italian. I shouted, '*Amici! Amici!*', etc. Then, after a little bit of discussion and explanation I persuaded them to take me in their transport into Rhodes to Italian headquarters. All this had taken the best part of an hour or so and the major had already been found and taken in and there he was with Admiral Campioni. We had a long discussion with the Italian Admiral. We talked to him for a large part of the next hour or two. He was very enthusiastic to begin with and thought we were the precursor to substantial reinforcements. Although I said that we had further Raiding Forces standing by, I really couldn't inflate their number. Accordingly I informed Campioni that in the next few days he could only expect some two hundred reinforcements. Thereafter it would be some days before additional forces could reach Rhodes. As this sank in Campioni's enthusiasm started to wane. All this time Captain Dolbey who had been speaking and interpreting so well and so nobly was in acute pain ...[10]

Dolbey, who had a compound fracture, was evacuated, first by fast craft to Symi, then by Italian seaplane to Kastellorizo and thence to Cyprus.

For the time being, Jellicoe and Kesterton remained in Rhodes and tried to stall Campioni, while in the Middle East frantic efforts were made to find enough landing craft to dispatch 234 Brigade. As this could not be achieved before 18 September, one battalion was stood by and ordered to embark in motor launches and RAF craft, while preparations continued for transporting the rest of the brigade. Jellicoe continues:

> I stayed all the next day [10th], seeing, when I could, Admiral Campioni, getting messages through to Cairo, explaining the position and saying it was highly desirable that it was necessary to provide substantial reinforcements within a few days if Campioni was to be persuaded to hold out. The most, however, that I was able to promise him was a non-assault-loaded brigade within six or seven days. Of course, the sudden transfer from one side to the other was asking a great deal of the Italians. So, although I spent all the next day, whenever I could, talking to Admiral Campioni, and although he remained extremely friendly, at the end of it he was convinced it was not on as far as they were concerned. He sent me [and Sergeant Kesterton] off in an Italian fast craft with his chief of staff with all the maps of their minefields to Kastellorizo, which, in fact, a squadron of mine had occupied that day.[11]

In the haste to occupy the Aegean, specialist troops, intelligence operatives and conventional forces were deployed by all available means. Poor communications, insufficient co-ordination and the actions of a few who seem to have treated the occasion as an adventurous outing meant that sometimes the same island was singled out by more than one interested party. On 8 September, Colonel L. F. R. Kenyon concluded his appointment on the General Staff of Force 292 and immediately joined the Aegean Mission as a representative of III Corps Commander, Lieutenant General Sir Desmond Anderson. He was at Kastellorizo when Jellicoe returned from Rhodes with his assessment of the situation. This failed to deter the colonel from intervening personally. On 11 September he set off in an RAF launch with Group Captain Harry Wheeler, senior RAF Staff Officer in Force 292 (and soon to be appointed senior RAF officer on Kos):

> On arrival we heard some AA fire and saw a number of craft 'swanning'

about outside Rhodes harbour (I found that on an air alarm craft were ordered out of the harbour). The Italians replied to our signal by a refusal to allow us into the harbour. I suggested asking the Italians to take off one officer in one of their own craft, and to this they agreed and shortly after a MAS [*Motoscafo Anti Sommergibile*: Italian motor torpedo boat] came alongside. No question had arisen as to who should go, and I transhipped. Wheeler had some doubts as to the advisability of my visit, but these were solved by a large bomb which fell on Rhodes. The commanders of both vessels had the same idea and the RAF launch drew off at speed to the East, while my MAS went to the West.

I was met by an Italian Naval Captain who at once struck me as being a good fighter, and who gave immediate evidence of his intense dislike for the Germans. He spoke good English and failed to conceal (or succeeded in conveying) his lack of confidence in the advice being tendered to Campioni by the senior Italian General in Rhodes.

As I drove up to the [Governor's] Palace, there was a fairly heavy air raid in progress. I was led through a number of kitchens and was presented to Campioni in a dark scullery. He seemed embarrassed and led me to his state reception room upstairs.

He informed me that his military advice was that the troops, having been pushed off the anti-tank obstacle covering Rhodes, could not survive another German attack. He understood that the British would reinforce in about five days time. He stated that the best he could do was to temporise with the Germans to gain time. This course was not possible if the enemy knew he had British officers with him and as the place was full of spies he wanted me to go.

At my request he then outlined the facts on which his military advice was given. The crux of the whole advice was the presence of the German tanks, which seems to have paralysed the entire Italian command. But for this factor, he said, he could fight on, and so on.

I knew something of Campioni's record and personality and formed the opinion, to which I still adhere, that in a difficult position he was playing an in and out game and halting between two policies. I was in some doubts as to whether the best course would be to compromise him thoroughly with the British, and so cut off his chances of making terms with the Germans and increasing the fighting spirit.

He then intimated that I must really be off as he was expecting some German officers at once with whom he was going to 'temporise'. He refused my suggestion that I should wait to hear the result of his Conference. He ordered an *MAS* to take me to Castelrosso [Kastellorizo] and I was disguised in a long black cloak and taken from the Palace to the port. By this time I was convinced that he was intending to capitulate and that his main preoccupation was to get rid of me before the Germans learned of my presence and insisted on his handing me over.

At the harbour I was entertained to a good and much needed English breakfast by my former contact, who now spoke much more frankly. He said the General had always wanted to surrender, but that there was considerable opposition from some of his officers. He said the troops were not good and were shockingly led. As for himself, he was going to set up in a small fort and kill as many Germans as he could. My own view was that we could do nothing to influence the general situation, but that we might save something out of the wreck. I told him, therefore, that it was his duty to arrange the total evacuation or destruction of all craft in the harbour and said that we should welcome him and the Naval craft particularly at Castelrosso or Leros. He promised to do all he could; some craft appeared later at Castelrosso and, I believe, more at Leros.

A further message then came from the Palace ordering me off at once and I went in an *MAS* ...

I wrote my report on the way back to Castelrosso and an hour or two after its dispatch we got news of the Italian capitulation.[12]

That day, *Sturmdivision Rhodos*, numbering approximately 7,500 men, seized control of Rhodes and took prisoner 35,000–40,000 Italians, ending British hopes of an assisted take-over. Rhodes had been the first 'Accolade' objective and involved considerable forces. Indeed, the very success of Aegean operations was dependant on acquiring the island, as explained by Colonel Kenyon:

It is significant that every plan, no matter how much the expected military opposition was written down, contemplated the capture of Rhodes as a preliminary to any extension to the north; and that every plan was profoundly influenced by the necessity of capturing at the earliest stage a number of Advanced Landing Grounds, and by the great difficulties to be overcome if this was to be possible.[13]

It therefore became necessary for the British to revise their planning and strategy. Future operations were to be on a reduced scale and, as it was essential to act quickly, they had to be improvised. German resources in the Aegean had been stretched by their deployments in Rhodes and Crete, and it seemed possible that by a rapid move the Middle East forces might obtain control elsewhere in the region and by doing so detract from recent enemy successes, enhance British prestige throughout the Middle East and act as a diversion for operations in Italy. In spite of the reluctance of Eisenhower to divert resources, there was hope in the British camp that even with the limited means at their disposal, the occupation of other islands such as Kos, Leros and Samos could still succeed. The number of German aircraft in Greece and Crete did not yet represent a serious threat and with British fighters operating from Kos, the possibility of major German seaborne or airborne operations seemed slight.[14]

It was thought that with Italian co-operation British forces might maintain themselves in Kos and Leros until an attack could be launched on Rhodes from the Middle East. The task of reinforcement and supply was to fall largely on the Royal Navy.[15]

On Friday, 10 September, Lieutenant Colonel David Pawson of MO4 (SOE) led a pre-emptive Anglo-Greek mission to Samos. After conferring with the Italian commander, *Generale* Mario Soldarelli, Pawson continued to Leros. He returned to Samos and was joined there on the 14th by Major-General Allan Arnold (Military Attaché in Ankara) who had been dispatched to foster Italo-Greek relations in order to form a united front against the Germans. During the night of 12–13 September, Lieutenant Commander Ramseyer in ML 349 also conveyed Major Sutherland and about ten of his men from 'S' Detachment to the island of Kos. They were accompanied by Major Jellicoe aboard the requisitioned Italian *MS 12*, who then proceeded to Leros and on to Astipalaea.

On 13 September, *Generale* Soldarelli received a message from Leros stating that a German mission wished to land there. Due primarily to the intervention of Lieutenant Colonel Pawson, a reply was sent ordering Leros not to co-operate. The enemy fully intended to occupy the island the next day, but postponed the operation until the 15th due to lack of air support, only to be pre-empted by the arrival of Major David Lloyd Owen with 'Y1' Patrol of the Long Range Desert Group (LRDG). The Majority of 'A' and 'B' Squadrons followed. It was also already too late for an unopposed take-over by the Germans of the nearby island of Kos.

Kos is centrally located among the Dodecanese and lies at the entrance to the Gulf of Kos. It is 26 and a half miles (42.7 kilometres) long with a width varying between just over a mile (1.75 kilometres) to 6.3 miles (10.2 kilometres). There is a rugged southern coastline with a hill range extending from Cape Foca in the east, west to Pili and beyond, with Mount Dicheo the highest peak at 846 metres. A series of lesser hills continues to the western end of the island. In the main, the precipitous southern slopes are rocky and barren, whereas the slightly gentler northern face descends to pine forests and a cultivated heartland. Sandy beaches abound and there are extensive salt flats on the northern coast at Lambi and Tingachi. The capital and main harbour is Kos, at the extreme eastern end of the island. A central road runs along the fertile coastal plain from Cefalo (Kefalos), in the west, all the way to Kos town.

By mid-September, 216 Group had assembled twenty (later increased to twenty-two) DC-3 Douglas Dakotas for Operation 'Accolade'. These included eight paratroop aircraft which, together with 120 men of 'A' Company, 11th Battalion The Parachute Regiment, were detached for training at Ramat David, near Haifa, in Palestine. On 14 September six Dakotas were ordered to Nicosia in Cyprus from where a drop on Kos was scheduled to take place that night. The same morning, a Beaufighter of 46 Squadron piloted by Squadron Leader W. A. Cuddie became the first Allied aircraft to land at Antimachia aerodrome where it offloaded an RAF wireless team. Beaufighters and Dakotas continued to arrive throughout the day.[16]

That evening, Lieutenant Colonel R. M. C. Thomas, commanding 11th Battalion The Parachute Regiment, together with an Advance Headquarters and 'A' Company under Major D. A. Gilchrist boarded the six Dakotas at Nicosia and squeezed into the tiny inward-facing seats along the walls of the narrow fuselage. Much of their equipment was packed into thirty-six bomb-rack containers but each man was weighed down with a bulky parachute pack which made it impossible to sit comfortably for any length of time. The aircraft took off at two-minute intervals and were airborne by 2241 hours. During their three hours' flight the Dakotas flew below 3,000 feet along Turkey's mountainous coastline in order to avoid detection by enemy radar. As they neared Kos, the pilots maintained a drop height of 500 feet above sea level. The leading machine reached the drop zone at 0145. The paratroopers stood at 'Action Stations', facing aft and with their parachute static lines secured to an overhead steel cable. A dispatcher also stood and watched the signal lamps above the open door in the port side of the fuselage. Final safety checks were carried out: helmet straps fastened, parachute harness, equipment and static line all secure. Airspeed was reduced to facilitate the men's exit. From the lead aircraft a red signal light was fired, which was duly answered from the ground by a green. With seconds to go, the captain gave the order 'Red light on', and the co-pilot flipped a switch on a facing panel. Above the doorway the red lamp snapped on. The dispatcher shouted 'Stand in the door!' and the number 1 stepped towards the opening. Moments later, the captain ordered 'Green light on', the co-pilot activated the green lamp and the first paratrooper leapt out into the night air. As always, there was a fleeting moment when everything seemed to be frozen in time, yet paradoxically there was an acute sensation of falling, an awareness of hurtling along an invisible slide that was the aircraft's slipstream. Then a sharp tug as the attached static line released the parachute and the canopy deployed with an audible snap. The sudden decrease in acceleration jerked the soldier upright, knocking the breath from his body. Most tend to jump with their eyes instinctively shut tight and only open them at this stage: a glance upward to check that the canopy had opened fully (if not, there was little time to rectify any problems); a quick look around to make sure the airspace was clear (it was a fine, clear night with a full moon) and then the anticipated landing. It is a curious fact that night jumps tend to produce gentler landings than those by day. One cannot see the 'ground rush' and is generally more relaxed at the moment of ground contact. The drop by 'A' Company some one and a half miles north-west of Kos town was no exception and only two men were slightly injured. All aircraft returned safely and were back at Nicosia by 0439 hours.

Once on the ground, the paratroopers retrieved their arms and equipment from their containers before gathering at a roadside rendezvous. Lieutenant Colonel Thomas was met by Major Sutherland according to plan, and after being briefed on the local situation arranged for his men to be deployed on Antimachia aerodrome.

On 15 September, Lieutenant Colonel R. F. Kirby of 1st Battalion The Durham Light Infantry was air-landed with the advance element of his command. Lieutenant General Anderson also arrived and instructed Ramseyer to take Sutherland and his SBS to Samos. Anderson followed the next day (16th) and continued with Ramseyer to Leros. On the 17th, 'A' and 'B' Companies of 2nd Battalion The Royal Irish Fusiliers with a communication party, base personnel and stores reached Leros on board the British destroyers *Hurworth* and *Croome*. Shortly afterwards, Ramseyer and Anderson returned to Kos where the former joined ML 354 and a detachment of SBS under Captain J. M. 'Jock' Lapraik who had been ordered to Symi. According to Ramseyer, 'I decided to fill in the night by occupying Simi [Symi]. The ML had no previous experience in this type of work and the waters were new to the Commanding Officer. At dusk we sailed South after embarking SBS and their equipment'.[17] The island was secured in the early hours of the 18th. The same day, four patrols of 'B' Squadron LRDG also left Leros for Astipalaea.

On 18 September, Pawson's mission left Samos for Ikaria on board *MAS 522*. Acting on orders of the boat commander, the crew disarmed and apprehended the team, which included Major Michael Parish of MI9 (who was shot and wounded) and *Pliarhos* Alex Levidis of the *Elliniko Vassiliko Naftiko* [Hellenic Royal Navy]. Soldarelli's second-in-command, *Generale* Pejrolo, was also taken prisoner. It was an unfortunate end to an otherwise successful operation.

On Kos, Anderson caught up with Colonel Kenyon and after the pair had discussed the general situation, the latter was appointed to command all troops on the island with Major C. F. Blagden in charge of Civil Affairs. Anderson and Ramseyer left for Cairo on the 18th and the next day Kenyon set to work reorganising the island defences. By this time, reinforcements, including 'B' Company 2nd Battalion The Queen's Own Royal West Kent Regiment, had arrived at Kastellorizo. The remainder of the Royal West Kents were deployed later in the month to garrison the island of Samos (a platoon subsequently occupied neighbouring Ikaria), while the LRDG set up base at Kalymnos and sent patrols as far west as the Cyclades. Meanwhile, at Nicosia, in Cyprus, an Advanced Air Defence Headquarters was established as a forward co-ordinating authority for offensive air operations in the Aegean and for fighter protection of shipping in the Levant.[18]

Churchill had bargained that even without Rhodes, the rest of the Dodecanese could be taken. So far, his gamble looked like paying off. But it was a dangerous game in which the players constantly raised the stakes. According to British intelligence, by 19 September, Axis forces occupied Thasos, Samothraki, Limnos, Lesbos, Chios, islands in the Sporades and the Cyclades, Kasos, Karpathos, Kythira and Antikythira as well as Crete and Rhodes.

CHAPTER 3

Reinforcements   September 1943

In the wake of the armistice, Italians were divided in their loyalties, but those who displayed a willingness to change sides ran a terrible risk. On 11 September, Adolf Hitler issued a directive outlining the fate of 'all Italian units which have allowed their weapons to fall into the hands of the insurgents or even collaborated with the insurgents'. Officers were to be shot 'in accordance with martial law' and their men 'transported directly to the east ... and placed at the disposal of Quartermaster General, Army General Staff for employment'.[1]

Two days later, at Kefallonia, in the Ionian Islands, Italian coastal batteries opened fire on two approaching German landing craft, sinking one and damaging the other. It was the beginning of a battle that would result in the deaths of many of the 12,000 officers and men who formed the island garrison: besides those killed in action, thousands were executed or perished en route to labour camps after their transport ships were lost to mines. Kefallonia was the worst massacre of pro-Badoglio Italians, but it was not unique. Italian officers would also be executed at other distant outposts, notably that of Kos, in the Aegean.

Men and matériel began to arrive by air at Kos as soon as Antimachia was secured. By 17 September, the paratroopers and Durham Light Infantry had been joined by army gunners (although their 40mm Bofors were still en route by sea), a detachment of 2909 Squadron RAF Regiment (equipped with 20mm Hispano cannon), RAF signallers and radar technicians as well as ground crew and pilots of 7 (SAAF) Squadron with Spitfire Vs. Until then the air defence had been reliant on a handful of assorted Italian fighters commanded by *Sottotenente* Giuseppe Morganti, of *396ª squadriglia*. The only untoward incidents occurred when the senior RAF officer on Kos, Group Captain Harry Wheeler, was fatally injured in a car accident on the 15th, whereupon he was superseded by the CO of 7 (SAAF) Squadron, Major Cornelius van Vliet; and on the 17th when Turkish light AA slightly damaged two aircraft on their way back to Ramat David. On the 18th, Wing Commander R. C. Love arrived to take charge of 243 (Fighter) Wing which had been formed at Antimachia. Headquarters was situated within a few hundred yards of the landing ground, while airfield personnel set up camp in a nearby wadi with a cookhouse and a water point but little else in the way of home comforts.

The Allies suffered their first major loss at sea on 14 September when the Greek submarine *Katsonis* was rammed and sunk by *UJ 2101* north of Triceri Strait. At least fourteen of her crew were taken prisoner. In the race to occupy the islands, both sides risked their naval forces to ferry troops and provisions. While en route from Piraeus to Rhodes on 17 September, a convoy consisting of the submarine-chaser *UJ 2104* and the steamers *Pluto* and *Paul*, was attacked south of Naxos by eight Beaufighters of 237 Wing out of Limassol. Of three Beaufighters damaged by *Flak*, two crash landed on returning to base (one with a dead navigator). In turn, at least one escorting Arado seaplane was shot down.[2] In the early hours of the 18th, the convoy was shelled by shore batteries on Astipalaea before being attacked by HM destroyers *Faulknor* and *Eclipse* and the Greek *Vasilissa [Queen] Olga*. The badly damaged escort vessel reached Astipalaea and foundered on the east coast of the islet of Glino where her crew was apprehended by the Italian garrison. Originally the Norwegian whaler *Darvik*, *UJ 2104* had been taken over by the British as HMS *Kos* before falling into enemy hands at Crete. In naval tradition it is unwise to rename a ship, but it was a case of third time lucky for *UJ 2104* which was the sole surviving vessel from the convoy. When initial reports mistakenly indicated that Astipalaea had been invaded, three Italian torpedo boats were sent on a fact-finding mission. Two were written off in an air attack and the third was damaged and beached at Astipalaea. The true nature of the situation was then realised and that evening troops of 'B' Squadron Long Range Desert Group (LRDG) were dispatched to the island where Major David Lloyd Owen took charge of several German officers (including a war correspondent) and accompanied them on board ML 355 to Leros. The remaining prisoners were evacuated in two batches during the next few days.[3]

On 23 September, the merchantman SS *Donizetti* with 1,576 Italian prisoners of war on board was sunk by HMS *Eclipse* off south-west Rhodes. An ex-Italian torpedo boat, the former French *La Pomone*, renamed *TA 10* by the Germans, was immobilised and drifted inshore where she was deliberately sunk by her crew. Allied aircraft also struck at a convoy bound for Crete, sinking the transport *Dithmarschen*.

The loss of the *Donizetti* was a tragedy that could probably have been avoided. According to one source[4] an Italian clandestine wireless station on Rhodes advised the British that the ship was transporting Italian prisoners, but the attack proceeded regardless. The enemy was justifiably concerned about British activity in the Aegean, not least because of the increased threat this posed for their convoys, the War Diary of the Operations Division of the German Naval Staff noting:

> The situation in the area of the Dodecanese has grown very serious since 18 September.[5]

Clearly, something had to be done. As had been demonstrated in the central Mediterranean, control of the sea lanes was dictated as much by air superiority as by naval power. Aircraft played an important transport and resupply role and were essential for any offensive operation. Air cover was also crucial for the safe passage of shipping. The British intended to use Kos as a base for single-engine fighters to provide short-range cover for a proposed landing at Rhodes, scheduled to commence in late October, and as protection for British warships operating out of Leros. By 17 September, the Germans had been alerted to the presence of British forces on Kos. Aware that without an air base, the British had no hope of maintaining their presence in the area, the enemy wasted little time before commencing bombing operations.

On Saturday morning, 18 September, Dakota FD806 of 216 Squadron was transporting soldiers of the Durham Light Infantry when it struck the water while low-flying and ditched off the Turkish island of Kara (the crew and passengers survived and were interned temporarily in Turkey). Further transports landed at Antimachia and had just been offloaded when Messerschmitt Bf 109s swept across the aerodrome in a low-level strafing attack. At least one soldier died and three were wounded; three Dakotas were burnt out and another badly damaged. Another Dakota that arrived during the raid made an emergency landing near Lambi, north of Kos town. On this date, 7 (SAAF) Squadron suffered its first combat casualties when Spitfires flown by Lieutenants A. G. Turner (in JK148) and A. E. F. Cheesman (JK140) were shot down offshore.[6] In turn, two Bf 109Gs of *IV./J.G.27* were lost and their pilots, *Oberfeldwebel* Wilhelm Morgenstern (10463/white 1) and *Unteroffizier* Gustav Dettmar (18470/white 5) reported as missing. The latter was, in fact, captured and during interrogation maintained that he had been hit by anti-aircraft fire. That night, two Beaufighters of 46 Squadron from Cyprus patrolled the skies over Kos without incident.

Thereafter, the *Luftwaffe* continued to target Kos, and Antimachia airfield in particular. The outnumbered South African Spitfire pilots flew one sortie after another, but whatever they achieved was outweighed by enemy successes. For those in the Durham Light Infantry, the experience was all too reminiscent of their time in Malta where the unit had endured nearly a year of air attacks. Then, as now, the men had been virtually powerless to fight back, having to rely instead on anti-aircraft gunners and whatever fighters could be mustered by the air force. For soldiers accustomed to facing the enemy on the ground, it was a frustrating and trying period. As in Malta, many were employed as labourers filling in bomb craters and otherwise helping to maintain the island as an air base – instead of concentrating on training in preparation for the inevitable German assault.

As a consequence of events on 18 September, the remainder of the Durham Light Infantry were transported to Kos by sea and daylight air deliveries were curtailed, but not in time to prevent two Dakotas from being dispatched from Nicosia on the morning of Sunday, the 19th. One was burnt out in a strafing attack within minutes of arrival and the wireless operator/air gunner, Sergeant Gerard Newall, killed. The other aircraft was refused permission to land and returned to Cyprus with its load. The Dakota damaged in the previous day's raid was hit again, caught fire and burnt out. Thereafter, supply flights were nearly all carried out under cover of darkness. Another South African pilot was also lost when a Spitfire flown by Lieutenant Isadore Seel crashed after failing to recover from a spin during a dogfight with Bf 109s.[7]

A new arrival on the 19th was an airfield engineer, Lieutenant Colonel W. J. McDowall. He was soon at work on a second landing ground at Lambi, inspired, no doubt, by the Dakota landing there the day before. With virtually no machinery for the job, his work force set to with picks and shovels. Until the delivery of two bulldozers a few days later, a tractor and oxen were also used to drag an improvised trammel! Nevertheless, an airstrip 1,100 yards long by 50 yards wide was ready by the morning of the 21st and by nightfall the width had been increased to 100 yards. It was an incredible feat, accomplished under the most trying conditions. The construction of a second strip, suitable for night-time landings by Dakotas, took some of the pressure off Antimachia, although its use necessitated considerable maintenance work the following day.

There was activity of a different kind in the Athens area as the *Luftwaffe* increased its bomber force. Notwithstanding Allied air attacks against enemy airfields, the *Luftwaffe* intensified its efforts against Kos during the last few days of September. Raids took on a depressingly similar pattern as enemy bombers pounded airfields and installations. On the 27th, a Spitfire was damaged at Antimachia by enemy bombers operating at an altitude beyond the range of Bofors guns which had recently been delivered and installed for airfield defence. In the course of the day, 7 (SAAF) Squadron accounted for at least one Bf 109 for three Spitfires shot down: Lieutenants Kenneth Prescott and John Hynd were killed during the first raid at about 1130 and in the afternoon Lieutenant A. L. Basson was forced to bale out over the sea, but was rescued by a caique manned by LRDG.[8] Another, unarmed, caique picked up a pilot of *IV./J.G.27* only to have him snatched at gunpoint by the crew of a German seaplane!

The next day, eight reinforcement Spitfire Vs of 74 Squadron arrived from Egypt via Cyprus; a ninth (ES204) developed engine trouble some 15 miles off Kastellorizo. Flight Lieutenant Albert 'Andy' Anderson, an experienced fighter pilot who had survived ten months in Malta in 1941–2, baled out too low for his parachute to open. His body was never found. Spitfires from both squadrons were soon in action, but again it was the hapless South Africans who came off worst when Lieutenant Taylor and Captain E. A. Rorvik were shot down. The former baled out and was rescued, and the latter (in EE786) was posted as missing.[9] On the same day, the *Luftwaffe* acknowledged the loss of a Bf 109G-6 of *III./J.G.27* (the pilot survived), although this was stated to have resulted from an engine problem.

Early on the 29th, three pilots of 74 Squadron were scrambled to intercept another raid. Flight Sergeant W. J. Wilson met three successive waves of Ju 88s over Antimachia. He was credited with shooting down one bomber in the first formation before diving through the second and third formations and damaging two more aircraft. He was then set upon by five Bf 109s, which he successfully evaded, causing two to collide, one of which allegedly fell in flames. In spite of the glowing report in the squadron Operations Record Book (ORB), *Luftwaffe* records fail to substantiate these claims: a Ju 88 of *II./K.G.6* was written off and two of the crew injured after crash landing at Larisa (Greece) with engine trouble, and at least three more Ju 88s and one Ju 87 are listed as having been damage in take-off or landing accidents. However, the destruction caused by the *Luftwaffe* is beyond doubt: Antimachia aerodrome was so damaged that two of the returning Spitfires had to land at an airstrip under construction at Tingachi salt pans. The airstrip at Lambi was also rendered unusable. Subsequent air deliveries had to be dropped by parachute, until the ground could be repaired sufficiently to allow Dakotas to land during the night of 2–3 October.

At the same time that 7 (SAAF) Squadron was being decimated on Kos, *Luftwaffe* strength in the Greece/Aegean area had increased to an estimated 362 operational aircraft.[10] The *Luftwaffe* had two good airfields on Rhodes, just 70 miles or so from Kos, and two more on Crete. There were also well-equipped bomber bases on the Greek mainland at Larisa and Salonika and in the Athens area, and dive bomber bases at Megara and Argos. As the number of German bombers in the region increased, so, too, did the risk to Allied warships. The British were disadvantaged in that most of their air and naval bases were situated far from the scene of operations. This placed an intolerable strain on destroyers, especially 'Hunt' class vessels, whose endurance was severely restricted by fuel limitations. Furthermore, effective air cover was impossible without long-range fighters due to the distances between the operational area and Allied airfields in Cyprus and at Gambut, in Libya. Not all aircraft types were affected, however, and during September, the southern Aegean was covered by frequent reconnaissance flights. Anti-shipping strikes were also undertaken and night raids carried out against land targets; airfields in Crete and Rhodes, which had received considerable reinforcements, were attacked frequently during the latter half of the month.

By 2 October, the air defence on Kos consisted of a handful of operational Spitfires. Air Force personnel numbered around 500 officers and men. Half were divided between 2901 and 2909 Squadrons of the RAF Regiment at Antimachia and Lambi. There were about 680 Army personnel on the island, including at least seventy-six officers and men of 4th Battery Light Anti-Aircraft Regiment Royal Artillery and 540 or so all ranks of the Durham Light Infantry. The latter had just been redeployed with 'A', 'B', and 'HQ' Companies and Battalion Headquarters disposed mainly in bivouac areas stretching from the northern coast south-east for nearly two kilometres to within 800 metres of Gherme (Platani). 'C' Company was allocated Kos town; the nearby landing ground at Lambi was held by the Anti-tank Platoon, and 'D' Company with two detachments of the Mortar Platoon and one section of the Carrier Platoon held Antimachia. The battalion was woefully under-equipped for its role, without its Bren gun carriers (instead, jeeps were made available for night patrols), anti-tank guns (but for some Boys anti-tank rifles) and most of its 3-inch mortars.

There were already on Kos 3,500–4,000 Italians comprising the majority of *II* and *III battaglione* (battalion) of *10° reggimento di fanteria* (infantry regiment) of *Divisione 'Regina'* with heavy weapons including a company of 81mm mortars of *I battaglione*; *252ª compagnia cannoni anticarro* (anti-tank company); *10ª compagnia mitraglieri costiera* (coastal machine-gun company) and *403ª compagnia mitraglieri ex-Milizia Volontaria per la Sicurezza Nazionale* (ex-'Blackshirts' machine-gun company). There were three units of *36° raggruppamento*: *XXXI gruppo artiglieria* (artillery group) and *LXXXII gruppo artiglieria contraerea* (anti-aircraft group), both with three additional batteries, and *136ª batteria* of *XXIX gruppo*. Also available was *295ª batteria mitragliere* (equipped with 20mm cannon) and various support units. The questionable effectiveness of Italian-manned coastal and anti-aircraft batteries meant that Kos had to rely instead on twenty-five British-manned 40mm Bofors and twenty-four 20mm Hispanos distributed mainly at Antimachia and around Kos town. Plans were afoot to improve the island's defence capabilities but any proposals were purely academic, for events were taking place that would soon place Kos firmly under German control.

CHAPTER 4

Operation 'Eisbär' 3 October 1943

ON 23 SEPTEMBER, *GENERALLEUTNANT* Friedrich-Wilhelm Müller, commanding 22. *Infanteriedivision*, was ordered by *Heeresgruppe E* [Army Group E] to make preparations for the seizure of Kos and Leros. Due to its importance as an offensive Allied air base, Kos was selected as the first objective. Müller's plan was to take the island in a surprise assault. A long, narrow beach at Marmari on the north coast was chosen as the landing site for his staff and *Kampfgruppe* [Battle Group] von Saldern, the latter commanded by *Major* Sylvester von Saldern, and comprising his own *II. Bataillon/Grenadierregiment 65 (II./Gren.Rgt.65)*, together with *III. Bataillon/Grenadierregiment 440 (III./Gren.Rgt.440*, with just 250 men), *3.* and *4. Batterien/Artillerieregiment 22 (3* and *4./Art.Rgt.22)*, *3. Batterie/Flakbataillon 22 (3./Fla.Btl.22)* and *2. Kompanie/Pionierbataillon 22 (2./Pi.Btl.22* less one *Zug)*. *II. Bataillon/Grenadierregiment 16 (II./Gren.Rgt.16)* with one *Pionier Zug*[1] under the former's CO, *Hauptmann* Philipp Aschoff, was to come ashore on the steep south coast below Point 428 (Eremita), with the primary task of destroying gun emplacements south of Platani which might otherwise be used against the main assault and to cover Kos town and port. Because the terrain was unsuitable for vehicles, the *Bataillon* 7.5cm *Paks (Panzerabwehrkanone* – anti-tank guns), tow-trucks and extra ammunition were to come ashore with *Kampfgruppe* von Saldern. Until the groups could link up, *II./Gren.Rgt.16* would have to rely on mules as their only means of transport. In order to neutralise Antimachia as an effective air base, a joint amphibious/air landing was to be made in the narrow southern coastal strip just east of Cape Tigani (today known as Paradise

Beach). The troops entrusted with the task were from *Abwehr* [military intelligence] units: *15. Kompanie (Fallschirmjäger)/4. Regiment Brandenburg (15./4.Rgt. Brandenburg)* commanded by *Oberleutnant* Oschatz and *1. Kompanie/Küstenjägerabteilung Brandenburg (1./Küstenjäger-Abt. Brandenburg)* led by *Hauptmann* Armin Kuhlmann and under whose authority the combined force, to be known as *Kampfgruppe* Kuhlmann, would operate.

As troop transports there were the steamships *Trapani, Catherine Schiaffino, Kari, Ingeborg* and the *Citta di Savona*, nine *Marinefährprähme* (*MFPs* or F-lighters) and three *Pioniersturmboote*. Escort vessels comprised the minelayers *Drache* and *Bulgaria*, five *Unterseebootjäger* (*U-Jäger* or submarine-chasers), three motorboats, two *Kriegsfischkutter* (*KFK* or motor fishing vessels) and four *G.A.-Boote* (coast defence vessels) under the command of *21. Unterseebootjagdflottille (21. U.-Jagdflottille)*, as well as three *Räumboote* (minesweepers) of *12. Räumbootflottille (12. R.-Flottille)*.

By Friday morning, 1 October 1943, the assault troops had gathered at their departure points: in Crete, *II./Gren.Rgt.16* and *Kampfgruppenführungsstab* (battle group staff officers) embarked at Heraklion, and *II./Gren.Rgt.65, 3* and *4./Art.Rgt.22, 3./Fla.Btl.22* and *2./Pi.Btl.22* at Suda. The remaining units assembled on the mainland near Athens; the amphibious element boarded their vessels at Piraeus, and *Fallschirmjägerkompanie Brandenburg* stood by to emplane at Athens-Tatoi aerodrome.

Embarkation was completed that evening and the vessels departed to rendezvous the next day in the Cyclades. There, the relatively inexperienced F-lighter crews carried out landing exercises in a last-minute effort to prepare them for the daunting task ahead. In the afternoon of the 2nd, the force divided and set deception courses for Rhodes and Ikaria. It was precisely the right move. Although the Germans were aware that their presence had been detected by Allied air reconnaissance, there was no way of knowing that the British had already fooled themselves into thinking that the convoy was Rhodes-bound. Only after dark did the convoy change direction towards Kos. An unexpected squall resulted in rough seas and a miserable passage and threatened to jeopardise the entire operation. However, early on the 3rd the weather improved. The convoy proceeded to their designated disembarkation points north and south of Kos, unimpeded either by Allied warships or submarines.

Late on 2 October, a signal was received by Force 292 from the then

Senior British Naval Officer (SBNO) in the Aegean, Captain Edmund Baker, RN, stating that during the afternoon an enemy convoy, including three transports, had been reported steering east south of Naxos. It was assumed that the vessels were heading for Rhodes. That night, five Dakotas of 216 Squadron took off from Lambi after offloading supplies. They left just in time. At 0300 on the 3rd, Major C. F. Blagden took a telephone call from RAF Headquarters at Antimachia. He was informed that an enemy convoy had been sighted at 1120 on 2 October approximately 12 miles south of Melos, heading east at 12 knots. Blagden could not have known that this was the flotilla from Suda. He, too, misinterpreted the enemy's intentions:

> Assuming the course and speed to have remained constant this should have brought the convoy to Rhodes during the night 2/3 October. I roused Colonel Kenyon immediately and passed on the information. After some discussion and in view of information contained in recent Force Sitreps [situation reports] coupled with the fact that no further news of the convoy had been received after 1120 hours on 2 October, in spite of ideal reconnaissance weather, Colonel Kenyon decided that it was a Rhodes reinforcement. I was in agreement – no action was taken other than repeating the message to Leros.[2]

For Kenyon, all was about to be made horribly clear:

> A few minutes later, Italian HQ asked if we were expecting a convoy, as shipping had been sighted near the salt pans. Unfortunately, much shipping arrived without notice in Cos [Kos], and we were expecting supplies. I decided however that we must risk that, and ordered the Italians to open fire. This they did very promptly, but without any effect.[3]

The first wave of *Kampfgruppe* von Saldern landed by *MFP* on schedule at 0500 hours.[4] After encountering minimal resistance *II./Gren.Rgt.65* established a beachhead while the F-lighters returned to the transports waiting with the next wave south of Pserimos. In *5. Kompanie* of *II./Gren. Rgt.65*, *Feldwebel* Gustav Wehrs had been nominated to supervise the transhipment of his soldiers:

> The three *Fährprähme* left first and after a while the sound of fighting could be heard coming from Marmari on the island of Kos – it was

still dark at this point. Our 'barge' anchored and had to wait until a *Fährprahm* returned. It came alongside and we began to transfer from the relatively high *Trapani* onto the flat *Fährprahm* down below which kept moving to and fro in the waves. With an MP [sub-machine-gun] or a rifle hanging around the neck, one had to climb down the rope ladder (or Jacob's ladder) on the outside of the ship and then try to pick the right moment to leap onto this wobbly thing. Surprisingly, it worked quite well; even with our lack of practice.[5]

From just offshore, *UJ 2110* and *UJ 2111* provided supporting fire and other escort vessels covered the area in smoke. Such was the speed of the German advance that six Spitfires at Tingachi salt pans were captured intact. Five pilots of 74 Squadron and three ground crew of 7 (SAAF) Squadron who fled to Kos town were advised to leave by the harbour master and taken on board the Italian water boat *Adda*. They were only just in time, for as soon as the vessel was clear, the jetty was destroyed by a direct hit.[6]

Troops of 1st Battalion The Durham Light Infantry had stood-to at 0445 as usual, when British Headquarters telephoned with news of two unidentified landing craft approaching Marmari. The commanding officer, Lieutenant Colonel R. F. Kirby, had recently been hospitalised with a knee infection and in his absence the unit was being run by the battalion second-in-command, Major Hugh Vaux. He readied the counter-attack force (predominantly 'A' and 'B' Companies) and dispatched the Carrier Platoon, under Captain George Sivewright, on a mobile patrol to the Marmari area. Shortly afterwards, the platoon commander's jeep ran into a burst of machine-gun fire. The result was spectacular: the rounds slammed home, causing the driver to lose control of the vehicle which somersaulted off the road in a cloud of dust. Minutes later, an NCO returned to report to Major Vaux that enemy forces had indeed come ashore in the Marmari area and were being engaged by the Carrier Platoon and that Sivewright's jeep had been shot up with unknown result.[7] In the face of superior odds, the Carrier Platoon broke contact and withdrew eastward along the main Antimachia–Kos road.

At 0610 'B' Company of the Durham Light Infantry was ordered to take up a defensive position astride the main road in the Ingurlichi region (west of Platani); 'HQ' Company was positioned to cover the ground north between 'B' Company and the coast; 'A' Company (with two officers and forty men) was held in reserve in the Andisli region (between Ingurlichi and Kos town); 'C' Company was held in reserve in Kos and Battalion Headquarters was located in an olive grove north-west of Platani.

With daylight came the first sorties by aircraft from both sides. All four aircraft returned from an initial low-level strike by 46 Squadron. The next attack by the Royal Air Force was carried out at about 0718 by three machines of 227 Squadron, one of which was shot down in flames. Just over an hour later, seven Beaufighters of 252 Squadron braved an intense anti-aircraft barrage to bomb and strafe shipping; four aircraft were damaged. Two aircraft of 89 Squadron and another of 46 were en route home after another attack when the latter was shot down and crashed off the Turkish coast, taking the pilot and unit CO, Wing Commander George Reid, to his death.[8]

The ferry lighter handlers were persuaded by attacking Beaufighters to commence their run-in prematurely, with the result that *Feldwebel* Wehrs found himself with only part of his *Kompanie* before the troops were eventually reunited:

> We reached the English field hospital which was based at Marmari. One medical officer stood outside with his arms crossed and asked cockily in German: 'What do you want from me?' 'To become my prisoner,' I replied. Later this field hospital proved very useful for us, the two surgeons deployed there taking care of all casualties.[9]

At around 0900, *III./Gren.Rgt.440* began to arrive, enabling *II./ Gren. Rgt.65* to push east. As they moved inland, the Germans silenced each gun battery until there remained only one whose fire was poorly co-ordinated and largely ineffective. The Germans also seized the Italian command post on Point 211 (Profeta Elia).

At Marmari, more and more troops poured ashore along with artillery and heavy weapons. On the south coast, 5. and 8. *Kompanien* of *II./ Gren. Rgt.16* arrived in two F-lighters, one of which temporarily ran aground, resulting in a delayed turn-around and late transhipment of 6. *Kompanie* (less 2. *Zug*) from *Citta di Savona*. During the run-in, the landing craft was attacked by four Beaufighters, which met with well-aimed anti-aircraft fire. 2. *Zug* and 7. *Kompanie* followed at 0800. Defensive artillery fire was inaccurate and failed to deter the troops during a tiring ascent on to a ridge dominated by Point 428 (Eremita), where they were presented with an impressive view of the rugged landscape separating them from their main objective two miles away. The batteries at Platani could be seen firing on the northern beaches; shells were also impacting on the Eremita ridge in the vicinity of 8. *Kompanie*.

An erroneous report of an enemy landing at Cape Foca had been relayed to the majority of the Durham Light Infantry, following which 'C' Company was deployed against the supposed threat east of Kos town. Due to a breakdown in communications, 'D' Company at Antimachia aerodrome could not be contacted and would remain out of touch for the duration of the battle. Before long, the area between Battalion Headquarters and the forward companies was taking mortar fire from the heights above Platani. At first, the explosions were mistaken for Italian shells falling short; it was then realised that enemy forces were in position on high ground south-west of the town.[10]

From his vantage point on the southern heights, *Hauptmann* Aschoff was ideally placed to assess the situation before organising his men into battle formation to attack Platani's batteries. 6. *Kompanie* was selected to lead the assault covered on the right flank by 5. *Kompanie* and supported by 7. *Kompanie* on its left, with 8. *Kompanie* following up as reserve on the extreme left. The troops began their descent under fire towards their objective.

Having discharged himself from hospital, Lieutenant Colonel Kirby had arrived on a motor cycle at Battalion Headquarters and resumed command. After inspecting 'B' Company area, the CO ordered 'A' Company to move 1,200 metres south-west to strengthen the line held by 'B' and 'HQ' Companies along Wadi (Valley) Dermen. At 0900, approximately eighteen *Stukas* attacked Platani and 'A' Company. The bombardment was closely followed by an infantry assault by the forward elements of *Major* von Saldern's *II./Gren.Rgt.65*. 'A' Company was pushed back 800 metres nearer Platani, with an estimated 50 per cent casualties. Subsequently, a joint British/Italian defence of the area was implemented between the company commander, Captain J. G. G. Gray, and *Capitano* Carlo Orlandi of *10° reggimento di fanteria*.

Having been delayed by rough seas and forced to abandon one boat,

Hauptmann Armin Kuhlmann's *Küstenjäger* had landed in daylight and under light artillery fire. Consequently, *Kampfgruppe* Kuhlmann was unable to secure the drop zone in time for the arrival soon after 0700 of the *Fallschirmjäger* who were subjected to heavy fire during and after their descent.[11] Unable to raise Battalion Headquarters by wireless or land-line, Captain J. H. Thorpe, commanding 'D' Company of the Durham Light Infantry at Antimachia, had no option but to send a situation report by dispatch rider. The messenger, Private James Buglass, was killed en route.

At approximately 0840 the *Brandenburger* linked up and subsequently repulsed an Italian counter-attack from the west. A number of paratroopers were dispatched towards the direction of enemy threat, while the majority of *Kampfgruppe* Kuhlmann gathered for an attack along the main road towards Antimachia. Advancing in the face of heavy fire from batteries in the Antimachia area, the *Brandenburger* overran infantry and gun positions until they reached a line three and a half kilometres west of the aerodrome. Here, they paused to regroup and to await ammunition resupply, forcing Italians captured en route to act as porters.[12]

Generalleutnant Müller and his staff were ferried ashore at 1000 hours. At about the same time, the transport flotilla waiting off Pserimos came under artillery fire. The vessels withdrew north where they continued to offload men and equipment. By evening most had completed their task and departed.

In the meantime, it was the turn of 'B' and 'HQ' Companies of the Durham Light Infantry to come up against *II./Gren.Rgt.65*. The German reliance on air support and heavy weapons had a predictably devastating effect. Snipers also took their toll after infiltrating the walled olive-grove area bordering the Dermen valley. To maintain the position, Lieutenant Colonel Kirby transferred thirty men of the Anti-Tank Platoon south from Lambi to the sector held by 'A' and 'B' Companies, and Colonel Kenyon moved across a detachment of the RAF Regiment (which turned up at the wrong location). When jittery troops in 'B' Company reported seeing tanks – actually German half-tracks – four Bofors guns were manhandled from Lambi to cover the Antimachia–Kos road. Between midday and 1400 two platoons of 'B' Company were overrun and the company commander, Captain J. E. Stafford, withdrew the survivors to the defence line of Battalion Headquarters. Half an hour later, Major Vaux ordered 'HQ' Company to fall back on Battalion Headquarters. Kirby, who was visiting companies and attempting to contact Italian forces, did not return until 1545 whereupon Vaux was dispatched to assist Lieutenant Colonel W. J. McDowall in the defence of Lambi and the northern flank.

In the Eremita area, *II./Gren.Rgt.16* had had a harrowing time. The move towards the northern plain was made under increasingly accurate artillery fire. As they dashed from cover to cover, the troops suffered their first casualties. Among the rugged, pine-covered slopes, it took 6. *Kompanie* two hours to reach their rendezvous with 7. *Kompanie*. 5. *Kompanie* had drifted east until it was separated from 6. *Kompanie* by enemy strongpoints and a nearby ammunition dump (believed to have been to the north of the ancient ruins of the Asklepieion). Furthermore, there were infantry positions just 200 metres along the line of advance of 6. *Kompanie*. Before the primary objective could be achieved, the immediate problem had to be resolved. With the support of all available heavy weapons and with 2. *Zug* providing covering fire and protection on the right, 1. *Zug* was tasked with spearheading a right-flanking attack against the ammunition dump.

The assault began at 1350 with the troops covering 150 metres before faltering in the face of heavy fire. One of the attacking infantry, *Gefreiter* Wiegard, was shot in the stomach and head and fell just short of the objective. The situation dictated a drastic approach and the troops were ordered to swing hard right towards the line of defence and punch straight through the dump: 2. *Zug* and support weapons were redeployed accordingly; *Gruppe* Kalsbach of 1. *Zug*, which had led the attack so far, was to maintain its present position, and two *Gruppen* under the command of *Feldwebel* Meyer were tasked with penetrating the dump via a depression that was covered by defensive mortar fire. The latter gained ground as far as a wire perimeter fence. Purely by chance, a gap was found, allowing Meyer to gain entry. 3. *Zug* and elements of 2. *Zug* followed, with machine-guns providing cover fire against defending machine-guns situated no more than 200 metres away. During the attack, *Unteroffizier* Bullman shot up an anti-tank gun, thereby preventing the crew from coming into action. Immediately afterwards, Bullman was seriously wounded by a mortar bomb. With 3. *Zug* as reserve, 1. *Zug* moved to seize the high ground within the compound, covered on the right by 2. *Zug*. Mortars provided fire support as the assault troops cleared ammunition huts and took care of resistance with hand grenades and explosives until the defending forces finally gave way.

If the Germans thought the battle was won they were immediately proved wrong. Their opponents, whoever they were, were brave and resolute men.[13] After withdrawing only a short distance, they halted along the edge of an olive grove behind the camp where two machine-guns were sited to prevent a follow-up attack. The first attempt to break through was made by *1. Zug* under *Leutnant* Schallau and involved a simple yet totally unexpected tactic. Accompanied by encouraging cries of 'Hurrah!' the troops charged, taking their enemy completely by surprise and making considerable headway. However, any further progress was thwarted with well-directed fire from just 70 metres away. The *Kompanie* was caught inside the camp, prevented from continuing by the perimeter fence and with mortar bombs landing dangerously close to ammunition crates. A mortar crew was ordered forward to destroy the defensive position. During the move, *Obergefreiter* Bielmeier was killed. He fell in open ground, making it impossible for anyone to reach him, or to recover the mortar bipod he had been carrying. Another strategy was called for: covered by machine-guns, *3. Zug* dashed forward in order to reinforce *1. Zug*. This resulted in several casualties, prompting the survivors to continue along a ditch and through drainage pipes in an effort to avoid further losses. In the meantime, the redoubtable *Feldwebel* Meyer had gone ahead and found a breach in the wire which he extended while under fire. He and *Leutnant* Schallau squeezed through and made for cover behind a nearby tool shed. Both *Züge* followed. They were joined two hours later by *2. Zug*. Their adversaries' machine-guns were still aimed towards the ammunition dump and away from the gathered German troops who were now in visual contact with *7. Kompanie*. To the right, the sound of firing indicated the whereabouts of *5. Kompanie* whose troops were also in contact with those defending the dump.

Offshore, Beaufighter crews persevered with near-suicidal attacks against German shipping. During a low-level strike in the afternoon by 46 Squadron, one aircraft was seen to hit its target, only to disappear in the explosion. Two more aircraft were severely damaged by *Flak* and came down in the sea off Turkey. Only one Beaufighter managed to return to base.[14]

West of Antimachia the German advance had resumed at 1400 with a *Zug* of *Fallschirmjäger* north of the main road and another of *Küstenjäger* on the south side. Italians who had surrendered a 7.5cm anti-aircraft battery supported the attack by firing at AA positions at the aerodrome. Taking advantage of the many ravines in the area, the paratroopers succeeded by late afternoon in reaching the high ground just north of their objective. Prevented by communication problems from contacting their comrades south of the road, the paratroopers launched a solo attack and by 1810 they had secured the airfield and taken thirty-three British prisoners.

According to Company Sergeant Major W. Carr of the Durham Light Infantry, at 1730 Captain Thorpe issued orders to destroy all documents immediately prior to withdrawing 'D' Company Headquarters from just north of the aerodrome to a nearby valley. At about this time, *Luftwaffe* bombers carried out the first of two raids on the aerodrome – to the consternation of German ground forces in the area, who suffered one casualty as a result of 'friendly fire'. Carr was part of a small group caught up in the second attack:

> At 1750, five 87s came over. They were diving to drop their bombs when the forward troops of Jerry put up a Verey light (white) so they banked and dropped the bombs, seven in all, a distance of six yards from us. The company commander was wounded in the small of the back – left side. The shrapnel passed through his web belt cutting the left buckle; wound did not bleed very much; put on a field dressing. This was the last raid of the day.[15]

At their beachhead at Cape Tigani, German troops were also in action as they held out against a series of infantry assaults supported by artillery fire against their hilltop positions on Annunziata. To the north, *III./Gren.Rgt.440* had established a line from the coastal region of Cara Mustafaina (west of Marmari) inland to Point 66 (Lacu) and north-east to Point 211. Pili, and the neighbouring hamlets of San Nicola and San Giorgio were taken without resistance and at 1300 *Kampfgruppe* Müller ordered the *Bataillon* to push towards Antimachia in order to link up with *Kampfgruppe* Kuhlmann. As an additional precaution, the *Bataillon* was to secure a plateau (Point 145) just east of the town. The task was carried out by a *Zug* of *10./Gren.Rgt.440* with mobile anti-aircraft and anti-tank guns.

In spite of strong opposition, *II./Gren.Rgt.65* had made good progress east along the coast road. Allied troops were powerless to defend themselves against German artillery and air support and accordingly Lieutenant Colonel Kirby issued orders to pull back at 1715 and to form a defence line around Kos. 'A' Company could not be contacted and remained in position until nightfall, before conducting an independent withdrawal to Kos town. This left *II./Gren.Rgt.65* holding a line from Platani, north-east to the town outskirts and north-west to the coast at Lambi. There were few options for the British holding the Kos perimeter: they could defend their positions to the last man; fall back on Kos and conduct a fighting withdrawal along the coastal corridor as far as Cape Foca; take to the hills to continue a pointless guerrilla action, or surrender. At the port of Kos, the crews of three tank landing craft (LCTs) were spared any such choice when their offer to help with the defence was declined by the Army. It was therefore decided to leave under cover of darkness for Turkish waters. Sub Lieutenant R. E. Fletcher was the commander of LCT 3:

> At approximately 1730 we were informed by soldiers from the firing line that the enemy was about one mile to our east and advancing rapidly. This information, together with the fact that our position was being ranged by mortar and 75mm fire, decided commanding officers [of the landing craft] to leave then rather than await the remaining one and a half hours until dusk.[16]

All three boats had experienced ongoing mechanical problems and due to a severe petrol leak, LCT 3 could not be started. A few men tried to get the craft underway, while the majority of the crew was ordered on to LCT 114. However, when the engine caught fire, Fletcher judged the situation to be hopeless and ordered all weapons to be dismantled. Small arms were disposed of by being thrown overboard; code books were destroyed and the sea-cocks opened in order to scuttle the craft. The motor mechanic, who had been issued with two grenades which were to have been placed in the engine room, had disappeared. Consequently, LCT 3 was later captured relatively intact by the enemy. The last of the crew transferred to LCT 139 which left under fire and with mortar bombs sending up huge geysers of seawater around LCT 3.

For RAF Lance Corporal William Johnston, it was a day he would never forget. With others from 123 Maintenance Unit he had earlier left their headquarters at the Asklepieion and attempted to reach Lambi. After surviving enemy mortar fire, strafing and bombing by Ju 87 *Stukas*, he decided to return to the Asklepieion to blow up nearby petrol and ammunition dumps. His efforts were interrupted by the arrival of *Stukas* whose bombs at least partially destroyed the site. Unable to add to the destruction, Johnston again set off towards Lambi. On the way, he joined a nine-man sniper group under Lance Corporal Newton of the Durham Light Infantry. For the next three hours the men held a position between Tingachi and Lambi, before they were forced to fall back on Kos town. By 1700 they were just 200 yards from the shore, where they remained for another one and a half hours. Eventually, with the enemy closing in, the men took advantage of their only chance of escape and ran to board a departing launch (HSL 2517).

For some, the sight of the departing vessels was altogether too much. Flying Officer B. W. Purcell had been employed on flying control duties with 243 Wing when he found himself in an unfamiliar and, one suspects, unwelcome role as an infantryman:

> I was ordered to look after a small party of men, and we established ourselves in a trench to give, if possible, all aid and covering fire to the Durham Light Infantry as they retired. In effect, however, this was not practical as the German tactics were to push back the troops by *Stuka* dive bombers and then their snipers would advance until the position was secure for a general advance. The *Stuka* bombing was intense and between 1600–1645 I obtained permission to retire. I split up my party, half to a trench with the DLI, and the remainder by a farm yard just outside the town. We were gradually driven back and I was attracted to shooting from the beach. There, several of our own soldiers were firing rifles trying to attract the attention of the RAF HSL [High Speed Launch] and seaplane tender who were evacuating, also there were two LCTs and one schooner. It looked like a general evacuation. I semaphored the launches but they cannot have seen me. Men were trying to paddle out on doors, pieces of wood, etc. I tried it myself and found it impossible. I ordered the men if they were leaving the Island to bury their rifles in the sand and take the bolts with them. I also ordered them to try and make the harbour and escape if possible in a small boat and some of them managed this.[17]

II./Gren.Rgt.16 had met with a varying degree of success. After forging ahead, *8. Kompanie* took the first battery at Platani during the afternoon, but near the Asklepieion the three remaining *Kompanien* continued to face tough resistance. As *6./Gren.Rgt.16* assembled south of Platani for a renewed attack, three *Stukas* were directed with signal flares on to the target. Immediately after the last bomb exploded, the *Kompanie* pushed forward 200 metres to the edge of the olive grove. The defending troops were undeterred. *1. Zug* broke left in an effort to avoid their fire, and those in *3. Zug* were forced to take cover behind a wall before resuming their advance at a crawl. In an attempt to circle their objective, the latter were redirected left into a ravine and advanced some 300 metres to within about 100 metres of a water reservoir – and another camp, with its entrance protected by bunkers and fortified towers.

Shortly before nightfall the *Grenadiere* launched one more attack against two well-defended positions 75 metres to their front and right and another 50 metres left. *2.* and *4. Züge* were tasked with securing the left and right flanks respectively, and *1. Zug* was ordered to cover the front and right. *3. Zug* was nominated for the assault. Just before Zero Hour, the *Kompanie* assembly area was mortared, resulting in such heavy casualties among *1.* and *2. Züge* that *3. Zug* had to be reassigned to fill the gaps in case there was a follow-up by infantry. No such attack materialised, allowing the wounded to be recovered and evacuated to the rear. Before the survivors could mount a renewed offensive they were pre-empted by a sudden withdrawal by their enemy from the olive grove. Taking full advantage of this unexpected development, the Germans inflicted heavy casualties among the fleeing troops. With the enemy threat removed from their right flank, further *Kompanie* attacks were postponed until the following day. Night-time positions were allocated and reconnaissance patrols sent out to establish contact with *5.* and *7. Kompanien*. At Platani, all the gun positions were taken by early evening. Fighting continued in the town, but by 2030 *8. Kompanie* was able to link up with *II./Gren.Rgt.65*.

That evening, Kirby called for an 'O' Group for 1900 hours. Five officers gathered near Paleologou Square in Kos and orders had just started when the place was shaken by the explosions of two mortar bombs. The CO was hit by shrapnel in the face and left knee; OC 'HQ' Company, Major K. M. W. Leather, was severely wounded in the left arm; OC 'B'

Company, Captain J. E. Stafford, sustained shrapnel wounds to the right thigh, and the quartermaster, Captain Frederick Bush, received fatal back injuries. All were rushed to the civil hospital. Having once again resumed command, Major Vaux was told by Colonel Kenyon to prepare for the possible arrival of British paratroopers and an infantry battalion. It was therefore proposed to withdraw to the hills south-east of the town to await reinforcements.

The British began their withdrawal shortly before midnight covered by part of the Anti-Tank Platoon and two platoons of 'C' Company under Captain F. W. Armitage. Each group of twenty or so passed through Kos to a rendezvous at Due Melini where Regimental Sergeant Major G. Flannigan was waiting with a resupply of food and ammunition. The men continued to a crossroads three kilometres further on before finally turning south towards Simpetro (Sympetres) heights. The ultimate objective was Asfendiu, where it was hoped to obtain a resupply at an Italian food dump.

In Kos town, Flying Officer Purcell had teamed up with a flight lieutenant. In a commandeered rowing boat and using two pieces of wood as oars, they paddled for an hour and a half before the shrapnel-damaged boat finally sank. With no other choice, the two men swam the remaining distance to Turkey.

The next day, *Kampfgruppe* Müller continued in its efforts to secure the three objectives: the town and port of Kos; the south-east region and Antimachia aerodrome. Apparently unaware that the British had abandoned their positions, at 0800 the *Luftwaffe* resumed its attacks, with *Stukas* concentrating on Kos and heavy bombers pounding gun batteries south-east of the town. The positions which had held up much of *II./Gren.Rgt.16* were also designated as a priority artillery target. With fire support provided by *3.* and *4./Art.Rgt.22*; *II./Gren.Rgt.65* and *II./Gren. Rgt.16* launched a lightning assault, and by 0900 had seized the town and nearby Lambi airfield. Among those captured were Kirby and an '*Oberst*' [colonel] in command of the Italians (presumably *Colonnello* Felice Leggio). *II./Gren.Rgt.65* cleared the area north of the town as far as the coast with hardly any resistance. After regrouping, *II./Gren.Rgt.16* pushed east along the British path of retreat towards Forbici Point (Cape Psalidi). The Germans were delayed by Italians near Cape Foca (probably in the area of Point 260/Crotiri) and by the British rearguard whose troops had withdrawn at 0400. However, by about 1800 *II./Gren.Rgt.16* was able to report that the coastal strip was clear as far as Cape Foca.

During the retreat, many were overwhelmed by the overnight trek and arduous ascent. Men who had fought bravely the previous day now seemed only too happy to be taken prisoner, as *Oberfeldwebel* Walter Lünsmann of *6./Gren.Rgt.16* recalled:

> We had reached Kos town. Now we received orders to comb through the mountains above the town. I suffered from malaria and was hardly able to go on. I sat down on a rock. Suddenly, something flashed in front of me – about 30 metres away. Shooting from the hip with my MP, I moved toward that point. There were about 40 English soldiers in a firing trench. They had attached a white flag to a rifle and were surrendering.[18]

Colonel Kenyon had joined a group led by an officer in the Durham Light Infantry:

> As soon as we reached the southern slopes of Simpetro and Truzzuli, I saw numerous parties emerging ahead and making off westwards. These parties were made up of the poorer elements of the garrison; many men had thrown off equipment and arms. Fatigue was telling, and in the absence of effective junior leadership, the men were gradually heading downhill. I was not disturbed by this, as our future task would clearly suffer from the inclusion of unsuitable troops in our force.[19]

In attempting to locate who were those following, Kenyon became separated and found himself alone and attracting the attention of a sniper:

> By about 1700 hours, moving in and out among the hilltops, I was approaching Asfendiu. The sniper had left me, and everything was quiet. I was able to locate myself accurately from my view of the winding road leading up to Asfendiu. I therefore decided it was time to leave the high ground and start for Asfendiu. The ground was precipitous in places, and I was not sorry on rounding a corner to find a group of Italians sitting about. As I was negotiating for a guide to take me on, I was gripped from behind and found myself literally in the hands of

a German sentry who had been sitting amongst the Italians whose surrender he had accepted.[20]

In the south-west, 9. *Kompanie* of *III./Gren.Rgt.440* had been left to secure the northern beachhead while 11. *Kompanie* advanced overnight to Point 145. In the morning, contact was established with a *Fallschirmjäger* reconnaissance patrol in Antimachia village and *Kampfgruppe* Kuhlmann came under the orders of *Hauptmann* Erwin Dörr, CO of *III./Gren.Rgt.440*. *Hauptmann* Kuhlmann and his *Küstenjäger* were tasked with holding the aerodrome, while *III.Gren.Rgt.440* (less 9. *Kompanie*), together with the *Fallschirmjäger* and supported by heavy weapons of *II./Gren.Rgt.16* and *3./Fla.Btl.22*, advanced south-west towards Kefalos which was defended by around 200 men under *Tenente* Francesco Di Giovanni of *10° reggimento di fanteria*. Their progress was delayed by fighting in the hills two kilometres north-east of the town, but by 1400 Kefalos was in German hands. The entire south-western region was cleared by nightfall.

The previous day, Captain Clark of MI14 had supervised the departure from Cardamena of several boatloads of evacuees; among those to escape was the CO of 7 (SAAF) Squadron, Major Cornelius van Vliet. To end the exodus, a motorised *Zug* of *II./Gren.Rgt.65* was dispatched with heavy weapons to clear the coastal area. According to Müller:

This resulted in the capture and disarming of several hundred English who had planned to escape from Cardamena in fishing boats.[21]

Among those who had earlier sought refuge in an orchard in the area was RAF Flight Sergeant R. S. Taylor. After spending a night in the open, he awoke at dawn on the 4th:

Me 109s flew directly over us and one Me 110 just scraped the top of the trees where we were hiding. We then saw two Me 109s carrying one big bomb each fly down the beach from the direction of the hills towards Cardamena ... Soon after, *Stukas* came and dive bombed the orchard; this raid lasted about five minutes. We were taking shelter behind a wall and men and women were running about with children all around us. There was a few minutes pause when a bigger number of *Stukas* came and dropped a lot of bombs on the same target, but we had split up to find better shelter this time. This heavy raid lasted about

15 minutes and bombs were bursting all around us. The air was filled with sand which smelt foul and I stumbled through it and then ran for the shelter of the hills. Bullets were flying about; some I could hear whistling close by, but keeping to the trees I got to the bottom of the hills. The peasants gave me water and an Italian water bottle.[22]

Equipped with the rubber inner tube from a car tyre, Taylor moved into the hills with the intention of making for the beach and swimming to Turkey. Before he could put his plan into action, he witnessed the mayhem on Cardamena Plain. His attention was drawn by the devastating effects of one gun in particular:

I could see it flash when it fired and shells burst at the bottom of the hills amongst men under trees with white flags. Then it fired at Italians about 100 yards from me who were making a raft and they ran. Men were running along the hillside above me and machine gun bullets whistled above my head. About ten minutes after dark all went quiet and I lay down under a big rock to sleep. I awoke later with the sound of aircraft flying about and saw flares up and down the beach. I decided not to try to swim with the rubber tube.[23]

Isolated parties of Allied soldiers and airmen remained in hiding on Kos for days after the battle. On 6 October, *Kampgruppe* Müller signalled *Heeresgruppe E*:

Mopping up of the island continued. Day passed quietly. Number of prisoners has increased to 886 English including 46 officers, 3,000 Italians. 89 Italian officers shot.[24]

Among those executed in compliance with the *Führer*'s directive, was *Colonnello* Felice Leggio. For the Italians, Kos was the latest in a series of defeats. For their new allies, the British, it was a minor disaster. Müller records that his battle group ultimately took prisoner 3,145 'Badoglio Italians' and 1,388 British together with forty guns ranging from 7.5 to 14.9 cm, sixteen anti-aircraft guns (2 to 4 cm), one LCT, twelve fishing boats, a luxury yacht (for the personal use of the *Generalleutnant*) eleven intact aircraft and enough infantry weapons for 5,000 men, in addition to vast stocks of ammunition, petrol and provisions. German losses amounted to fourteen or fifteen dead and at least seventy wounded (it is not stated whether these figures include five killed and eighteen wounded during naval operations on 3 October).

On 4 October, a composite patrol ('X1') of the LRDG under a New Zealander, Captain R. A. Tinker, was evacuated by caique after several days on Pserimos. All except Driver Al Lawrence, who was presumed captured, reached nearby Kalymnos in time for a general withdrawal that night; 350 or so Italians were left to their inevitable fate. On the 7th, the garrison surrendered without a fight enabling *III./Gren.Rgt.440* and *Küstenjägerkompanie Brandenburg* to occupy the island in preparation for the next phase of Müller's plan: Operation *'Leopard'*, the invasion of Leros.

CHAPTER 5

The War on Land   October 1943

At the end of the first day of the battle for Kos, Captain J. H. Thorpe, CSM W. Carr and Private Proudlock of the Durham Light Infantry had travelled by jeep towards Cardamena. After halting for the night, they reached the town outskirts in the morning of Monday, 4 October, to find some forty stragglers, including four officers of the Royal Artillery. Dissuaded by attacking *Stukas* from proceeding further, Captain Thorpe and his two comrades left soon after, initially heading for the foothills north of Cardamena and eventually reaching the heights overlooking Asfendiu. During the next few days they were looked after by Greeks whose selflessness would have cost them dearly if discovered by the Germans. It was a familiar story all over the island.

Another party managed to escape under fortuitous circumstances when, during the night of 3–4 October, Wing Commander R. C. Love led the men to an RV on the south coast:

> About an hour before dawn, we detected a small boat lying offshore within about a hundred yards of our position. We watched very carefully and detected a number of men coming ashore on what appeared to be some form of raft. We were very doubtful as to whether the party was British or German and after considering the problem for a while, I decided to approach one man who appeared to be standing as sentry on the beach. I discovered that it was a small detachment of SBS under Captain [Walter] Milner-Barry. He told me that he had been sent to discover the situation on Cos and to carry out some demolitions if possible.[1]

Milner-Barry remained to arrange the evacuation of other evaders, while Love and his party were taken in the tiny SBS caique (LS 2) to Turkey. During the next few days, the SBS rescued many including a number of officers, among them Lieutenant Colonel Orme, Royal Artillery; Squadron Leader J. C. F. Hayter, commanding 74 Squadron; Squadron Leader Morgan (33 Sector Operations Room); Major H. M. Vaux and Lieutenant Colonel W. J. McDowall.

On the 5th, Thorpe's party were asked to identify themselves in a message delivered by a Greek woman from 'Private Walters of the SAS Regiment'. Carr sent a reply, stating that they were three English soldiers, but nothing further was heard. That morning, Flight Sergeant R. S. Taylor was found by two boys from whom he learned about other '*Inglesi*' in the vicinity. The youngsters departed and returned later in the day with a SNCO and two soldiers of the Royal Artillery and nine members of the RAF Regiment.[2] Subsequently, the men were joined by RAF Sergeant Philpotts who led Taylor to the hiding place of two RAF officers, Flight Lieutenant Allan and Flying Officer C. T. Hyland. Hyland revealed that he had established contact with a 'commando' and was hopeful that a boat might be arranged to evacuate them from the island within the next two nights. This was not to be. At about this time, a member of the SBS patrol, Private Watler (undoubtedly the same Private 'Walters' referred to by Carr and, possibly, also Hyland's contact), was taken prisoner and incarcerated in Kos castle.

On 10 October, Thorpe's party agreed to split up. The officer's wound had become gangrenous and Proudlock was suffering from suspected sandfly fever. Carr left them in the care of some Greeks and then struck out alone towards Cardamena. Two days later, he was taken to a house where he met Taylor and his party. Carr was quick to ingratiate himself, as Taylor recalled:

> A DLI Sergeant Major came up to the house with some peasants and joined us. He had a tin of tea and shared it out; the first hot drink we had so far.[3]

Carr seemed less than impressed by the conduct of the RAF officers who, having taken up residence in a nearby cave, gave the impression that they wanted little to do with anybody else. On 14 October, Hyland paid the men a visit and was told that a shepherd was to lead them to a boat that night. He left to fetch Flight Lieutenant Allan, but by the time the officers arrived, the others had already gone. According to Taylor:

> We waited for the Sergeant AA and DLI CSM, who had gone off earlier to see a peasant about food. The Sergeant and CSM returned, but the officers had still not arrived and as the shepherd was in a hurry and it being a five mile walk across the mountains we left.[4]

When the expected boat failed to materialise, the men were taken to a cave in the hills. Taylor maintains that on the 17th he dispatched a shepherd with instructions for the officers to follow him to their location. The message does not appear to have reached its destination. Hyland merely states that on the 19th, they encountered a Greek and an Italian soldier who told them that a party of British soldiers were in hiding on the coast. The officers were led to 'the party that left us on the 14th' and were informed that the men had been obliged to do so when the departure time was unexpectedly brought forward. It must have seemed to everybody that they were destined to remain on Kos for ever, until a Greek offered to take a makeshift raft to Turkey and fetch help. It was a journey fraught with danger and took eighteen hours to complete. Presumably as a result of this brave effort, shortly before 0200 on 22 October, a caique arrived and embarked a total of seventeen Army and RAF personnel, eight Italians and two Greeks. The vessel reached Turkish waters without incident a few hours later.

It was at Leros where the enemy's main efforts were next concentrated. According to Italian sources, there were thirty-two raids involving 410 sorties by the *Luftwaffe* in the week following the fall of Kos.[5] On Tuesday morning, 5 October, Lakki was attacked by 29 Ju 88s, 34 Ju 87s and four He 111s which dropped a total of 67 tons of high explosive. A vivid account of what it was like to be caught up in such a raid is provided by an unidentified member of the Long Range Desert Group (LRDG) who arrived from Kalymnos on the night of 4–5 October:

> Our orders were to evacuate to Leros using any local form of transport. All that evening [4th] we loaded caiques with stores in preparation for our move at night. By dark all was ready, and our curious looking fleet of motley craft crept silently into the darkness. The night was calm and one by one the various small craft drew alongside the quay in

the main harbour at Leros. The men were tired out, but it was decided to get the stores unloaded so that the ships could be dispersed at dawn. By dawn all was unloaded on to the quay but the shambles of kit and equipment was awful ... We did not know why we had come to Leros again, and the CO had no news. He had left us to try and get some orders and shortly afterwards we heard the drone of bombers and the deep crack of heavy AA guns. Our next sensation was of terrific machine gun fire, whipped up in a fury and joined by rifle fire, until it reached a shattering crescendo, then a high pitched whine, when seconds are counted, before the ear splitting crash of bursting bombs. We fell on our faces and counted the seconds and suffered the din, surprised to be alive. Then there was silence; silence and the smell of cordite and the rising smell of dust which billowed up and heightened the eerie gloom. The bombs had fallen close, and at first we had thoughts only for the others. Casualties were slight but the grim reality of death was vile; one felt sickened and enraged and quite helpless. This raid was only a taste of worse to come, but we had enough time to disperse the men and get a few light automatic weapons on the hill – and then it came again, first the noise of diving aircraft, then the piercing whistle before the unnatural thunder. This time a ship was hit and there was indescribable chaos as our stores were scattered. Clouds of black oily smoke swirled into the sky as the other AA guns followed the departing raiders. We did not know how long this continued, but we often dived for cover before emerging from a hole to see if the others were alright. Our machine gunners stood their ground magnificently and fired unceasingly at *Stukas* which seemed to dive right down the barrels of the guns ...[6]

During a lull in the bombing, the men gathered their kit and moved inland, away from the docks:

The fine streets were turned into a mass of rubble and drooping telephone wires lay across charred and blackened craters. The piles of rations and ammunition were a mess of broken tins and exploded cartridges. Much was still burning and so were many hearts as we saw the destruction of so much fine equipment ...[7]

By this time, the SBS – numbering some twenty-six men under Captain Jock Lapraik – had turned Symi into a base from which to infiltrate enemy-held islands. A patrol led by Danish Lieutenant Anders Lassen had also briefly occupied Halki. The SBS on Symi were joined by a six-man LRDG patrol led by Captain Alan Redfern and unexpectedly reinforced on 3 October by forty ground-crew of 74 Squadron, who called at the island en route to join their unit on Kos, unaware that the island had already fallen. The original Italian garrison of approximately 140 men completed the mixed force. Early on Thursday morning, 7 October, a large caique was allowed to enter Pedi Bay and before the mistake was realised offloaded around ninety German troops and some Italian Fascists. These pushed inland towards the outskirts of Symi town (Yalos/Chorio) before the advance faltered. Fighting continued until mid-afternoon, when the order was given to withdraw. Three Ju 87 *Stukas* carried out a diversionary raid as the troops, including an estimated thirty wounded, re-embarked. They left behind six prisoners and sixteen confirmed dead. According to an unsubstantiated account, others were butchered by local Greeks. In turn, the SBS suffered one fatality (Private William Morrison) and an officer and at least one OR were wounded, as were several Italians. A number of civilians were also killed during the bombing.

The next day, three Ju 87s arrived to bomb Symi. After one was reportedly shot down off the coast (unconfirmed by *Luftwaffe* records), the remaining pair harassed the island defenders throughout the day, returning to nearby Rhodes to rearm and refuel. During one raid, there was a direct hit on British Headquarters and two men were killed outright (Leading Aircraftman Norman Gay and Lance Corporal Robert McKendrick). Corporal Sydney Greaves and Guardsman Langslow Bishop were trapped in the debris, the former with a great weight on his stomach and the latter held by his foot. Any attempt to shift Greaves meant transferring wreckage on to Bishop. Efforts to free the men continued all day and into the night. Eventually, Bishop agreed to the amputation of his foot. Prevented by a wrist injury from personally carrying out the procedure, the medical officer of 74 Squadron, Flight Lieutenant R. J. L. Ferris, supervised as Private Porter 'Joe' Jarrell (an American volunteer medic attached to the SBS) performed the task in the worst of conditions; working in a confined space by candlelight and using the most rudimentary equipment. This allowed Bishop to be extricated, but not surprisingly the former LRDG man did not survive the ordeal. After twenty-nine hours, Greaves was also lifted clear, and immediately succumbed to his injuries. Jarrell was later awarded the George Medal for his part in the rescue effort.

On the 11th, the little town of Symi was severely bombed and all but destroyed, prompting the evacuation of the British forces from the island. Captain Redfern had already left by caique when news of the withdrawal reached him:

> Petrol and Naptha dumps were destroyed but all other stores loaded into caiques. Some drunken Italians were not helping matters by firing at the working parties and throwing grenades at them under the impression they were Germans. So ended the occupation of Simi [sic]. We left behind us some 4,500 unfortunate people, terrified, homeless and foodless. Their town gutted and on fire, and smelling from dead bodies in the wreckage. We also evacuated all caiques, to prevent enemy from getting hold of them, so there is little they can do about it.[8]

On Thursday, 14 October, the trawler *Hedgehog* of the Levant Schooner Flotilla sailed from Leros under the command of Sub Lieutenant D. N. Harding to supply 'M2' Patrol of the LRDG on Astipalaea. She was expected to return with injured and up to ten unwounded survivors from the German *Olympos* convoy (see Chapter 6). Exceeding his orders, Harding embarked some fifty prisoners. After *Hedgehog* left Astipalaea, a message was transmitted to Leros that she had developed engine trouble and was putting in at Levitha. There, the prisoners allegedly overpowered their captors and established radio contact with their forces. Certainly, their plight had been reported by German air-sea reconnaissance by Sunday, 17 October. Consequently, that same evening, *Oberleutnant* Oschatz commanding *15./4. Rgt Brandenburg* was ordered to prepare part of his *Kompanie* for an operation with the primary task of seizing Levitha and of freeing and evacuating any German prisoners. Early the next morning, the assault force was airlifted from Athens-Phaleron in two Ju 52 seaplanes and a Dornier flyingboat with three Arados as escort and three more providing forward reconnaissance. The transport aircraft landed according to plan and the troops prepared rubber dinghies for the short trip ashore. As it was being released from the Dornier one of the inflatables capsized and an occupant,

Obergefreiter Bruhn, was dragged under water by the weight of ammunition boxes and equipment. After resurfacing two or three times, the unfortunate Bruhn disappeared altogether. He was to be the only German fatality of the operation.

The landing and subsequent sweep through the island was unopposed. One of two Italian wireless stations was taken after being shot up and bombed by Arados. Two Italians there were fatally wounded; the remainder of the crew fled. Contact was established with the prisoners and by 1330, just four and a half hours after their arrival, the *Brandenburger* had secured the island. Sub Lieutenant Harding and the eight men under his command were captured together with eleven Italians who had manned the wireless stations. That afternoon, the British prisoners were evacuated and most of the assault unit departed after being relieved by troops of *11. Luftwaffen-felddivision.* The remaining *Brandenburger* were withdrawn by Ju 52 the next day. The trawler *Hedgehog* was destroyed by fire either just before or during the assault.

As the *Brandenburger* were congratulating themselves, a comparatively modest infiltration of Kalymnos was in preparation by the LRDG. During the night of 18–19 October, three ORs and the Greek intelligence officer of 'A' Squadron, Second Lieutenant G. V. ('Pav') Pavlides, set out from Leros in a rowing boat. On reaching their destination, two men stayed with the boat while Pavlides and Sergeant D. Bassett left on reconnaissance. Shortly after daybreak they were surprised by a small group of Germans, one of whom was shot in the ensuing fire-fight. Pavlides and Bassett withdrew and that night returned to their boat, whereupon the patrol returned without further mishap to Leros.

Another patrol ('S2') under Lieutenant Stan Eastwood was less successful. After arriving by caique off the west coast, the five men transferred to a rowing boat for the final approach. They were to report on enemy shipping and, if possible, ascertain when the Germans intended to invade Leros. The mission had barely begun before the patrol commander, Lance Corporal A. I. Curle and Private Reed were captured. Gunner Richard Edwards was seized soon after as was an LRDG SNCO, Sergeant R. Tant, who came ashore on the night of 21–22 October in an attempt to locate Eastwood's party. Only Lance Corporal W. F. Whitehead evaded capture. The remainder were removed to Kos for transportation to the mainland with other prisoners of war. At a holding area at Antimachia, Curle discussed the possibility of escape with an Austrian guard who agreed to co-operate provided he could come too! The plan was abandoned when the guard was changed that evening. The next night, Curle, Sergeant Tant and a fellow prisoner, Lance Sergeant G. Morley of the Durham Light Infantry, engaged another guard in conversation. When Curle went to bed, the three continued chatting. Sergeant Tant recalled:

> In the evening I sat at the entrance to our compound talking to Lance Sergeant Morley (DLI) until everybody had gone to bed. One of the sentries came over and started talking to us. He was very friendly and spoke the whole time of his hatred of the Nazis. Eventually we asked him what he would do if we attempted to escape, to which he replied he would shoot, but in the air. We told him there would be no need to shoot at night and he agreed, saying that perhaps we could escape one night. We immediately said 'What is wrong with tonight?' and he said 'Nothing', but we must wait until he came on guard again at 0100 hours as there was only five minutes to go before the guard would be changed. We then convinced him that we would have little time to travel before light. He said he would ask his fellow guards (two) if they would permit us to go and in the meantime Sergeant Morley gathered our belongings, while I tried to find Lance Corporal Curle …

Tant was still searching for his friend when the guard returned and announced that if they intended to go they had to leave immediately:

> I was still unable to find Lance Corporal Curle. We walked out of the stables carrying our kit and supplied with the password '*Königsberg*'. After covering about 100 yards we stopped to 'muffle' our boots and then continued on through the area, circled the village on the west side, and made towards the west point of the mountains.[9]

Curle gave his captors the slip the next morning and with the help of an Italian evader was soon reunited with Tant and Morley. On 4 November all four were taken in a Greek caique to Turkey. Tant and Curle continued by caique to Leros where they arrived at dawn on the 5th. That night, Lance Corporal Whitehead arrived from Kalymnos after an islander, Zacharias

Tyliacos, swam to Leros to fetch help. Eastwood, Edwards and Reed also managed to escape and all three eventually reached Turkey.

By 24 September, within days of occupying Astipalaea with its garrison of several hundred Italians, three LRDG patrols had returned to Leros, leaving 'M2' Patrol under Captain Ken Lazarus to report on enemy aircraft and shipping movements. For the most part, this small party, numbering no more than sixteen men, operated alone, but for a brief period when they were joined by a platoon of the Royal Irish Fusiliers. On 12 October, the patrol commander was asked if he wished to be relieved. Rhodesian Captain John Olivey, who was then on Leros, recalled:

> He wisely replied that he would rather be bored on his island than bored on ours. But his boredom did not last too long as Jerry captured the island ... about a month [sic] later.[10]

Just three days after its last troops left Levitha, *15./4.Rgt. Brandenburg* mounted a parachute assault against Astipalaea in conjunction with air-sea landings by *1. Kompanie/Küstenjägerabteilung Brandenburg*, the latter arriving in seaplanes and paddling ashore in dinghies. The impressions of a *Luftwaffe* officer who flew the men into battle were recorded in a *Brandenburg* report:

> The *1./1. Regiment Brandenburg* behaved impeccably on the 'plane during the flight to Stampalia [Astipalaea]. The *Jäger* were in high spirits and sang all the way. The pilot was particularly impressed that, given the coming landing on the occupied island, '*Kameraden*, today there is no going back' was sung. The pilot's report finished with the comment that he had never before flown such a *Truppe* in his life.[11]

As a preliminary to the invasion, the *Luftwaffe* targeted key installations, destroying an Italian wireless station at Porto Scala. At approximately 0915 on 22 October, *15./4.Rgt. Brandenburg* was dropped at Maltezana, in the middle of the island. The paratroopers were followed by the *Küstenjäger* who landed along the south-west coast. As they advanced, the Germans freed forty-eight prisoners, most or all of whom were from the ill-fated *Olympos* convoy. The Italians put up little, if any, resistance, and were soon rounded up so that by 1400 hours the Germans were already in control of the island.

'M2' Patrol was divided between three locations, with Lazarus and five men manning a wireless post at Assitia. Judging the situation to be hopeless, the OC decided to disperse the troops and to meet later at a prearranged rendezvous (RV) for evacuation by sea. By evening of the 26th, Lazarus and four of his men had gathered at a hideout where they were looked after by islanders. The wireless set, which had been concealed following the German landing, was recovered, but it proved impossible to reach anyone outside Astipalaea. When the battery ran down, a ten-volt replacement was found in the wreckage of the wireless station at Porto Scala. This was insufficient to power the transmitter, but enabled the men to tune in to the BBC, from where they subsequently heard about the fall of Leros. The party was evacuated to Turkey by a Greek-manned caique towards the end of November and reached Haifa on 8 December. None of the remaining patrol members seem to have evaded capture.

On Saturday, 23 October, the day after radio contact ceased between Astipalaea and Leros, a Fascist radio broadcast announced that prisoners of war in Levitha had overpowered their captors. Faced with the loss of two key outposts, the commander of 234 Brigade on Leros, Major-General F. G. R. ('Ben') Brittorous, decided to mount an operation to retake Levitha. On Saturday evening, ML 579 and ML 836, with twenty-four and twenty-five LRDG troops respectively, set out from Leros. The men were equipped and organised along infantry lines into two sections, each comprising three detachments and a headquarters, with Captain John Olivey in overall command and OC Section 1, and with Lieutenant Jack Sutherland OC Section 2. The whole was designated 'Olforce'. This was an unusual and unwelcome role for such a specialist unit which had been formed in North Africa primarily to gather intelligence and to undertake deep-penetration mobile patrols. As recorded in an LRDG report:

> The plan for the attack on Levita [sic] was difficult to form since there was little accurate information available of enemy strength or disposition. Consequently it was with great misgivings that 50 men [sic] of LRDG were embarked on such a foolish operation, but no appeal to the GOC would rescind his orders that it was vital to the Navy that the enemy garrison should be liquidated ...[12]

The main joint objective was the high central ground which overlooked the port of Levitha and from where it was proposed to deny the rest of the island to the enemy. Essentially, the plan required each section to establish its own headquarters and for the remaining troops to clear the surrounding area. At dawn, the two sections were to link up while retaining any commanding positions occupied during the night. At 2200, the two MLs would return and depending on the situation either offload stores or disembark an Italian garrison force. In the event of failure, both sections were to make for the western end of the island for evacuation by sea.

As planned, the two MLs approached their respective disembarkation points and the troops went ashore in assault boats which were then collapsed and concealed along with each section's 2-inch mortar, extra ammunition and stores. Neither landing was opposed, but as per operation instructions, the MLs engaged likely shore targets before they withdrew. It is doubtful whether this preliminary action achieved anything other than to alert the island garrison. After ascending Mount Vardia, Olivey pushed on towards Segnale. Headquarters was set up on a plateau on the summit where prepared defence works surrounded the buildings of an unmanned Italian meteorological station. By this time, Sutherland's party was already in action and taking casualties, with a New Zealander seriously injured in the face by an exploding grenade. As he had not yet been detected, Olivey decided to seize their next objectives before dawn and slightly ahead of schedule. Two patrols under Sergeant Harris and Corporal Thomas Bradfield were each tasked with occupying nearby hills, but at first light both detachments came under rifle and machine-gun fire. At least one man was captured. According to Olivey:

> Just before sunrise about twelve Germans appeared on their hill and with them a soldier in British uniform who commenced signalling in semaphore. At first his signals were readable, but shortly [afterwards] they got very erratic and quite unreadable. Jerry was obviously up to his old games of asking us to surrender ... My reply to his signals was a few rifle shots in the direction and he and his prisoner scattered to their trenches.[13]

At about this time, Corporal Bradfield was brought back with a serious arm wound. Although the two sections were prevented by communication problems from maintaining wireless contact, the noise of battle indicated that Sutherland's men were also busy. In fact, the latter had made good progress against well dug-in positions and taken thirty-five prisoners, but at the cost of another New Zealander who also received facial injuries from grenade fragments. From their hilltop position and now under effective mortar fire, Olivey's party could do little. At 600 yards, even the nearest enemy troops presented a difficult target. The LRDG, on the other hand, were easily seen from the air, as daylight brought the first sorties by enemy aircraft. Morale received a much-needed boost when an Arado seaplane made a forced landing several miles offshore after being shot up by both sections. A while later, two patrols were deployed by Olivey to prevent enemy infiltration and two Rhodesian soldiers were sent to retrieve the section 2-inch mortar and to bring up extra ammunition. The latter returned at 1230 with three prisoners. (These were sent back under escort and later escaped after overpowering one of two guards; the other somehow avoided the same embarrassing fate.)[14]

In the afternoon, the three detachments were re-deployed as fighting patrols. Gunner James Patch was one of the patrol leaders whose task it was to attack an enemy-occupied hill:

I took the patrol round to the flank keeping the objective under observation, but from that direction there was no possible means of approach as we would have had to cross 400 yards of open ground and the hill upon which the enemy was established was sheer on this side. I therefore decided to approach from the rear, but at this time more enemy aircraft appeared and began ranging the whole island. These aircraft numbered, as far as I could judge, eight *Stukas* and four two-seater seaplanes. We advanced with much caution in order not to be spotted by these 'planes and as we approached the rear of our objective a column of the enemy was observed filing in twos and threes and at very wide intervals along a ridge towards their position on the hill – our objective. They seemed to number about thirty men. We were then placed in an unfortunate position. We were 200 yards range from the enemy in very open country with bushes only one foot high and no rocks. The enemy 'planes had now spotted us and the column had withdrawn to the other side of the ridge. The aircraft flew over us one by one, never firing, but coming within ten feet of our heads while a machine gun post now established among rocks on the ridge kept us occupied with spasmodic fire. I therefore decided to withdraw. This was accomplished very slowly as the enemy had us under continuous observation and fire and a wide stretch of open country had to be traversed in this manner.[15]

At about 1815, Captain Olivey was hailed by a familiar voice calling on him to surrender. Seeing one of his officers, Lieutenant Francis Kay, escorted by two Germans, Olivey drew his revolver and opened fire before fleeing with Rhodesian, Gunner Jack Rupping. They took only their rifles, a set of binoculars and a map case. The position was immediately occupied by German troops who then proceeded to ambush a returning patrol led by an unsuspecting Gunner Patch:

> As we approached our HQ at about 4.30 pm [1830C: for an explanation of time zones see Appendix B], we observed some of our own men walking freely about round the outside wall of the house and therefore approached without caution. As we drew near, however, we found ourselves covered by two spandau MGs manned by Germans who had been concealed behind a low wall. A German then came out of the building and called upon us to surrender and at the same time the rest of the enemy party numbering about fifteen men appeared from their hiding places. The men from our own party whom we had seen near the building were Lieutenant Kay and three or four Rhodesians who were already prisoners ...[16]

After enduring mortar and machine-gun fire as well as attacking Ju 87 *Stukas* and Arado seaplanes, those in Section 2 had been fought almost to a standstill. According to Trooper Ronald Hill:

> Captain [sic] Sutherland then said he would surrender to save further bloodshed as no useful purpose could be served by holding on ... Our ammunition had also been expended and we were by this time using captured arms. By the time Captain Sutherland made this decision it was too late for anyone in our party to take evasive action, especially as our position was in full view of the enemy prisoners. Captain Sutherland thereupon sent out a German prisoner to inform the attackers and displayed a white flag. Whilst this was going on, I threw what arms

I could including the captured machine gun and mortar over the cliffs into the sea. The German prisoners we had taken earlier in the day then took over and we were taken to the German HQ where we met most of Captain Olivey's party.[17]

After dark, Olivey and Rupping made their way to the coast where, at around midnight, they were rescued by a motor launch. Five other LRDG men were picked up, all from Olivey's section, including Bradfield, Captain Dick Lawson (medical officer) and one of the former prisoner escort.

Olivey returned to Levitha by ML the next night, but failed to locate any more survivors. Besides those taken prisoner, at least four ORs were killed: an Englishman, Gunner Herbert Federmann and three New Zealanders, Troopers Hector Mallett, John Bowler and Archibald Penhall (who was mortally wounded and died in captivity).[18] The select and highly specialist Long Range Desert Group never fully recovered from the disaster of Levitha, which was to result in far-reaching repercussions for the unit's remaining New Zealanders.

CHAPTER 6

The War at Sea October 1943

ON 1 OCTOBER, THE ROYAL NAVY dispatched from Alexandria all available 'Fleet' destroyers to escort to Malta HMS *Howe* and *King George V*. This left only 'Hunt' class destroyers in the Aegean at a time when it was known from intelligence reports that a German invasion of Kos was likely. Only after the German landing were the destroyers and other warships at Malta and Taranto ordered to proceed to the Levant. Six Lightning squadrons of the United States Twelfth Air Force were also released from the central Mediterranean and based at Gambut, in Libya, in support of the Royal Navy. This draining of resources from the main theatre of operations was precisely what General Eisenhower had hoped to avoid. On 6 October, he wrote to Air Chief Marshal Tedder, agreeing to continue to support the bombing of enemy airfields in Greece, which was beneficial both to Allied operations in the Aegean and the security of Adriatic ports in Italy, but stressed that he was currently unable to make further commitments to the Middle East:

> Since the matter of assisting the Middle East has not been referred to me by the Combined Chiefs of Staff but has been handled as a matter of co-operation and upon suggestions from London, I suggest that you explain to the Chief of the Air Staff our whole situation so that he will understand that we are sympathetic to the needs of the Middle East but cannot possibly afford to meet them at the expense of jeopardising our own important campaign in Italy. If the decision to undertake Accolade depends upon a firm commitment for the diversion from our

own operations of a material portion of our air force, then Accolade will have to be postponed. We will be inferior to the enemy in ground strength throughout the winter. Our air force is the asset that we count on to permit us taking the offensive in spite of this fact. Our first purpose must remain.[1]

The next day, the British Prime Minister cabled President Roosevelt of the United States to outline his concerns and to petition American support for British efforts in the Aegean:

I believe it will be found that the Italian and Balkan peninsulas are militarily and politically united and that really it is one theatre with which we have to deal. It may indeed not be possible to conduct a successful Italian campaign ignoring what happens in the Aegean ...

I have never wished to send an army into the Balkans but only by agents and commandos to stimulate the intense guerrilla activity prevailing there. This may yield results measureless in their consequence at very small cost to main operations. What I ask for is the capture of Rhodes and the other islands of the Dodecanese. The movement northward of our Middle Eastern Air Forces and their establishment in these islands and possibly on the Turkish shore which last might well be obtained would force a diversion on the enemy far greater than that required of us. It would also offer the opportunity of engaging the enemy's waning air power and wearing it down in a new region. This air power is all one and the more continually it can be fought the better.

Rhodes is the key to all this. I do not feel the present plan of taking it is good enough. It will require and is worth at least up to a first class division which can of course be replaced by static troops once the place is ours. Leros which for the moment we hold so precariously is an important naval fortress and once we are ensconced in this area air and light naval forces would have a most fruitful part to play. The policy should certainly not be pursued unless done with vigour and celerity requiring the best troops and adequate means. In this way the diversion from the main theatre would only be temporary while the results may well be of profound and lasting importance.

I beg you to consider this and not let it be brushed aside and all these possibilities lost to us in the critical months that lie ahead. Even if landing craft and assault ships on the scale of a division were withheld from the build-up of OVERLORD for a few weeks without altering the zero date it would be worth while. I feel we may easily throw away an immense but fleeting opportunity ...[2]

Two days later, at a meeting between Eisenhower and the Commanders-in-Chief in the Mediterranean and Levant,[3] it was argued that resources in the Mediterranean were insufficient to allow the Allies to undertake the capture of Rhodes and at the same time secure their immediate objectives in Italy. The postponement of 'Accolade' was recommended until such time as weather conditions were favourable and sufficient forces became available subsequent to the capture of Rome. As to be expected, there were dissenters in the British camp who believed that Leros, Samos and Kastellorizo should continue to be held, together with other island outposts. However, by 10 October even the British Prime Minister had dramatically altered his stance. In a message to Roosevelt and Eisenhower, in which he reluctantly concurred with the overriding view, he appears to have virtually written off Leros:

I have now to face the situation in the Aegean. Even if we had decided to attack Rhodes on the 23rd [as General Wilson intended] Leros might well have fallen before that date. I have asked Eden to examine with General Wilson and Admiral Sir Andrew Cunningham whether with resources still belonging to the Middle East anything can be done to regain Kos on the basis that Turkey lets us use the landing grounds close by. If nothing can be worked out on these lines and unless we have luck tonight or tomorrow night in destroying one of the assaulting convoys, the fate of Leros is sealed.

I propose therefore to tell General Wilson that he is free if he judges the position hopeless, to order the garrison to evacuate by night taking with them all Italian officers and as many other Italians as possible and destroying the guns and defences. The Italians cannot be relied upon to fight and we have only 1200 men, quite insufficient to man even a small portion of the necessary batteries, let alone the perimeter. Internment in Turkey is not strict and may not last long; or they may get out along the Turkish coast.

I will not waste words in explaining how painful this decision is to me.[4]

While Allied military commanders and politicians debated, the German High Command concentrated on the practicalities of securing the rest of the Aegean. On the successful conclusion of Operation *'Eisbär'* ('Polar Bear'), *Generalleutnant* Müller prepared for Operation *'Leopard'* – the assault on Leros – using essentially the same units already on Kos. However, before they could be redeployed, the assault troops had to be relieved. Accordingly, on Wednesday, 6 October, *IX./Festungsinfanteriebataillon/999* embarked on the steamship *Olympos* and six *Marinefährprähme* and set sail from Piraeus with the submarine-chaser *UJ 2111* as escort. They were spotted by Allied aircraft shortly afterwards. An enemy report was also transmitted by 'T1' Patrol of the LRDG from an OP on Kythnos in the Cyclades. At 0401 hours on the 7th, HM submarine *Unruly* sighted the convoy off Kos and proceeded to Diving Stations. Exactly one hour later she fired four torpedoes, all of which missed their target. *Unruly* surfaced and at 0600 opened fire with her deck gun. Fifty-four high explosive rounds were expended; up to three landing craft were thought to have been sunk, and hits were registered on at least two other vessels.

According to the after-action report of *Oberleutnant zur See* Schunack, commanding *UJ 2111*, the *Olympos* and an *MFP* were hit whereupon the former veered away and the latter was set on fire and immobilised. When the rest of the convoy came under fire from the port side, the escort vessel led the five remaining landing craft in taking avoiding action by turning to starboard. Air support was called for, although the attacker had not yet been identified. Minutes later, the escort vessel began taking hits resulting in a number of casualties. It was not until first light, some sixteen minutes after the first shots were fired, that two submarines were reported on the surface close to Levitha at a distance of 7,500 metres. They were engaged by an *MFP* and *UJ 2111* and ceased firing when one was apparently hit and began to emit smoke. The other dived (*Unruly*'s Log records that she dived at 0705 when four aircraft were reported overhead – if there was a second submarine, her identity remains a mystery)[5]. *UJ 2111* and the five undamaged *MFPs* continued at speed towards Kos, by which time neither the *Olympos* nor the damaged landing craft were visible.

Meanwhile, the Royal Navy cruisers *Sirius* and *Penelope* in company with the destroyers *Faulknor* and *Fury* were racing towards the scene in response to an enemy report by *Unruly*. The destroyers intercepted and sunk *Olympos* and rejoined the cruisers in attacking the rest of the convoy. Schunack was alerted to the sight of the four warships approaching through the morning mist; *UJ 2111* opened fire minutes later. The British warships responded by pairing off for a flanking attack. *UJ 2111* continued firing, this time concentrating on the cruisers, before Schunack realised the hopelessness of the situation and gave the order to divert to Astipalaea in order to use the coast as cover. It was already too late. The cruisers concentrated on the *U-Jäger* while the destroyers turned their guns on the *MFPs*. In desperation, the Germans ignited a smoke buoy, which did little to conceal their movements. *UJ 2111* swerved as shells landed 200 metres on either side. The situation on board was desperate. The vessel was severely damaged and with so much shrapnel covering the decks, it was impossible to carry ammunition forward to keep the last remaining gun firing. The noise of battle was such that shouted orders could no longer be heard. As the opposing forces closed to within 700 metres of each other, Schunack had to accept the inevitable:

> Now, with all of our weapons silent, and under constant enemy fire, I give the order: 'Open sea-cocks. Everybody abandon ship.'
>
> After reassuring with the *I.W.O.* [*Erster Wachoffizier* – First Officer of the Watch] that the order has been carried out properly, I intend to leave the ship as well. However, I then notice that the men in the water are being shot at with tracer rounds from close range and I remain on board until [the] ammunition is hit by further firing and explodes.
>
> As the sea-cocks seemed to be covered by heavy [marine] growth on the ship's hull and let water in only with difficulty, the ship remains floating in the water for about another two hours burning and exploding.[6]

During the engagement, the cruisers had been subjected to air attack by Ju 88s and shot at by a shore battery on Astipalaea, albeit without effect. At 0810 the unit turned south-east and departed at speed, still firing at those foundering in the water. In addition to those vessels sunk, a landing craft (*F 496*) was badly damaged and later arrived at Astipalaea. On board were at least eighty personnel, three trucks and two 7.5cm guns all of which were captured by Italian troops and the resident LRDG 'M2' Patrol under Captain Ken Lazarus.[7]

After withdrawing, the British warships were harassed by Ju 88s and Bf 109s, until the appearance of eight Lightnings. These jettisoned their long-range fuel tanks and swept in for the kill. At least one of the attackers was shot down before the American fighters had to return to base to refuel. Following an ineffectual attack by three Ju 88s at 1130, a dozen Ju 87 *Stukas* commenced a dive-bombing and machine-gun attack at 1213. By this time, the force had rendezvoused with the destroyers HMS *Rockwood* and the Greek *Miaoulis*. *Sirius* and *Rockwood* were narrowly missed as was *Penelope* who was also struck by a bomb that passed straight through the port side without exploding but nevertheless caused the deaths of one officer and nine ratings and injured twenty-eight others.[8] In turn, one more enemy aircraft was reported to have crashed.[9] For most of the afternoon until early evening, air cover was provided mainly by Beaufighters, one of which was lost when it was shot down by a Messerschmitt Bf 109.[10] The force remained together until clear of the Crete–Rhodes area, when *Miaoulis* and *Rockwood* were detached to Limassol leaving the remaining ships to continue to Alexandria.

On 7 October, *Vizeadmiral* Werner Lange and *Generalleutnant* Müller were ordered by *Heeresgruppe E* to carry out Operation 'Leopard' by the 9th irrespective of the destruction of the *Olympos* convoy. Müller requested a twenty-four hour postponement due to the unavailability of sufficient landing craft. Sightings of British warships and unsuitable weather conditions resulted in further delays, which were to continue for the next four weeks.

Following her successful action on the 7th, *Unruly* went on to torpedo and sink a minelayer south of Amorgos on 8 October: the *Bulgaria*, with a crew of eighty-one, was bound for Kos with 285 men, this time of X./*Festungsinfanteriebataillon/999*.[11]

A day later, the cruiser *Carlisle* withdrew south with HM ships *Panther*, *Petard*, *Rockwood* and the *Miaoules*. At 0750, on Saturday, 9 October, two low-flying Arados were sighted, evidently shadowing the warships. One aircraft was claimed damaged and the other driven off by an escorting Beaufighter which then returned to base. The vessels were without escort for forty minutes until the arrival of several Lightnings. Thereafter, air cover was provided for the rest of the morning with each formation remaining until after the arrival of their relief flight. At one point, three Beaufighters of 252 Squadron had just arrived in the area when, it is claimed, they were attacked by three Lightnings. One machine, hit in both engines and the hydraulic system, crash-landed on returning to Lakatamia; none of the crew was injured.

Towards midday, several minutes elapsed during which there was no air cover. The *Luftwaffe* chose this moment to attack. One *Stuka* after another dived almost vertically on to their chosen targets, the banshee wail of their sirens barely audible above the tremendous barrage put up by the ships' guns. But help was on its way as Lightnings of 37th Fighter Squadron approached under the command of Major William Leverette:

> ... our Squadron took off at 1030 with nine planes ... Two planes were forced to return to base because of engine trouble shortly after take off, leaving seven planes – a four ship Flight led by the undersigned [Leverette] and a three ship Flight led by Lieutenant [Wayne] Blue. We sighted the convoy at 1200 hours, approximately fifteen miles east of Cape Valoca on Island of Scarpanto [Karpathos]. The convoy had been attacked and the cruiser was smoking from the stern.[12]

HMS *Carlisle* survived, unlike the 'Fleet' destroyer *Panther*, which received a direct hit, broke in two and quickly sank. Electrical artificer, Chief Petty Officer Frank Forster, recalled his ship's final moments:

> I ran to my action station and as I looked at the switchboards, there was a very heavy explosion and the ship lurched ... a few seconds later all power failed, the lights went out and the ship began to flood. The ship had been damaged in a previous action by enemy bombs and we had brought her back to port but this was much worse and my torpedo-man and I decided to make our way to the upper deck. We splashed through the water to the first ladder and climbed it by the light of an emergency lamp. I had almost reached the top of the ladder when the ship lurched again and I grabbed the ankle of the man above instead of the hatch coaming. The man screamed in terror from fear of being dragged back into the flooding compartment and as I regained my foothold I released his ankle.
>
> I made my way along the port passage to the break of the fo'c'sle and joined a group of men who were afraid to abandon the ship because of the gaping hole which yawned in front of them. I gave a push

to those in front and was about to follow when a heavy inrush of water caught me unaware and carried me back into the darkness of the ship ...

Now I had to decide very quickly whether I should allow the force of the water to carry me into the darkness of the forward compartments and hope to make my way out by opening a hatch, or try to fight the rush of sea water and reach the upper deck again. I decided to fight and hung on grimly to the rifle racks – I remember thinking how sad this would be for my wife, whom I had married six months previously, if I didn't escape. My half-prayer was answered immediately: the inrush of water subsided for a few moments and the terrifying noise abated as the lower compartments filled up. There was about a foot to spare between the water level and the deck head. I lay on my back on the surface of the water and slowly hauled myself out hand over hand on the cable carrier plate. The way out from the passage was by now completely submerged and I was compelled to try the cross passage to the starboard side. I reached the exit to the upper deck and saw that the ship had broken in two with the stern rising high in the air. The sea was warm and calm and the bright sunshine welcomed me back to safety. I could hear the cries of someone down below but did not have the stomach to go back for anyone and I was the last man out.[13]

The crews of *II./St.G.3* were to pay dearly for their success. The slower and less manoeuvrable *Stukas* were no match for the American Lightnings, as testified by Major Leverette:

During our first orbit around the convoy, while flying a south-westerly course at 8,000 feet, Lieutenant [Homer] Sprinkle called out 'Bogeys at one o'clock, slightly high, approaching the convoy from the northwest.' We immediately changed course to pass behind the bogeys and began a gradual climb. Shortly thereafter, we identified the bogeys as Ju 87s, in three flights, totalling approximately twenty-five. Lieutenant Blue implicitly followed instructions to maintain his flight of three planes at altitude to cover my flight as we attacked the Ju 87s at about 1215. My flight immediately dived to the left and attacked the Ju 87s from the left quarter. I attacked an E/A [enemy aircraft] in the rear of the formation, fired at about 20° and observed smoke pouring from left side of engine. I broke away to the left and upward, attacking a second E/A from rear and slightly below. After a short burst at about 200 yards this enemy aircraft rolled over and spiralled steeply downward. After breaking away to the left again and turning back toward the formation of Ju 87s, I saw both E/A strike the water. Apparently neither rear gunner fired at me. I attacked another E/A from slight angle, left rear, firing just after rear gunner opened fire. He ceased firing immediately and pilot jumped out, although I did not see the chute open. I continued into the formation, attacked another E/A from 30°, observing cannon and machine gun hits in engine. Large pieces of cowling and parts flew off and engine immediately began smoking profusely as the E/A started down. Breaking away and upward to the left, I re-entered the formation and opened fire with cannon and machine guns on another E/A at approximately 15°. The canopy and parts flew off and a long flame immediately shot out from rear of engine and left wing root, rear gunner jumping clear of E/A. Continuing into formation and attacking another E/A from slight angle to left rear and below, I was forced to roll partially on my back to the left to bring my sight on to the E/A, opening fire at close range. I observed full hits in right upper side of engine which immediately began to smoke. I broke away slightly to the left, and my Element Leader, Lieutenant Hanna, saw the enemy aircraft strike the water. Attacking another aircraft from behind and slightly below, the rear gunner ceased firing after I opened a short burst. The enemy aircraft nosed downward slightly and I closed to minimum range, setting the engine on fire with full burst into the bottom of fuselage. The enemy aircraft dived abruptly and I was unable to break away upward and in attempting to pass under right wing of the aircraft, three feet of my left propeller sliced through the enemy aircraft. We engaged the Ju 87s until they passed over the south coast of Rhodes at approximately 1230 hours.[14]

Sixteen *Stukas* and a Ju 88 were claimed by the American pilots: in addition to Major Leverette's seven kills, five Ju 87s were claimed by Lieutenant Troy Hanna; three more and one probable by Lieutenant Homer Sprinkle; Lieutenant Wayne Blue was credited with the Ju 88 and Lieutenant Robert Margison (Blue's wingman) with one other Ju 87.[15]

HMS *Carlisle* was taken in tow by *Rockwood* and brought back to Alexandria, but her damage was such that she would never again put to sea. Such costly efforts by the British only served to delay the inevitable. The situation might have been very different if the Americans had agreed to extend their air support, for, in addition to providing cover for the Royal Navy, Lightnings also carried out shipping sweeps and strafing attacks and bombing raids against Kos. However, just when they were making their presence felt, the Lightning squadrons were recalled. For the British in the Aegean, the loss of these superb machines was a devastating blow that would have fateful repercussions.

Notwithstanding the misgivings expressed by Churchill in his correspondence with Roosevelt and Eisenhower, Leros was retained as a British base. At Cairo on 12 October, the Foreign Secretary presided over a high-level conference in which the recapture of Kos was ruled out, not least because of the massive use of air power this would entail. However, it was agreed that the garrison on Leros would greatly benefit by the destruction of just some of the landing craft known to have been assembled for a German assault against the island. Accordingly, the Mediterranean Air Command was requested to carry out a large-scale attack the following day. The reply was disappointing: unsuitable weather conditions, distances to be covered, and insufficient time to transfer the necessary aircraft made such a strike impracticable. It was recommended that Beaufighters and other available aircraft be used instead. By this time, the two Lightning groups at Gambut had already been withdrawn. As some compensation, Air Chief Marshal Tedder provided a squadron of B-25 Mitchell bombers armed with 75mm cannon for shipping strikes. However, the Mediterranean Air Command refused to divert its heavy bombers in order to extend the bombing of enemy airfields in Greece. While Tedder fully appreciated the importance of air superiority for a successful conclusion to operations in the Aegean, Italy remained the priority, and clearly it was felt that enough had been done to assist the Middle East.

Beaufighters, Baltimores and Mitchells all took part in shipping strikes and a number of vessels were damaged, while on the night of 18–19 October, some 40 miles east of Antikythira Channel, Wellingtons of 38 Squadron torpedoed and sank the merchantman *Sinfra*, carrying 204 German troops, 2,389 Italian and seventy-one Greek prisoners.[16] The coast patrol boat *GK*

51 was also sunk by air attack, and Allied aircraft hit at troops and ground targets on Kos. The Royal Navy conducted offensive patrols against German ports and achieved significant results at sea, although what should have been the first major success of the month was anything but when, on the night of 8–9 October, ML *835* attacked and drove ashore what turned out to be an Italian Navy auxiliary vessel, SS *Alessandro Volta* (she was later destroyed by German aircraft). A number of caiques and other vessels were sunk by submarines including, off Kinaros on 16 October, the steamship *Kari* with 500 troops, by HMS/M *Torbay*.[17] During the night of 16–17 October, UJ *2109* (formerly HMS *Widnes*) was destroyed and F *338* was burned out aft as a result of attacks by destroyers at Kalymnos and a steamship, *Santorini,* was badly damaged. The next night, the merchantman *Trapani* was set alight by naval gunfire. Off the north coast of Kos two nights later, motor torpedo boats (MTBs) attacked a patrol boat (*LS 5*) and a landing craft (F *131*), destroying the latter. North of Kos port another landing craft (F *330*) was burnt out when on-board ammunition detonated. On the 29th, HMS/M *Unsparing* torpedoed the troopship *Ingeborg* south of Amorgos and later sank a rescue vessel (*Nioi*) loaded with survivors.[18] Warships also carried out offensive patrols against German ports.

According to the *Kriegsmarine*, by 22 October, 29,454 Italian and British prisoners of war had been evacuated from the Aegean to the mainland. An other 6,000 mainly Italian prisoners perished when their transport vessels were lost through Allied action.

In addition to Allied ships damaged or sunk during the period 7–9 October, the abandoned LCT *3* had been captured during the German invasion of Kos and a few days later, ML *835* was destroyed in an air raid at Levitha. In mid-October, the trawler *Hedgehog* was lost; on the night of 16–17 October, the destroyer *Hursley* was damaged by return fire; the cruiser *Sirius* was damaged and nearly fifty of her crew were killed or wounded in an attack by Ju 88s on the 17th, and on the same day MTB *313* also sustained damage. At about this time HM submarine *Trooper* disappeared east of Leros, probably after striking a mine. A few days later ML *1015* foundered in heavy seas. On the night of 22–23 October, many lives were lost when mines claimed HMS *Hurworth* and blew away the forecastle of the Greek destroyer *Adrias,* to the east of Kalymnos. The minelayer responsible was almost certainly the German *Drache*. In the early hours of the 24th, the same minefield claimed HMS *Eclipse* while she was en route to Leros. On the 24th, the merchantman SS *Taganrog* was bombed and sunk at Samos and two days later, ML 579 was destroyed and four of the crew killed in an air raid at Arki. LCT 115 was lost together with twenty-two men and four heavy anti-aircraft guns some 35 miles off Kastellorizo on the 28th. More than five dozen of her crew were reported killed and wounded when HMS *Aurora* was severely damaged in an air attack on the 30th; another destroyer, HMS *Belvoir*, had a lucky escape when she was struck by a bomb that failed to explode, and the Italian *Morrhua* was sunk at Samos. (The *Luftwaffe* lost at least three Ju 88s during the day's attacks.) Many more Italian ships and small craft were crippled or sunk during the same period including, in just two weeks, at least seven vessels at Leros. (see Chapter 7)

Any voyage was a potentially hazardous undertaking. Sea mines, used by both sides, added to the danger. Some victims vanished without trace; others stayed afloat long enough to allow all or some of the crew to escape, and many vessels sustained crippling damage, leaving them drifting and helpless in an unforgiving sea. The destroyers *Hurworth* and *Adrias* had been on a fairly routine operation when they sailed into a minefield on the night of Friday, 22 October. They were to have provided a diversionary bombardment while HM ships *Jervis* and *Pathfinder* made a delivery run to Leros. The captain of the Greek *Adrias* was Commander J. N. Toumbas:

> I was standing on the right side of the gyro compass when at 2156 a tremendous double tremor shook the ship. I just had time to ask myself what was happening when I felt myself being lifted in the air before falling with all my weight on the bridge face down. Simultaneously, all sorts of things started falling on me. At the same time a big explosion was heard followed by a series of noises of rending metal. I did not lose consciousness and with superhuman effort managed to disentangle myself from the debris which was covering me. When I finally got up I perceived that I was wounded in different places. I saw the 4-inch guns of Number 1 turret over the bridge. The bridge appeared to be deserted, bodies were lying all over the place. I called to the wheel house without getting any answer. I then saw the BNLO [British Naval Liaison Officer], Lieutenant Walkinshaw, and a British signalman

getting up. A small fire started on the bridge due to a short circuit which was immediately extinguished by the BNLO. The whole of the forecastle had been cut off and I thought that we had been torpedoed and ordered a signal saying so to be passed to D.22 [Commander R. H. Wright on HMS *Hurworth*]. At that time I vomited blood. I told the BNLO that I was going to control the ship from the after steering position (searchlight).

I ordered Sub Lieutenant Sotirion who was at the time getting out of the rangefinder director to follow me. As I was descending from the bridge I met the First Lieutenant who, having tried to communicate with the bridge without any result, had come up to see what was happening and I ordered him to report to me the state and water-tightness of the ship. I then went quickly to the searchlight where I found the Quartermaster. The Navigating Officer, Sub Lieutenant S. Moyrikis, came a few minutes later. Change over to after steering position was effected immediately and at the same time I got the report of the Chief Engineer that the boilers and engines were in working order. I then ordered the Second Engineer to take every possible measure for the safety of the ship and told the Chief Engineer to shove up with baulks from the inside all the damaged watertight compartments. The crew were very cool and everybody was at action stations. I started to move the engines astern and the ship started turning to port. The First Lieutenant reported to me that the wardroom and the low power room were flooded. The ship listed 10–12° to starboard sagging by the head. The explosion was seen by HMS *Hurworth* who immediately turned and started flashing. Communication was impossible as all the lights were in pieces. We tried to get through with a torch. HMS *Hurworth* came near to us and D.22 himself passed the following signal by voice: 'Am coming alongside to take your crew and then sink the ship.' I answered through the BNLO that I did not agree with sinking the ship and that I was going to ground her in Turkish territorial waters. The above order was repeated twice and each time my answer was negative. The only thing that I agreed to was to allow a certain number of the crew whose presence was unnecessary to be transferred on board HMS *Hurworth* before proceeding to Turkish territorial waters ...

HMS *Hurworth* was manoeuvring to come alongside us, to take over those of the crew which were not needed, and was approximately 200 yards on our starboard side. It was 2210 when a terrific explosion was seen on the *Hurworth*, on her starboard side as high as the Captain's cabin. Loud whistling noises were heard and a flash seen which reached a height of at least 100 yards. HMS *Hurworth* was blown into the air and the ship disappeared instantly ...[19]

Commander Royston Wright recalled that HMS *Hurworth* broke in two, with the fore-part remaining afloat for about three minutes and the aft end for a few minutes longer:

The explosion threw me off the bridge and into the sea, in which I landed on my back. After surfacing I first grabbed a float, then, finding myself close to the after part of the ship, I clambered back to investigate. This part was listed perhaps 15° to starboard, was down by the 'bows' and was sinking quite slowly. Two of the Hands were getting out the motorboat but nothing was happening around the whaler, in fact I doubt whether there was anyone else on board. In any case had there been anyone, I was quite useless either to give a lead or an order having a mildly fractured spine and being able only to crawl. Someone gave me a cork lifebelt, which I donned and waited for the ship to sink. She did so after about ten minutes, very smoothly and with a great hissing of air ...[20]

The account by Commander Toumbas continues:

Voices were heard from the sea aft. We picked up Petty Officer Chatizikonjtantinoj, who was wounded, and as we thought that more voices were heard, I ordered a raft to be thrown overboard. The ship was not obeying the rudder, I therefore steered by engines.

I had no hope, nor had anybody else who was on the searchlight platform, that anybody from the *Hurworth* had survived after the terrific explosion that we had witnessed. I tried, though, to get near the place of the explosion which was in complete darkness. The terrible end of HMS *Hurworth*, the ship with which for half a year we had side by side performed splendidly such pleasant tasks under the command of her gallant and heroic Captain D.22 Commander Wright moved us deeply. Everybody from the *Adrias* loved her and we considered, as we say in the Greek Navy, that she was our friendly ship ...[21]

Although there was nothing to indicate that anyone had survived, Toumbas ordered that life buoys and floats be thrown overboard before he attempted to take his ship into Turkish waters:

> I decided to move forward despite danger of the watertight bulkheads giving way and new leaks developing. I decided this firstly in order to extinguish, by the bow wave, forward fires that were burning in the wreckage below the bridge and secondly in the unfortunate event of hitting a second mine. If such a thing happened whilst the ship was moving astern then the majority of the crew which were concentrated aft on the quarter deck would have met with certain death. The fires were extinguished after the ship had gone ahead for a while ...
>
> I had no charts and no compass. The small magnetic compass of the searchlight was broken to pieces. With the Polar Star and the high mountains of Kalymno [Kalymnos] as guides, I steered the ship to where I thought the Turkish coast was ... I felt that I was losing consciousness, but soon recovered my senses, under the strong slapping of the Quartermaster, who I hope was not very pleased with the opportunity that was given to him. I was assured that I had been unconscious for two minutes only, during which time the Quartermaster, Leading Seaman P. Pavlou, took the initiative and ordered a correct movement of the engines ...[22]

It was still dark when *Adrias* arrived at Gumusluk Bay, Turkey, with forty-nine dead, wounded or missing. It would be December by the time she was able to continue to Alexandria.

The ship's crew would have been amazed and, no doubt, appalled had they known that there were survivors from *Hurworth*. Many owed their lives to Able Seaman Charles Russell. He had been helping to unshackle *Hurworth*'s motor boat in order to pick up survivors from *Adrias* when his own ship was blown up. Russell remained calm, released the boat and with four others took it inshore and lay up for the night. At dawn the men realised they were among enemy shipping in an unfamiliar harbour. In spite of suffering from serious burns, Russell took charge and the boat slipped unnoticed from the port. The five then returned to the scene of the sinking and in two trips collected thirty-eight survivors who were ferried to an island near the Turkish coast.

Lieutenant H. C. A. Middleton was on the ship's bridge when *Hurworth* was mined. The force of the explosion flung him into the sea and left him with a dozen or so others clinging to a Carley float:

Although every effort was made to keep together, a floating mine forced the party to divide into two groups. At this time I was with Lieutenant Pearce and about eight ratings, half of whom were wounded; we were supported on two Denton rafts and a cargo chute. The water was warm and the night fine with a breeze from the northward; very slow southerly progress was made by paddling and swimming. Several dark shapes of boats or ships appeared and were hailed by everyone shouting in unison, but it was difficult to determine how far away they were, or to distinguish their type as everybody had their eyes coated with oil fuel.

At about 0200 the party became split up, Lieutenant Pearce, Joiner Ferguson, AB Underwood, Stoker O'Donnell [sic: Stoker Albert Donnelly] and myself on a Denton raft continued to make towards Pserimos, but at dawn it was obvious that Kalymnos was the closest island and we made for a headland which appeared to be about 2–2½ miles away, just north of Port Vathi. Our method of progress was for O'Donnell and myself to swim ahead towing the raft behind us, while the other three supported their bodies on it, kicking with their feet and paddling with their hands. Progress, to begin with, was fairly good, but became slower towards the end of the forenoon. Underwood, who although unwounded, had failed to assist our movements in any way and was becoming increasingly pessimistic, after repeated warnings was told either to 'get on or get off'. At 1100 he was left behind. Soon after this, O'Donnell drowned. He had been outstandingly cheerful and hardworking, but throughout the night and day he had inhaled small quantities of seawater and it was obvious that he would not survive. Although by 1500 the shore was only about one mile distant it did not appear to be getting any closer and everyone was becoming exhausted. By 1700 Lieutenant Pearce and Ferguson were too weak to paddle and not being strong enough myself to tow them ashore I left the raft and swam about ¾ mile to the rocky coast line which I reached about an hour later. After wringing out my battledress I slept during the night on the rocks just clear of the sea.[23]

With the help of islanders, Middleton remained in hiding for ten days until he was able to swim to Leros and safety. Stoker Donnelly was posted missing, together with Lieutenant Anthony Pearce, Joiner Duncan Ferguson and Able Seaman Arnold Underwood. Another party, consisting of two officers and nine ratings, clung to a Carley float and paddled ashore at enemy-occupied Pserimos, where they were hidden and cared for by local Greeks before being smuggled to the Turkish mainland. Two more seamen made their way to an island where they were rescued by the crew of a caique, and five survivors were taken on board the German *GA 45*. As for Commander Wright:

> From past experience of picking up survivors in the dark, I knew that it was the noisiest who got rescued and this theory I therefore applied. After perhaps 15 minutes a Carley float appeared and into this I was dragged. My rescuer was Leading Gunner E. Savakis of HHMS *Adrias*, and of his subsequent determination and endurance I cannot speak too highly. I must emphasise that I was a complete passenger. We agreed that we would avoid Pserimos and Savakis therefore set about paddling us to a group of islands off the Turkish coast. I doubt whether we were making a half knot but Savakis pulled almost without stopping for 18 hours until we landed on the uninhabited and completely barren island of Lodo at about 1700 [on the 23rd].
>
> We intended to rest for the night and to endeavour to make the Turkish mainland the following day. Unfortunately, during the night the Carley float broke up and in the morning it was obvious that we were a long way clear of the sailing caique route and that the chances of attracting attention were nil. Savakis now volunteered to swim to the next island, a much larger one, from which it might be possible to obtain help. It was a long swim, the weather was not entirely favourable and Savakis was already weakened by his previous efforts. But at 1120 he set out and within six hours was returning with an indescribably welcome caique.[24]

Wright was taken on board the caique, part of a clandestine force operating under Commander V. Wolfson RNVR, and with twenty-two badly injured men, including some who were transferred from the *Adrias* at Gumusluk, eventually reached Izmir on the morning of Tuesday, 26 October.

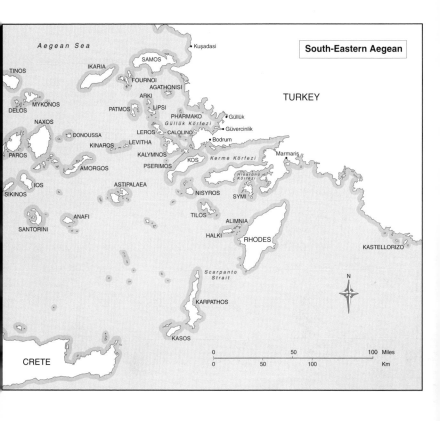

South-Eastern Aegean

Aegean Sea

• Kuşadasi

SAMOS

TINOS

IKARIA

FOURNOI

AGATHONISI

ARKI

MYKONOS

DELOS

PATMOS

LIPSI

TURKEY

NAXOS

PHARMAKO

• Güllük

Güllük Körfezi

DONOUSSA

LEROS

CALOLINO

• Güvercinlik

KINAROS

LEVITHA

• Bodrum

PAROS

KALYMNOS

Kerme Körfezi

Marmaris

AMORGOS

PSERIMOS

KOS

Hisaronü

Körfezi

IOS

ASTIPALAEA

NISYROS

SYMI

SIKINOS

ANAFI

TILOS

ALIMNIA

SANTORINI

HALKI

RHODES

KASTELLORIZO

Scarpanto
Strait

N

KARPATHOS

KASOS

CRETE

| 0 | | 50 | | 100 | Miles |
| 0 | 50 | | 100 | | Km |

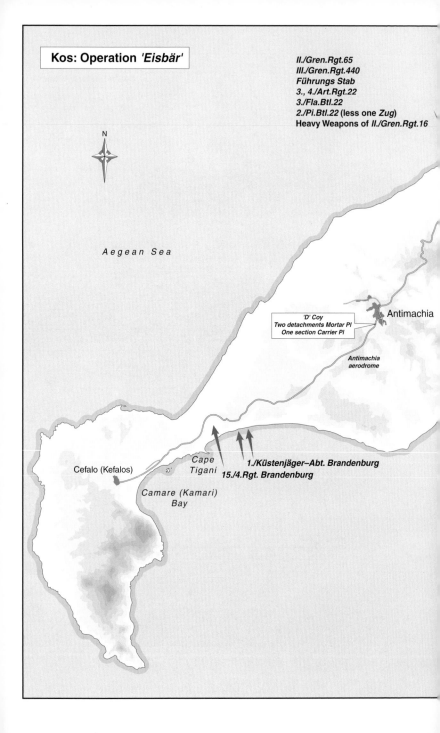

Kos: Operation *'Eisbär'*

II./Gren.Rgt.65
III./Gren.Rgt.440
Führungs Stab
3., 4./Art.Rgt.22
3./Fla.Btl.22
2./Pi.Btl.22 (less one *Zug*)
Heavy Weapons of II./Gren.Rgt.16

Aegean Sea

N

'D' Coy
Two detachments Mortar Pl
One section Carrier Pl

Antimachia

*Antimachia
aerodrome*

Cefalo (Kefalos)

*Cape
Tigani*

1./Küstenjäger–Abt. Brandenburg

15./4.Rgt. Brandenburg

*Camare (Kamari)
Bay*

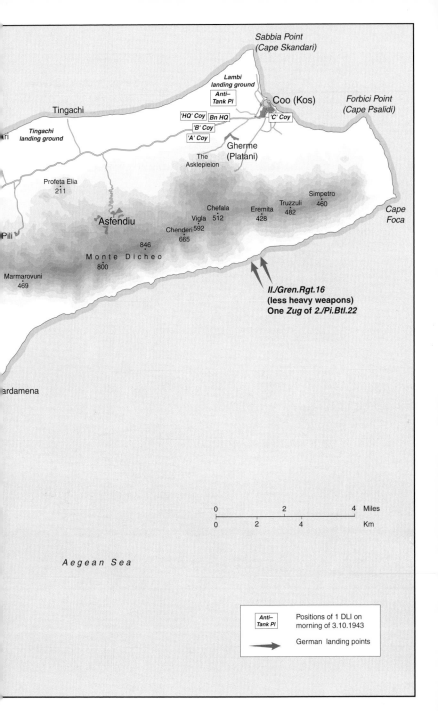

Sabbia Point
(Cape Skandari)

Lambi
landing ground

Anti–
Tank Pl

Coo (Kos)

Forbici Point
(Cape Psalidi)

Tingachi

Tingachi
landing ground

'HQ' Coy   Bn HQ

'B' Coy   'C' Coy

'A' Coy

Gherme
(Platani)

The
Asklepieion

Profeta Elia
211

Chefala
Vigla 512

Eremita
428

Truzzuli
482

Simpetro
460

Cape
Foca

Asfendiu

Chenderi 592
665

846

Pili

Monte Dicheo
800

Marmarovuni
469

II./Gren.Rgt.16
(less heavy weapons)
One Zug of 2./Pi.Btl.22

ardamena

0   2   4   Miles

0   2   4   Km

Aegean Sea

Anti– Tank Pl	Positions of 1 DLI on morning of 3.10.1943
→	German landing points

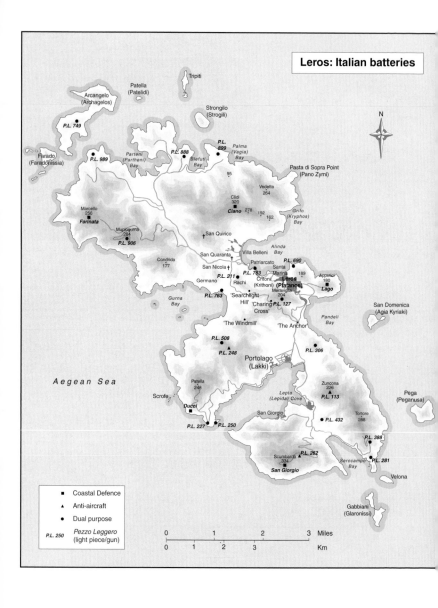

Leros: Italian batteries

Tripiti

Arcangelo
(Archagelos)

Patella
(Patelidi)

P.L. 749

Strongilo
(Strogili)

Farado
(Faradonissia)

P.L. 989

Parteni
(Partheni)
Bay

P.L. 888

Blefuti
Bay

P.L.
899

Palma
(Vagia)
Bay

Pasta di Sopra Point
(Pano Zymi)

95

Vedetta
264

Marcello
256
Farinata

Muplogurna
284
P.L. 906

Clidi
320
Clano 278   192

162

Grifo
(Kryphos)
Bay

San Quirico

Condrida
177

San Quaranta

San Nicola

Germano

P.L. 763

Alinda
Bay

Villa Belleni

Patriarcato
Santa
Marina
Critoni
(Krithoni)
Rachi

P.L. 211

P.L. 763

Gurna
Bay

P.L. 690

189

Appetici
180
Lago

**Leros
(Platanos)**

Meraviglia
204

'Searchlight
Hill'

'Charing **P.L. 127**
Cross'

'The Windmill'

'The Anchor'

Pandeli
Bay

San Domenica
(Agia Kyriaki)

P.L. 508

P.L. 248

P.L. 306

A e g e a n   S e a

Portolago
(Lakki)

Patella
246

Scrofe

Ducei

P.L. 227   P.L. 250

San Giorgio

Lepta
(Lepida) Cove

Zuncona
226
P.L. 113

P.L. 432

Tortore
288

Pega
(Peganusa)

P.L. 388

P.L. 262

Scumbardi
334
San Giorgio

Serocampo
Bay **P.L. 281**

Velona

Gabbiani
(Glaronissi)

N

■	Coastal Defence
▲	Anti-aircraft
●	Dual purpose
P.L. 250	*Pezzo Leggero* (light piece/gun)

0   1   2   3   Miles

0   1   2   3   Km

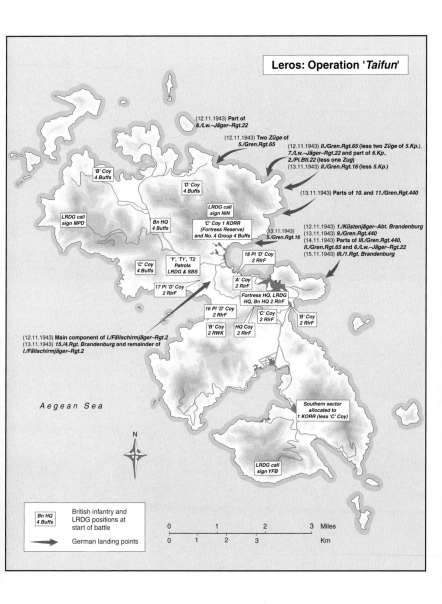

Leros: Operation 'Taifun'

(12.11.1943) Part of
8./Lw.–Jäger–Rgt.22

(12.11.1943) Two *Züge* of
5./Gren.Rgt.65

(12.11.1943) II./Gren.Rgt.65 (less two *Züge* of 5.Kp.),
7./Lw.–Jäger–Rgt.22 and part of 6.Kp.,
2./Pi.Btl.22 (less one *Zug*)
(13.11.1943) II./Gren.Rgt.16 (less 5.Kp.)

(13.11.1943) Parts of 10. and 11./Gren.Rgt.440

'B' Coy
4 Buffs

'D' Coy
4 Buffs

LRDG call
sign MPD

LRDG call
sign NIN

Bn HQ
4 Buffs

'C' Coy 1 KORR
(Fortress Reserve)
and No. 4 Group 4 Buffs

(13.11.1943)
5./Gren.Rgt.16

(12.11.1943) 1./Küstenjäger–Abt. Brandenburg
(13.11.1943) 9./Gren.Rgt.440
(14.11.1943) Parts of III./Gren.Rgt.440,
II./Gren.Rgt.65 and 6./Lw.–Jäger–Rgt.22
(15.11.1943) III./1.Rgt. Brandenburg

'C' Coy
4 Buffs

'Y', 'T1', 'T2'
Patrols
LRDG & SBS

18 Pl 'D' Coy
2 RIrF

17 Pl 'D' Coy
2 RIrF

'A' Coy
2 RIrF

Fortress HQ, LRDG
HQ, Bn HQ 2 RIrF

'B' Coy
2 RIrF

16 Pl 'D' Coy
2 RIrF

'C' Coy
2 RIrF

'B' Coy
2 RWK

HQ Coy
2 RIrF

(12.11.1943) Main component of I./Fällschirmjäger–Rgt.2
(13.11.1943) 15./4.Rgt. Brandenburg and remainder of
I./Fällschirmjäger–Rgt.2

Aegean Sea

Southern sector
allocated to
1 KORR (less 'C' Coy)

N

LRDG call
sign YFB

Bn HQ
4 Buffs

British infantry and
LRDG positions at
start of battle

German landing points

| 0 | 1 | 2 | 3 | Miles |
| 0 | 1 | 2 | 3 | Km |

Feldwebel Gustav Wehrs (centre) with members of *5./Gren.Rgt.65* at Suda Bay, Crete, prior to boarding the *Trapani* for Kos. This *Kompanie* sustained heavy losses during the subsequent landing at Leros. (*G. Wehrs*)

BELOW Troops from an unidentified German unit just before going into action on Kos. (*G. Symonds*)

TOP 3 October 1943: during the German invasion of Kos, a vessel undergoes an attack by three Bristol Beaufighters, possibly of 227 Squadron. According to the original caption the lead aircraft has just been shot down.
(H. Weissenborn)

3 October 1943: troops come ashore from a *Marinefährprahm* near Marmari.
(G. Symonds)

OPPOSITE A truck-towed *Pak* on Kos. (*G. Symonds*)

LEFT 4 October 1943: German troops in the deserted streets of Kos town. (*G. Symonds*)

BELOW The advance continues along the harbour road. (*G. Symonds*)

OPPOSITE Ju 87 *Stukas* over Point 482 (Truzzuli). (*G. Symonds*)

ABOVE 4 October 1943: pockets of resistance are mopped up towards the end of the German advance in north-east Kos. (*G. Symonds*)

Kos: British prisoners are put to work helping their German captors. (*G. Symonds*)

ABOVE Troops of *1./Küstenjäger-Abt. Brandenburg* about to land at Astipalaea on 22 October 1943. (*G. Symonds*)

BELOW A *Flak* crew at Astipalaea. (*G. Symonds*)

OPPOSITE ABOVE Leros from the south as seen by the *Luftwaffe*. (*G. Symonds*)

OPPOSITE BELOW Leros, with Alinda Bay in the foreground and, behind, Gurna Bay. The narrow strip of land between was used as the drop zone for German paratroopers on 12 and 13 November 1943. Rachi Ridge and Meraviglia, overlooking Leros town (Platanos), are clearly visible. Appetici is just out of view in the bottom left corner. (*G. Symonds*)

TOP Scumbarda under aerial bombardment. (*H. Weissenborn*)

German paratroopers exit from Ju 52 transports between Gurna and Alinda bays. (*E. Johnson*)

TOP MG-42 team in action on the eastern slope of Appetici. (*E. Johnson*)

German assault troops ascend Appetici. (*E. Johnson*)

Members of the *Nachrichtenzug* (signal platoon) of *I./Fallschirmjäger-Rgt.2* at a house within the drop zone at San Nicola. (*H. Weiser via P. Schenk*)

BELOW Italian bunker on the north-west shore of Alinda Bay. This was cleared by a *Fallschirmjäger* patrol in the early hours of 13 November. Point 278 is in the background. (*W. Keller*)

No less tragic was the loss of HMS *Eclipse*. The destroyer sailed from Alexandria in the early hours of Saturday, 23 October, together with HM ships *Petard*, *Exmoor* and *Rockwood*. *Eclipse* and *Petard* had each embarked around 200 Army personnel (mainly 4th Battalion The Buffs)[25] and ten tons of stores. It was intended to rendezvous in Turkish waters twenty-four hours later and transfer passengers and stores to small craft for onward passage to Leros. At about 1400 hours on the 23rd, *Rockwood* reported water contamination in her forward tanks and returned to Egypt in company with *Exmoor*. *Eclipse* and *Petard* passed through Kos Straits at 2330 that night. Half an hour later, HMS *Eclipse* was rocked by two almost simultaneous explosions. The ship listed to port until she lay on her beam and sank within minutes. Her captain, Commander E. Mack, reported:

> Amidships, the soldiers were fallen in a hundred each side, having just come out from forward mess decks. They were carrying their life belts and were receiving their final instructions for disembarking. Only three officers and 40 men (approximately) escaped. It is thought that the heavy casualties amongst them may have been partly caused by those on the port side becoming jammed against the guard rails by falling stores as the ship listed.
>
> Of the *Eclipse* ships' company, only six Officers and 68 ratings are known to be safe out of a complement of ten Officers and 190 ratings. It is thought that there was a considerably larger number in the water at the time, but many may have perished while waiting to be picked up.
>
> HMS *Petard* picked up three Officers and 29 ratings and about ten soldiers before having to leave the scene …[26]

Among the survivors was Sergeant Albert Lukehurst of the Buffs:

'Shortly after midnight', our instructions stated, 'and some ten miles from your destination, you will tranship into native boats which will convey you to Leros. The time allowed for the changeover will be one hour only; at the end of this time the destroyer will return. A hot drink will be served to all at 2330 hours.'

After partaking of the ship's hospitality we came up on deck and were instructed to stand by our kits. I recall coming back to mine and glancing at my watch – it was two minutes past midnight. We were going at full speed, a little over 30 knots. I sat down on my lifebelt and what happened after that is only a ghastly nightmare. I sat there dozing when suddenly, without the slightest warning, the whole deck seemed enveloped in a gigantic flash of flame. The blast that followed the explosion picked me up as a giant hand and I was thrown across the deck. I remember hitting something very hard at the entrance to the hatchway leading to the boilers. Here all was flame and scalding steam and falling metal as the ship broke up. The force of the explosion turned the destroyer on its side and the screws at the rear for one moment threshed the air.

The first explosion had barely died away when another followed ... By this time I was trapped among the falling metal and struggle as I may, and struggle I most certainly did, I was firmly held by something across my back. This second explosion, killing as it undoubtedly did many of my comrades, certainly saved my life as it freed my back and allowed me to slip into the sea. As I was sitting on my lifebelt at the time of the first explosion it is hardly necessary to say that by the time I reached the water I no longer had it with me ...

Fortunately I managed to get clear before the ill-fated destroyer disappeared beneath the waves – my recollection of those few moments is very dim. Quickly, my battledress became sodden and my boots felt like leaden weights; however, floating beside me in the water were several panniers in which our stores were packed and one of these gave me a welcome breather but it soon became obvious that they were rapidly becoming waterlogged and must soon sink.[27]

One of the rescuers was Sub Lieutenant Peter Wood, on board the *Petard*:

When we stopped, our Asdic [sonar] disclosed that there were mines all around us. We managed to clear the minefield and lowered two boats to pick up survivors. I took one of the whalers and made several trips into the oil-covered area and filled the boat with survivors, most of whom were desperately wounded and suffering terribly from oil in their lungs. In the middle of this operation, when we were about 300 yards from *Petard*, we heard the sound of German E-boat engines approaching. We held our breath as we watched the phosphorescent wakes of three craft pass within 100 yards of us ...[28]

According to Lieutenant Commander R. C. Egan on *Petard*, just one unidentified craft was reported in the immediate vicinity. Even so, this was sufficient to prompt the ship's departure. Initially, Lukehurst was unaware that he had been abandoned:

Object after object floated by all covered like myself in black oil and unrecognisable. Fate was kind to me that night because just when my pannier was almost submerged a small object floated by and in desperation I transferred my grip – words cannot express my feelings when I discovered it to be a lifebelt.

For a time I hung over my cork life-saver and endeavoured to remove my boots. It was a deadly job for each time I leaned forward to untie my laces I overbalanced and somersaulted. Eventually the job was accomplished and the lifebelt adjusted; it was slightly damaged but good enough for me. Next I emptied my pockets of anything weighty, but as the water was cold I retained my clothing.

While all this had been going on I had seen no one in the water, absolutely no one ... I was not alone in the water however, as all around I could hear the most pitiful cries for help ...

I swam around endeavouring to contact someone – when someone shouted I would swim in that direction but would find nothing. After several such fruitless efforts I decided that I was wasting my time and strength and the only thing to do was to try and make the Turkish coast on my own. In the distance I could see a light and taking a rough bearing by the stars to avoid swimming round in circles I began slowly to make my way towards it. After about a quarter of an hour had gone by I heard a shout close by and on investigation found a fellow supported by a couple of oars. I explained to him what I was attempting and we agreed to continue together. Accordingly he went to the front of the oars and put the blades beneath his armpits whilst I went to the rear and endeavoured to steer and thus swimming with our legs only we continued.[29]

After being in the water for four and a half hours, Lukehurst and his companion were spotted by an observant crewman on ML 337. After responding to the distress signal transmitted by *Petard*, the boat was en route to Turkish waters with survivors, including the commanding officer of the Buffs, Lieutenant Colonel Douglas Iggulden. When he was hauled on board the rescue vessel Lukehurst promptly passed out:

> When I came to under the warming influence of rum I found that Colonel Iggulden was in the same cabin; his first words sent a thrill of satisfaction through me – 'Well done, Lukehurst.' We spent that day anchored in neutral waters and the following night went through to Leros.[30]

There, they were reunited with survivors who had been picked up by an RAF rescue launch. As Lukehurst and his fellow soldiers recovered, none could have known that they would soon have to face another ordeal – of a very different kind.

CHAPTER 7

Leros Prelude to Battle

LEROS LIES BEYOND KALYMNOS NEAR the northern extremity of the Dodecanese. Of irregular shape, it is approximately 9 miles (14.4 kilometres) in length and varies in width from 0.65 miles (1.05 kilometres) to a little over 4 miles (6.8 kilometres), with several islets just off the mainland. Leros is predominantly rocky and characterised by narrow valleys and grey, windswept hills, the highest of which is Scumbarda in the south (334 metres). The island has a much indented and fairly inhospitable coastline, dominated by steep cliffs. The few sandy beaches tend to be in the central region, notably in the bays of Grifo, Alinda and Gurna. The capital and main residential area (called Leros in 1943, since renamed Platanos) is situated in a narrow coastal valley in the north-central part of the island, overlooked on one side by the promontory of Appetici with its ancient castle (at 180 metres) and on the south by Meraviglia (204 metres). A road runs through the centre of the island, linking the town with the chief port (Portolago/Lakki), and with branches leading to Italian gun positions on the heights. The Italians on Leros enjoyed a comfortable existence, a privileged few even residing with their families. Local Greeks led a more austere lifestyle and existed by farming small terraced plots on hillside slopes, as goatherds and as fishermen. After more than twenty years of Italian rule, both nationalities had learned to tolerate each other and, so far, Leros had escaped the fate of other disputed islands in the Mediterranean. This was soon to change.

When the advance party of the Royal Irish Fusiliers arrived at Lakki on the morning of 17 September, no one was sure how they would be received by the Italian garrison. As their destroyer approached the jetty, the commanding officer of the Faughs, Lieutenant Colonel Maurice French, prepared to disembark accompanied by his brigade liaison officer, Lieutenant Frank Smith:

> Our CO said to me: 'You and I will go ashore first, Smith, but we don't want to look too warlike, you know. I don't think we'll wear steel helmets, we'll wear caps and just carry side-arms.' Well, as we rounded the entrance to the harbour we were amazed to find that most of the Italians seemed to be congregating on the quayside – it was a reception party. A band played and gold-braided officers greeted the Colonel and I as we walked down the gang-plank. They thought it was a celebration, rather than a take-over ... I accompanied various officers who were taking over the different command posts and defence sites and at each one we visited, bottles of vermouth appeared and before the day was over we were in quite high spirits ourselves.[1]

More troops and equipment followed, including 'C', 'D' and 'HQ' Companies of the Faughs. The inevitable German reaction to the British build-up was not long in coming. Soon after arriving at Lakki on Sunday morning, 26 September, HMS *Intrepid* and the Greek *Vasilissa Olga* were attacked at their moorings with devastating results. *Intrepid*'s Captain, Commander C. A. de W. Kitcat, RN, had just left his ship when the attack developed:

> At about 0915 I set out for shore by motor boat ... When approaching the jetty I heard the sound of aeroplane motors overhead, and looking up saw a large formation of Ju 88s at about 5,000 feet. As I watched they commenced to dive, directing their attacks on the two destroyers. I at once returned to the ship, but before reaching it HMS *Intrepid* had received a hit on the bulkhead between No. 3 Boiler room and the Engine room port side and within half a minute HHMS *Queen Olga* received a hit in the after magazine. No warning whatever of attack was received; no Italian guns opened fire. Anti-aircraft armament of HMS *Intrepid* was at five minutes notice but was in full operation before the first bomb had dropped. I saw pieces fly from one machine, obviously hit by her fire, and am informed that this machine crashed on the island.
>
> HHMS *Queen Olga* rapidly filled, heeled over and sank. It is

regretted that loss of life was considerable. Her Captain, Commander Blessas, was wounded when the bomb struck and was subsequently killed by cannon shell from an aircraft ...[2]

Naval Lieutenant G. W. Searle was on board his vessel, ML 355, on the south side of the harbour:

With a shattering explosion the stern of the *Queen Olga* blew off. She had a direct hit in the after-magazine. One destroyer sunk, the other was badly damaged. The repair shops, the barracks and the southern jetties were hit with considerable destruction. The German pilots could be proud of their precision but the defences should have done better. MLs 351 and 355 both claimed hits on the planes but could not claim that any were brought down ...

The *Queen Olga* had gone down with great loss of life. First there was the explosion itself; then as oil from the ship spread over the water, it ignited and the place where she had been lying at a buoy became a patch of blazing oil around which MLs 836, 356 and 354 circled as they tried to pick up survivors. MLs 356 and 354 had actually been alongside *Queen Olga* when the raid started and had only just cast off in time to avoid destruction themselves. Astern of us, only some fifty yards away, were the smashed remains of two Italian *MS* boats which had suffered direct hits by bombs. Ashore, the workshops and barracks were on fire and bodies were being carried out.[3]

The *Intrepid* was towed inshore where it was hoped that the rugged shoreline would offer some protection against air attack, and allow emergency repairs to be carried out. But when the Germans returned in the afternoon the destroyer was struck again. Among the casualties was her commander, who was knocked unconscious (and remained so for three days). A young Lerian, Athanasios Paraponiaris, watched with his father and an Italian soldier as five bombers commenced their attack from out of the sun:

The first aircraft dropped its bombs in the sea by mistake. So did the second and third. The fourth aircraft in the formation was hit by ground fire and blown to pieces. The Italian soldier cried, '*L'hanno battuto!*' [They got him]; 'Oh, shut up!' my father told him.[4]

The *Intrepid* was seriously damaged and in the early hours of Monday, 27 September, she finally sank. Paraponiaris recollected the devastating results of the continuing air attacks:

They [the aircraft] came from the direction of Tsigounas [San Giovanni], again using the sun to blind the ground defences. The Italians scattered. Only those manning the hilltop batteries remained at their posts. Up there, the British used whistles because their alarm wasn't working. Nothing remained standing. Everything was destroyed. They bombed everything from one end of the island to the other; they bombed until dusk. There were eight to ten air raids from morning until midday.[5]

Within less than a fortnight, the *Luftwaffe* would account for the Italian *MAS 534*, the steamer *Prode*, destroyer *Euro*, minelayer *Legnano*, landing craft *MZ 730*, landing ship *Porto di Roma* and the refrigerator ship *Ivorea*. Few Lerians had anticipated anything like this. The bombing resulted in an exodus to outlying areas. Shallow caves which had until then been used as goat pens, were taken over as makeshift shelters by terrified civilians. Women huddled together and prayed for deliverance. When the bombing got close, they crossed themselves and moaned and trembled uncontrollably. It was Malta all over again, or so it must have seemed to many, including the commander of 234 Brigade, Brigadier Ben Brittorous, who had recently arrived to take charge, leaving Lieutenant Colonel French to concentrate on the island defences. Previously, Brittorous had commanded 8th (Ardwick) Battalion The Manchester Regiment (TA) in Malta. If he had then been a popular and well-respected figure, on Leros Brittorous was almost universally loathed by officers and men alike. Major G. J. Ryan DAQMG (Deputy Assistant Quartermaster General) had an early introduction following his own arrival at Leros:

I had heard a great deal about Brittorous – his fire eating propensities and his violent insistence upon being saluted on every possible occasion – and it was with some trepidation that I went to meet him. However, I had one card up my sleeve. I was to be the first to inform him of his local promotion, congratulate him and present him with his Major General's regalia, and most men would find it difficult to be officious with the bringer of such news. I found him to be a short,

red-faced man with a thick growth of dark curly hair and the most
enormous black moustache, the ends of which he constantly twirled. He
was very pleasant and was tickled to death to hear of his promotion.
Our chat was general and I remember little of it except when I raised the
question of our relations with the Italians and our need to know exactly
what stores they had on the island. 'Now look here Ryan,' he snapped,
'I won't have you upsetting the Italians or demanding things from them.
Our relations with them are excellent at present and I will not have
them upset. If there is anything you want, ask them for it and if you
have difficulty come to me. Is that clear?' From my recent conversa-
tions with Dickson [sic: Major Richard Dixon] and Boyd (the Staff
Captain) I was not very happy about these 'relations' but as they were
both in the room and said nothing, and as I was very much the
newcomer, I thought it best to acquiesce and say nothing too.[6]

Ryan set to work supervising the delivery and distribution of supplies,
but his authority was constantly undermined by the brigade commander.

It soon became apparent that Italian co-operation was not what it
should be. They were stalling. If one went to them with a direct request
(not demand, mark you) it would probably be granted, but they made
no attempt to offer assistance or to advise about the facilities available
on Leros. If we were to conserve and make maximum use of our meagre
resources, it was essential that we should know what was available
locally. The British were responsible for the total defence and administration of Leros – British and Italian garrisons and the civil population.
If we were to carry out our responsibilities, then we must know what
stocks of food, petrol, oil, ammunition and general stores were available
so that we could reinforce where necessary and with maximum economy.
But we did not know and the Italians would not tell us. I went to the
General time and time again. 'The Italians have promised us this information, Ryan, and we will get it in time,' he replied. 'Our relations
with them are perfect – [the Italian commander, *Contrammiraglio*
Luigi] Mascherpa and I are the best of friends – and I will not have
them bloody well upset, d'you understand?'[7]

In spite of the difficulties, Leros and Samos continued to be supplied by sea and, to a lesser degree, by parachute drops, with dumps established at Alexandria, Beirut and Haifa and in Cyprus and neutral Turkey. All kinds of vessels were pressed into service to deliver cargo to the islands:

> The speed with which these ships were unloaded was remarkable. Two or three destroyers each carrying 40 or 50 tons were in and away in 30 or 40 minutes. I think the record was 25 minutes. Speed was essential. Every night, enemy aircraft were over the island dropping flares in search of shipping. More often than not the destroyers had an air battle when leaving the island and sometimes they were spotted as they approached and had to turn away signalling that they would try again the following evening ... Submarines remained longer. They would come in after dark and if necessary remain to the last hour of darkness before slipping away to submerge in some sheltered spot for the day until the journey could be continued the next night. Caiques were easier. They were local craft and common to the islands. It did not much matter if they were seen during the day but their unloading, too, had to be carried out during darkness.[8]

Captain John Olivey, who had recently arrived with the LRDG from Kalymnos, encountered Brittorous a few days after settling in at his post atop Point 320 (Clidi). To his surprise, he was berated for having a grimy cap badge and for allowing his men to go on watch wearing just shorts and without having weapons immediately to hand.

> I passed on all these rockets and from that moment on my cap badge was ever shining, though some of the men, I noticed, preferred to lose theirs thinking, perhaps, that the glint attracted bullets![9]

Initially, a combined Naval and Brigade Headquarters was established in a building in Lakki. As the bombing of the port intensified, Brigade Headquarters shifted to San Nicola, and was followed by Naval Headquarters two days later, on 6 October. When bombs began to fall dangerously close to San Nicola, Brittorous relocated his staff to its Battle Headquarters in a tunnel on top of Meraviglia, in the centre of the island. The increasing attention of the *Luftwaffe* affected everyone, even those who had experienced the worst of the bombing in Malta. Most managed to control their fear and simply carried on with their work. A few succumbed and were evacuated.

If anyone should have been an inspiration for others during this trying time, it was Brittorous. Yet, according to Major Ryan:

> The General had by now lost the little respect or confidence which may have at one time rested in him. He left the entire responsibility for the defence of Leros to Lieutenant Colonel French, made no effort to advise, visit the defences or contact his officers and men. On the occasions he met the men, who were tired out and sweating at their digging, he did nothing but curse them in lurid language for not saluting him properly. He lived in the tunnel where he slept on a ledge on one side of the HQ alcove and where his batman would wake him at 0400 hours with shaving water and breakfast. Woe betide everybody if he had been disturbed during the night or if his breakfast was not 'just so'. Well before it was light and before the daily bombing was likely to start, he would leave in his Jeep with batman and driver for a shady tree conveniently situated near another bomb-proof tunnel and far away from any habitation, on the Parteni road. There he would stay for the rest of the day.
>
> If one wanted to consult him on any question – and after all he was the General, GOC-in-C Aegean Forces – to the tree one would have to go, being very careful to park one's Jeep or motor cycle a good 200 yards away from his 'domain'. On one occasion Owen Gethin, the RE officer, failed to do this and left wheel tracks on the verge opposite the tree. Bedlam was let loose. To the accompaniment of oaths, the Officer was compelled to find a rake and immediately scrub out the offending tracks which would have told the *Luftwaffe* exactly where the GOC Aegean was hiding.[10]

Another with vivid memories of the irascible commander was the commanding officer of 3rd Light Anti-Aircraft Battery, Major J. M. 'Pat' McSwiney. During a quiet period, he decided to take a swim in Partheni Bay:

> I was riding a motor-bike at a reasonable speed when I noticed, out of the corner of my eye, an officer, with a red band to his cap, sitting some distance off the road. I heard a shout, which I felt inclined to ignore, but decided not to be 'bolshie' so I turned the bike round and walked back to where the Brigadier [sic] and his ADC were sitting under the

shade of a juniper tree. I saluted. 'Who are you?' said the Brigadier and 'Why didn't you salute me as you passed?' Both seemed rather strange questions. I felt like asking him who he was, and why we had never met before, considering the part I had already played as one of his senior officers. I thought he must be a bit 'loony', so I played along with his questions, and apologised for not having saluted him before. He offered me a drink of whisky, which I declined as it was barely mid-day. 'Where are you going?' was his next question. 'To reconnoitre, sir' was the obvious reply. I saluted again, got on my bike, had my swim and returned the way I had come, remembering to salute as I passed. After I got back to Battery HQ (in a dugout on the side of Mer-aviglia) I went down into the operations room deep underground in Meraviglia itself. I found the senior Staff Officer (a GSO 2, the same rank as myself) and asked him who the 'old boy' was. He was aston-ished that I had never met him before, but from what he told me then, I realised that the Senior Officer on the island was this extraordinary man, who had completely lost his nerve, and therefore spent most of his time drinking the island's few bottles of whisky. It appeared that he retired to his juniper tree, from where he could observe the bombing by day, and at dusk took sanctuary in the hill fortress.[11]

As a young infantry officer on the Western Front in World War One, Brittorous had won the Military Cross and was twice Mentioned in Dis-patches; more recently, he was awarded the Distinguished Service Order for his role in the disastrous operations in France in 1940. But all men have a breaking point. In the evening Brittorous would return to Fortress Head-quarters to receive the daily situation reports:

Reports finished, he would dictate a signal to Cairo, most of it based upon our reports and pertinent, but always exaggerated – 80 sorties by the *Luftwaffe* would become 280 and the damage done exagger-ated proportionally. They were always toned down by Dick [Major Dixon] before dispatch ... Contempt for the General was becoming very noticeable, so much so that Lieutenant Colonel [W. R.] Brackett, the gunner expert on the island, left for Cairo ostensibly to report on the defences of Leros, but in reality to convey the feelings of the officers towards the Command to higher authority.[12]

The major-general's good friend, *Contrammiraglio* Mascherpa, set no less of an example for the Italians. It was noted that his morale had deteriorated to such a degree that he 'spends most of his time in a tunnel in the rocks, exhibiting every symptom of anxiety neurosis ...'[13]

Up to the end of October, operations in the Aegean had been controlled by Middle East Command through III Corps Headquarters (Force 292) and 234 Brigade (under Brittorous) on Leros. With developments dictating the necessity for a separate command to handle operations in the area, on 1 November, Major General H. R. Hall was appointed General Officer Commanding Aegean, with the specific task of holding Leros and Samos in order to cause maximum disruption to the enemy's lines of communication in the Aegean. In addition, he was given command of all Allied (including Italian) land forces in the area as well as of naval personnel in shore establishments which did not come under the Commander-in-Chief Levant or the Senior British Naval Officer Aegean. On 5 November, Major General Hall and Brigadier R. A. G. 'Dolly' Tilney arrived at Leros and Headquarters Aegean assumed control of operations. Hall decided to make Samos his headquarters and departed on 11 November, leaving on Leros Tilney who relieved Major-General Brittorous as fortress commander. Presumably, Lieutenant Colonel Brackett's report had made an impression. For many, the departure of Brittorous was long overdue. This did not necessarily mean that everyone was satisfied with his replacement. Typical were the misgivings echoed by Lieutenant E. B. W. (Ted) Johnson of 2nd Battalion The Royal Irish Fusiliers:

> The new commander turned out to be an old acquaintance of ours – newly promoted Brigadier Robert Tilney, late CO of the Leicestershire Yeomanry, a gunner regiment, whom we last met in our mountain warfare training in the Lebanon. As he arrived we wondered how well equipped he would be as a Gunner to organise the fight which would be an infantry battle.[14]

Originally, it had been decided by Lieutenant Colonel Maurice French to concentrate the Royal Irish Fusiliers on high ground in the centre of Leros. Lack of numbers precluded wider dispersal. (At the time, rifle companies averaged about sixty 'other ranks' although this number would fluctuate due to unit requirements and the arrival in October of the battalion rear party and reinforcements from the Middle East). By early October, Battalion Headquarters had been established on Meraviglia, close to Brigade, or Fortress, Headquarters; 'A' Company was positioned on the northern slopes, covering Gurna and Alinda Bays and Rachi Ridge; 'B' Company (less one platoon temporarily on Astipalaea in support of the LRDG) occupied the 'Windmill' area (San Giovanni) overlooking Gurna Bay and low ground to the west; 'C' Company, as mobile reserve, was south of Meraviglia, covering the 'Anchor' area (Porta Vecchia) and Pandeli Bay; 'D' Company held Rachi, between Gurna and Alinda Bays, and 'HQ' Company (part of which had been siphoned off to strengthen the rifle companies) was situated in the area of 'Charing Cross' (near Point 132 south of Meraviglia).

The north and south of the island were allocated mainly to patrols of the Long Range Desert Group, with the task of manning observation posts and with a wireless link to unit headquarters on Meraviglia.

During the night of 16–17 October, the Faughs were reunited with the battalion's rear party from Egypt. After being withdrawn from Kastellorizo, 'B' Company of 2nd Battalion The Queen's Own Royal West Kent Regiment also arrived and was retained on Leros. A few days later, the first troops of the depleted 4th Battalion The Royal East Kent Regiment (The Buffs) also landed, followed on 5 November by 1st Battalion The King's Own Royal Regiment (Lancaster)[15]. By this time, the infantry had been joined by 3rd Battery (less one troop) 1st Light Anti-Aircraft Regiment Royal Artillery (equipped with twelve 40mm Bofors guns); one troop of field artillery (with four 18/25-pounder anti-tank guns which had found their way on to Samos after being captured by the Germans in France in 1940), additional detachments of the LRDG and Special Boat Squadron, and supporting sub-units including Royal Army Medical Corps and Royal Engineers; a total of just over 2,900 officers and men.[16]

Accurate figures are difficult to come by, but the Italian garrison on Leros probably totalled 5,500 personnel; this included *I battaglione* (battalion) of *10° reggimento di fanteria* (infantry regiment) of *Divisione 'Regina'; 8ª compagnia mitraglieri da posizione costiera* (coastal machine-gun company); *402ª compagnia mitraglieriex-Milizia Volontaria per la Sicurezza Nazionale* (ex-'Blackshirts' machine-gun company); part of *147ª squadriglia* (maritime reconnaissance squadron) equipped with Cant seaplanes, and mainly unarmed workers and survivors of sunken ships. The Italians occupied positions overlooking likely landing areas including the bays of Blefuti, Lakki (where Italian Headquarters was situated), Gurna and Serocampo. They also manned hilltop gun sites. For a small island, Leros possessed an astounding number of heavy weapons.[17] Unfortunately, however, effective gun control was virtually non-existent. According to Tilney:

> There were no Fixed Signal Services on the island. It seems almost inconceivable that the Italians can have regarded Leros as a powerfully defended base and yet refrained from installing any form of buried communications or any fire control system with buried cables. A most elaborate gun control centre existed on Patella but communications from this centre to AA and coastal batteries were by air lines which were destroyed beyond hope or repair in the early stages of the enemy air offensive. Only three batteries were equipped with wireless sets, most indifferent ones that were rarely in contact, and there was no visual signalling equipment on the island …[18]

In the days to follow, communications generally were to present a serious problem due to insufficient and inadequate equipment in a terrain that allowed only restricted wireless links at the best of times. Fortress Headquarters remained on Meraviglia. Men and equipment were crammed into a tunnel which ran through the hilltop, with an entrance at each end and a vertical shaft providing access to an observation post. When Tilney took over his predecessor's command centre, he was unimpressed. In his after-action report, the brigadier, writing in the third person, described the place as being wholly unsuitable:

> Apart from being in a most conspicuous place which came in for almost incessant bombing, the tunnel itself was dark and narrow with only three small bays built off it. It was far too small and became hopelessly congested. The most suitable alternative would have been to have occupied the Italian HQ in Portolago [Lakki] but the Commander appreciated that he could not afford to upset the Italians when by firmness and tact good progress was being made with them; in any event the static wireless sets and the field telephone exchange had previously

been installed in the tunnel and there was neither time nor sufficient spare cable to allow of a move to a more suitable locality.[19]

Acting on instructions from Major-General Hall, Tilney quickly made himself unpopular by ordering a drastic shake-up of the established defence plan. Johnson recalled:

> Brigadier Tilney gave his orders to his COs for the new plan of defence on 6th November and the Faughs buckled down to move stores, weapons and ammunition to the new positions. This was a tiring and tedious job with little or no transport. Time for sleep was short. During the day one dug or blasted holes in the rock and carried stores. During the night fatigue parties became stevedores unloading precious cargo from anxious Royal Navy ships and submarines who were champing at the bit to get away to the Turkish coast before dawn and the inevitable *Stuka* sortie.[20]

The revised strategy was based on the principle of denying the beaches to the enemy. It was a plan flawed in design and, ultimately, in practice. A problem was lack of transport, which prevented Tilney from maintaining a strong central reserve. Instead, troops were to be deployed on a dangerously wide front (thereby aggravating the already poor line of communications). The priority was to destroy the enemy as quickly as possible, ideally before he could land and consolidate any initial gains. Accordingly, the island was divided into three sectors: the Buffs were deployed in the North, the Faughs (with 'B' Company of the Royal West Kents) in the Centre, and the King's Own (less one company) in the South. Each battalion, with one company held as local reserve, was sited to cover potential landing places on the coast. Units also had to be ready to move into any sector and under the authority of the area commander. Fortress reserve ('C' Company of the King's Own) was held just east of San Quaranta with the primary task of counter-attacking paratroopers who might be dropped in the North Sector. Medium machine-guns were sited to sweep likely landing areas; the four 18/25-pounders from Samos were placed on a feature in the Blacutera area (between San Giovanni and Meraviglia), and 2-pounder anti-tank guns and 40mm Bofors were installed at strategic points in and around the centre of the island. The loyalty and fighting quality of the

Italians had always been in doubt. Dispersed throughout the island, they were destined to play a comparatively minor role, enforced by Tilney's decision to restrict their movement when battle commenced:

> To ensure that they did not leave their positions it was ordered that, to avoid confusion between German and Italian troops, the Italians could only leave their positions at the risk of being shot unless they were wearing the distinguishing sign as issued, ie signal armlets.[21]

In the first days of November, Allied warships and aircraft searched for shipping gathering for the impending German assault against Leros. When moving between staging points in daylight, the enemy vessels were heavily escorted by fighters and when dispersed at night they were virtually impossible to detect. The Royal Navy achieved a rare success in the early hours of 7 November when the coast patrol vessel *GA 45* was sunk by HM ships *Penn* and *Pathfinder*. Submarines also took their toll on German-commandeered sailing vessels and some enemy small craft were damaged in air attacks, but at a cost. On 5 November alone, Beaufighter units lost six aircraft and four crews during Aegean operations: Bf 109s of *8./J.G.27* accounted for four machines of 227 Squadron which were engaged on an offensive sweep around Rhodes, and at Lavrion Bay, off the Greek mainland, two crews of 47 Squadron were taken prisoner when their aircraft were shot down by ship's *Flak*. Two pilots of *7./J.G.27* were each credited with a Beaufighter destroyed on the 6th: 603 and 47 Squadrons lost one and two machines respectively (the latter with one crew) in a low-level shipping strike which left the German *R 34* and *R 194* disabled and at least three killed and many more wounded; another aircraft belly-landed on returning to Gambut. On the 7th, a Beaufighter of 252 Squadron was written-off and the crew injured in a take-off accident. Three days later, a pilot in 47 Squadron died and a 603 Squadron crew was captured when two more Beaufighters fell to Messerschmitts of *III./J.G.27*.

As well as shipping strikes, Allied aircraft flew numerous reconnaissance sorties; Wellingtons undertook mine-laying operations in the Aegean, and Hudsons carried out regular night-bombing raids on Antimachia aerodrome. Overall, the effect on the enemy was minimal: without long-range fighters little could be done to prevent the *Luftwaffe* from maintaining air superiority, or from continuing to threaten Allied warships.

After considering the risks and taking into account the prevailing problem of fuel limitations, it was decided on 10 November not to allow British destroyers to operate against enemy invasion forces by day unless specifically ordered to do so by the Commander-in-Chief, Levant. Motor launches (MLs), motor torpedo boats (MTBs) and motor gun boats (MGBs) operating under the SBNO Aegean had to lay up in Turkish territorial waters during daylight hours. At night, the MLs were to carry out anti-invasion patrols, while the MTBs and MGBs remained in harbour at immediate notice to act on enemy reports. The Germans, too, feared being caught in the open. Around Leros, the *Kriegsmarine* was dissuaded from using its own destroyers by day due to the very real danger presented by coastal batteries and the threat posed by the Royal Navy. More than ever, the day really did belong to the *Luftwaffe*.

As a result of enemy activity, the British expected the invasion craft to assemble at Kos and Kalymnos after dark on 10–11 November and to spend at least one night to refuel and prepare to move to departure points in northern Kalymnos. Accordingly, Kalymnos harbour was bombarded by the destroyers *Petard* and *Rockwood* and the Polish *Krakowiak*. At least two escort vessels (*UJ 2101* and *UJ 2102*) sustained splinter damage and the already damaged merchantman *Trapani* was set on fire and capsized, but no landing craft were hit. While withdrawing, HMS *Rockwood* was damaged when she was struck by a glider bomb that, luckily, failed to explode. She was taken in tow by *Petard* under constant air attack to the Gulf of Doris.[22] Under Captain M. S. Thomas (Captain (D), 8th Destroyer Flotilla), HM ships *Faulknor*, *Beaufort* and the Greek *Pindos* bombarded Kos harbour a few hours later, with little effect. Originally, this force was to have withdrawn to Mandelyah Gulf but in order to place himself in a position to assist *Rockwood* and *Petard* if required, Thomas ordered his ships to make for Port Deremen, in the Gulf of Kos.

Earlier, four minesweepers had left Kastellorizo for Leros with reinforcements including the Buffs rear party from Egypt. Two of the vessels, BYMS 72 and BYMS 73, reached their destination without mishap, but the former could not be offloaded in time and departed still carrying essential stores. She would return the next night – with far-reaching consequences for the proposed German landing.

In the early hours of 10 November, MMS *102* ran aground off enemy-occupied Kos. On board was Leonard Marsland Gander, a correspondent with the *Daily Telegraph*; his conducting officer, Captain David Crichton of Army Public Relations and Sergeant Wood of the Army Photographic Unit. To avoid running the risk of another beaching, the accompanying minesweeper (MMS *103*) was discouraged from staying to assist. Daylight brought help from an unexpected quarter with the arrival of a caique whose crew included two naval officers; one British, the other American. They took on themselves the responsibility for freeing the stranded minesweeper, and in the meantime arranged for the transfer of her passengers by motor launch and caiques to the damaged *Adrias* off Turkey. The following evening, all personnel transhipped from *Adrias* to motor launches *456* and *461* for onward passage to Leros. Marsland Gander and those on board ML *461* disembarked at Alinda Bay, while ML *456* proceeded to Lakki. Within hours both boats would be back at sea, but under very different circumstances.

Throughout the war, the Germans relied on a coding machine known as Enigma for sending secret transmissions. These were duly intercepted and passed on to cryptanalysts and translators at Bletchley Park in Buckinghamshire, England. When, on 7 November, a German signaller keyed into his Enigma machine: 'Owing to compromise of code word *"Leopard"*, new code word *"Taifun"* ('Typhoon') is to be used from now on'[23], he was not only informing German commanders! Yet, those privy to 'Ultra', as the decoding operation was called, did not always take full advantage of their unique position. Ultimately, any advance knowledge of German intentions had little effect on the outcome of the war in the Aegean in 1943. On 11 November, 'Ultra' revealed that Operation *'Taifun'* was to commence the following day. Air reconnaissance also showed considerable movement of landing craft between Kos and Kalymnos. However, as relief destroyers were not expected until late on 12–13 November, it was essential for those in the area to conserve fuel. Accordingly, Captain Thomas was ordered to move to an anchorage nearer the Kos Channel from where *Beaufort* and *Pindos* could be sent to attack any landing craft reported off Kos. The force shifted berth to Alakishli Bay and arrived at 0157 hours on Friday, 12 November.

CHAPTER 8

Operation '*Taifun*'
Day 1: Friday, 12 November 1943

ON THE EVE OF OPERATION '*Taifun*', *Generalleutnant* Müller had at his disposal a battle group of experienced and motivated combat troops, most of whom had already seen action against the British on Kos. They were divided into three subdivisions, the largest of which was the eastern landing force. This comprised *Kampfgruppe* Schädlich with *Leutnant* Hans Schädlich in command of *1./Küstenjäger-Abt. Brandenburg* (*Hauptmann* Armin Kuhlmann had been severely wounded in an air raid at Kalymnos); *Kampfgruppe* von Saldern under *Major* Sylvester von Saldern with *II./Gren.Rgt.65*; *II. Bataillon/Luftwaffenjägerregiment 22 (II./Lw.-Jäger-Rgt.22)* and *2./Pi.Btl.22*; *Kampfgruppe* Dörr with *Hauptmann* Erwin Dörr and *III./Gren.Rgt.440*. The western landing force, or *Kampfgruppe* Aschoff, was provided by *II./Gren.Rgt.16* commanded by *Hauptmann* Philipp Aschoff. The third, airborne element, was designated *Kampfgruppe* Kühne with *Hauptmann* Martin Kühne commanding *I. Bataillon/Fallschirmjägerregiment 2 (I./Fallschirmjäger-Rgt.2)* of the *Luftwaffe*. Transport for the amphibious element was provided mainly by the *Kriegsmarine* and *Pionierlandungskompanie 780 (Pi.Ldgs.Kp.780)* with the *Küstenjäger* providing their own *Pioniersturmboote*. A second wave comprised *3./Fla.Btl.22* and *3.* and *4./Art.Rgt.22* together with heavy weapons of *II./Gren.Rgt.16* and *II./Gren.Rgt.65*. *III. Bataillon/Jägerregiment 1 Brandenburg (III./1. Rgt. Brandenburg)* and *15./4.Rgt. Brandenburg* were held in reserve near Athens.

It was assumed by the Germans that virtually the whole of Leros could be targeted by different batteries, and that potential landing sites along the coast were especially well covered. Vulnerable stretches of coastline were also expected to be fortified and mined. To minimise losses during the assault, a number of less heavily defended, but unlikely, landing sites were selected. It was intended for the first wave to secure these areas and to neutralise local defensive positions. Although the troops would only be lightly armed pending the arrival of heavy weapons with the second wave, they could rely on air support throughout the operation. Much depended on close inter-service co-operation.

The original battle plan had allowed for both the first and second waves to embark simultaneously with the latter ready to follow up when required. However, enemy action, bad weather and unavoidable delays had reduced the availability of transport vessels for the troops and their equipment to five *MFPs*; four *Infanterieboote (I-Boote)*; ten *Pionierlandungsboote (Pi-La-Boote)*, nine of which appear to have taken part in the initial landing; one *Pionierführungsboot (Pi-Führungsboot)* and the two *Küstenjäger Sturmboote*. Close escort was to be provided by two *R-Boote* and three submarine-chasers.

This meant that there was now only sufficient craft to embark the first wave following which the vessels would have to return for the second wave. It was imperative to accomplish the initial assault before daylight, but with a full moon adding to the problems, Y-Time (H-Hour) could not be scheduled any earlier than 0430. In order to reduce further delays, elements of the second wave were transferred to Kalymnos, the nearest German-occupied island to Leros. On X-1 (D-1) the headquarters staff of *Kampfgruppe* Müller moved to Isolavecchia Bay, in Kalymnos, the chosen location for the command post (CP) during the first stage of the battle. It was intended to transfer the CP to Leros once a beachhead had been established.

Three embarkation points were allocated for the assault units, depending on their areas of deployment. These were: the port of Kos; at Marmari on the north coast of Kos; and at Kalymnos harbour. At 2100 *II./ Gren. Rgt.65* was to be transported from the port of Kos, eastwards past the islands of Pserimos and Kalmynos to rendezvous at Calolino with *III./Gren. Rgt.440*, *II./Lw.-Jäger-Rgt.22* and *1. Küstenjägerkompanie* following their departure from Kalymnos at 2200. After continuing to a pre-selected point the combined eastern force was to divide into their individual landing

groups for the final approach to Leros. At 2300 the western force with
II./Gren.Rgt.16 was to proceed from Marmari along the west coast of
Kalymnos towards the island of Telendo and on to a pre-selected nautical
point for the final approach.

Generalleutnant Müller had impressed upon the naval officer commanding the invasion fleet, *Korvettenkapitän* Dr Günther Brandt of the
21. U-Jagd-Flottille, the importance of continuing once the operation had
started regardless of the appearance of British destroyers and regardless of
any losses. An aborted or delayed landing by any of the units could jeopardise the entire mission.

Embarkation was carried out according to plan and completed by about
2000 hours on Thursday, 11 November. At the same time, some two to
three miles from Leros, BYMS 72 was on a second delivery run when she
was attacked by Dornier Do 217s and struck by a glider bomb. With her
mast toppled, the port Oerlikon knocked out and the steering damaged,
the ship was left circling helplessly: two men were killed, five were injured
and one was reported missing. From Leros, ML 299 and MTB 315 hurried
to assist. Travelling on the latter was Lieutenant Commander Frank
Ramseyer. He boarded the minesweeper and assumed control and, with
the steering gear temporarily repaired, managed to pilot her in to Alinda
Bay.

The Kalymnos convoy had just got under way when two destroyers
were sighted between Kos and Kalymnos. Their identity could not be
ascertained (in fact, they were almost certainly German), but as an hour's
contingency had been included in the planning of *'Taifun'*, Müller agreed
to a request by Brandt to use this time to allow the destroyers to clear
the area; Y-Time was to remain unchanged. Accordingly the Kos convoy
departed at 2300 with *R 195* leading the way. After an uneventful
start a caique was seen at 0040 approaching from the east. As a precaution, this was intercepted, the crew was apprehended and the boat left to
drift.

At 0110 and 0115, two Wellingtons of 38 Squadron made several
attack runs during which a total of thirty-two 250 lb bombs were dropped
around the Kos flotilla, albeit without effect. Soon after, at 0120 and 0122,
Allied air reconnaissance – presumably the same Wellingtons – reported
two groups of eight and seven 'barges' respectively steering north-west

from Kappari (Pserimos), inside the minefield to the east of Kalymnos. It was assumed that the enemy was assembling in preparation for a daylight assault, but the threat posed by mines precluded a pre-emptive strike by the Royal Navy. That this was the main (eastern) force en route to Leros was not appreciated until it was far too late. It has been since argued that even if the Navy had reacted, the enemy would have received sufficient warning to avoid an attack and to respond with retaliatory action. The only certainty is that the last real chance of halting the invasion was now irrevocably lost.[1] The Kos flotilla reached the rendezvous at Calolino and was joined by the delayed force from Kalymnos about an hour later, at 0220. Both units then proceeded on course for Leros. Minutes later, the convoy was again bombed, this time by a high-flying unidentified aircraft, and once more without result.

After unloading her dead and injured at Alinda, BYMS 72 was again also under way, having been ordered to Lakki for immediate repairs. At 0205, ML 456 was just leaving the port when she was hailed by Lieutenant T. G. Fuller, commanding MTB 313, and informed that the minesweeper had bypassed the entrance and was continuing down the coast towards Kalymnos. ML 456 immediately set off in pursuit, her captain, Lieutenant Commander F. P. Monckton, later reporting:

> At 0247 off Argynondas Bay considerable crossfire was observed in the bay and a short burst of answering fire. The crossfire, which consisted of a quantity of tracer from small calibre guns, continued for two minutes.[2]

Having concluded that the minesweeper had been overwhelmed by superior forces and there was nothing he could do, Monckton returned to Lakki. One of the crew of BYMS 72 was Leading Wireman Crichton:

> We steamed for 16 miles and were intercepted by ships which we thought were English. The ships told us to follow them in and they would show us an anchorage. We had only started to follow them in when they gathered round us and opened fire on us. There were two E-boats, four large landing craft and three trawlers. They kept up their fire until the ship caught fire. The skipper ordered 'abandon ship'. Three men swam to the island and the rest were picked up by the

Germans. The BYMS 72 was seen being towed around the end of Salina [sic] Bay by the German ships.[3]

In fact, the ship had been hailed in English by *Oberleutnant zur See* Hansjürgen Weissenborn aboard *R 210* with the western landing force:

Ahead, a shadow which is approaching the convoy at high speed (20 knots). As I suspect an enemy destroyer, I turn our boats towards land with the intention of covering the convoy in smoke. As there is no shooting, however, I head towards him with my guns ready. I ... call out: 'Hello, what ship?' He replies in English that he is an English minesweeper and readily answers all my questions.

According to statements made later by prisoners, he thought that we were English; later, after opening fire, Italian. When told to follow me, he did so. However, as his guns, which were protected by shields, were pointing at me all the time and as his artillery was far superior to mine, I guided him to within range of the passing *U-Jäger 2101* and *2102* and used morse to advise them of the situation. After a joint attack, I again drew up alongside the English in order to clarify matters. From their questions I could see that they still could not comprehend the situation ...[4]

Three of those aboard the BYMS had been killed and several were wounded including the commanding officer and first lieutenant. Both officers together with fourteen ratings were taken prisoner and their ship, apparently with code books intact, was taken under tow to Kalymnos by *UJ 2102* with *UJ 2101* as escort. Several men tried to escape, but only Crichton, Stoker I. Yuill and Able Seaman Mariner, who had been shot through both knees, succeeded after slipping overboard and swimming to Linaria Bay on the west coast of Kalymnos.

Off Kalymnos at 0330 there was further action when the British MTB *307*, on passage from Kastellorizo to Leros, challenged two German destroyers which responded with gunfire. After taking avoiding action, the MTB arrived at her destination at 0415. Half an hour later, she joined MTBs *315*, *266* and *263* in a search for an enemy vessel reported south-east of Leros. Finding nothing, the force continued northward and off Pharmako Island misidentified as British what were probably the same two destroyers, this time without incident, before withdrawing to lie up in Turkish waters.

At 0456, ML 456, sighted while on patrol the eastern invasion force 12 miles east of Leros, heading north. After warning the SBNO, the launch approached the vessels for a closer inspection. At the same time the escort/pilot vessel *R 195*, having also observed the motor launch, signalled the leading F-lighter:

> *MFP 370* to take over navigational command. I will go ahead and attack. If attacked directly, surround landing unit in smoke and head off at 180 degrees.[5]

Lieutenant Commander F. P. Monckton recalled:

> The first burst of fire from the R-boat went over the top of ML 456 but with the second burst, which was prolonged, the midship Oerlikon received a direct hit and the leading number [AB Joseph McRobert] was killed and gunner [believed to be AB C. King] severely wounded. The after Oerlikon loading [number] was wounded and the gun misfired owing to Oerlikon splinters striking the magazine. The signalman on the bridge manning the G.O. Vickers .303 guns was badly hit by splinters from a cannon shell which struck the flag locker, the coxswain was also wounded in the arm.
>
> With the same burst, a shell hit the port ammunition locker of the midship Oerlikon gun and set it on fire and a cannon shell incendiary entered the engine room on the water line and started a fire.
>
> I withdrew towards Leros when I realised that my guns were not firing and my ship was on fire.[6]

While the battle raged, a number of landing craft commanders, having misunderstood the message from *R 195*, turned their boats around and began to head south so that the convoy ended up in total disarray. It was only after the *R-Boot* returned that order was restored, enabling the vessels to continue.

Of the seventeen-man crew aboard the British vessel, six had been wounded and one killed. On arrival at Alinda Bay, the launch landed four of the more seriously injured and the body of McRobert before making for the Turkish coast. ML 456 was barely two miles from Leros when she was targeted by the island's shore batteries. As the launch zigzagged and made smoke in an effort to avoid the fire, she was hit in the tiller flat by a shell and severely damaged. Nevertheless, the battered little vessel struggled on to arrive in Turkish waters at 0745. The ferocity of the brief action may be gauged by the reaction of the survivors, three of whom were reported to be 'in a very serious nervous condition'. A third 'had lost his best friend and had had his workmate severely wounded ... He got over it in five to six days.'[7]

The Royal Navy suffered an additional loss after three motor launches were ordered to proceed from Leros to the safety of Turkish waters. MLs 299 and 461 reached their destination without mishap but at 0515 the latter received a signal from ML 358 that she was being fired on by a convoy. She was not heard from again and is assumed to have been caught between the crossfire of the invasion fleet and the shore batteries. Further clues to her fate may be found in German after-action reports. The commander of R 195, *Leutnant zur See* von Zatorski, recorded that at 0500 hours:

Position four nautical miles off Alinda Bay. A *Schnellbootrotte* [fast boat section] sighted approaching the convoy. Again, navigational command is passed to *MFP 370*. *R 195* heads towards the *S-Boote*. It seems the enemy mistakes us for his own units, as he signals the letter X as identification and shows multi-coloured lights. *R 195* repeats X a number of times. The enemy units can be made out clearly as they are lit by the moon. Approached to 100 metres and opened fire with all weapons. Due to the short distance almost all shots landed on target. Heavy damage observed. It was not seen to sink, as enemy disappeared in fog. No own casualties ...[8]

A second boat fled the scene, apparently unharmed. Before engaging the enemy, the commander of *R 195* had ordered the rest of the flotilla to stay on course. This failed to prevent further chaos:

Confusion ensued. All the boats headed in every direction, surrounded themselves with smoke and came close to ramming each other. The sharp intervention of the convoy leader was again required for a second time. This meant that a considerable amount of time was lost.[9]

To make matters worse, the assault craft had missed the next navigation point so that new courses had to be plotted for each coxswain. It was already 0621 and nearly daylight when the eastern force began to land. On nearing Leros, it had split into three groups with *Kampfgruppe* Dörr making for Vagia Bay, *Kampfgruppe* von Saldern heading towards Grifo Bay and *Kampfgruppe* Schädlich steering for Appetici. When the latter reached the rocky shore below the imposing heights of Point 180, the *Küstenjäger* scrambled from their assault boats, out of sight and virtually unopposed by the Italians above. However, due to engine trouble, an *I-Boot* was forced to take up the rear and came under heavy artillery fire from the battery on Mount Vigla. With no other option, the coxswain persevered and manoeuvred the craft inshore. No sooner had the troops disembarked than the vessel was hit and caught fire which resulted in the *Küstenjäger* losing their entire stock of spare ammunition. With the blazing hulk emitting plumes of swirling smoke behind, and the grey cliff face before them, the troops prepared to ascend Appetici and assault Battery Lago. The Italians manning the coastal batteries have since been criticised for putting up a poor performance. Clearly, such accusations are not entirely justified.[10]

At dawn, *II./Gren.Rgt.65* (less two *Züge* of *5. Kompanie*), 131 officers and men of *II./Lw.-Jäger-Rgt.22* and *2./Pi.Btl.22* (less one *Zug*) came ashore between Pasta di Sopra Point and Grifo Bay, where landing craft engaged an already battle-damaged British 'gunboat' (presumably ML 358) and captured the Italian *MAS 555* and *MAS 559*. At Alinda the Germans also seized the British LCM 923. *MAS 555* was commandeered with her crew to ferry troops and ammunition to Appetici. It is alleged that the skipper, *Sottotenente* Calabrese, attempted the short but perilous passage using auxiliary engines, thus presenting the guns with a slow-moving target which resulted in the troops having to disembark at Santa Madonne, only a short distance from Grifo Bay. The vessel was eventually sunk, either by fire from shore or as a result of air attack by the *Luftwaffe*. *MAS 559* was lost a day later when she was boarded and scuttled by her commander, *Nocchiere* Alberto Baldelli.

After the troops had disembarked, the empty landing craft faced a hazardous return trip to Kalymnos. Some were unable to break out and instead had to seek shelter close to the coast where, at least, they were safe from artillery fire. The remainder of *Kampfgruppe* von Saldern attempted to force a landing in the Blefuti Bay area, directly under the Ciano coastal defence battery atop Point 320 (Clidi). The post was defended by fifteen men of 'B' Squadron LRDG under Captain John Olivey, and the four Italian 152mm artillery pieces supplemented by British 25-pounder field guns directed by a forward observation officer of the Royal Artillery, Lieutenant Harold Price. At dawn the British and Italian crews had stood-to and followed the engagement between the invasion fleet and ML 456 before waiting for the enemy to approach to within effective range. Captain Olivey had positioned himself behind one of the big guns:

> All the ships were making zigzag courses and gradually coming towards the cove which was below our gun depression.
>
> There was suddenly a tremendous bang and number 2 gun had fired its first round at a destroyer which was close in by now. This boat immediately turned about and went out to sea as fast as it could, putting down smoke as it went. The enemy's objectives were obvious, the cove below us already mentioned [Blefuti Bay] and the dead ground behind the hill to our north-east [Pasta di Sopra]. All guns were now firing and we could hear the 25-pounder shells as they whistled over-head. Our own Italian guns were doing splendid work and the shells went away with a tremendous rush. One could watch them for some way, they seemed to travel so slowly. It was all very exciting and we could only watch as everything was still well out of range. I think the Italians had the first hit and sank a landing craft just as it was about to disappear out of sight behind the headland. This made the enemy hesitate and one or two of the landing craft then turned about.[11]

Pionierlandungsboot 'H' was damaged by shell fire and drifted close to the islet of Strongilo, just off the north coast. The British gunners on Clidi could hardly believe their luck, for they had ranged their 25-pounders on the rock just days before:

> There was a tremendous explosion ... I think this boat must have con-tained transport of some sort, as it was obviously making for a small road which comes in close to the shore a few hundred yards further up the beach. I do not know if anyone was saved from this boat. They may have reached the shore of the island as they were close enough.[12]

Two officers and fifty-one ORs of *II./Lw.-Jäger-Rgt.22* were on board the landing craft. At least two ORs were killed, four were wounded and one officer and thirty-one ORs were taken prisoner. Most, if not all, were from 8. *Kompanie*. Four more ORs were accounted for after the fighting was over. 6. *Kompanie* of II./*Gren.Rgt.65* also suffered substantial losses when an *MFP* took a direct hit; only part of 5.*Kompanie* got ashore at Vagia Bay below Clidi and within Bren gun range of Olivey's force atop the height. For *Feldwebel* Gustav Wehrs and his comrades, the invasion of Leros was to be altogether different to that of Kos:

> We steamed up and down at a safe distance from the coast when suddenly a *Schnellboot* rushed past and we were told through a megaphone: 'Head for shore and follow the lead boat!' We immediately turned 90° and headed toward the island. Instantly, we were bombarded with heavy defensive fire. The enemy guns were in part openly visible on the rocky heights with the crews who were operating them. Our brave *Pioniere* with their twin 2-centimetre machine-guns fired back in turn but of course could not deal with all of them at the same time. Consequently, our landing craft was struck a number of times. One of our men appeared to be hit, but the blood he was splattered with was that of the [pack] mule which had been standing behind him. Unfortunately, the heavy fire caused our boat to veer off course and away from the main group of our assault fleet. We took cover behind the boat's bulwark and temporarily gave up our cover only when we fired our rifles, MPs and machine-guns; then the boat beached briefly and we jumped overboard onto land. The radio operator was in front of me – I gave him a nudge as he was not moving: he had been hit, and to top it all, our second radio operator also got hit when he jumped. So all contact to the battalion was cut off. Apart from these two, other comrades had fallen victim to the enemy defences. When I tried, as requested by the *Kompanieführer, Leutnant* Drabant, to assess our numbers I could account for only sixteen. However, in the heat of the moment I had missed a few as each man had to look out for himself and find cover behind little rocky ledges. Our *Fährprahm* withdrew and we were left behind – a small group in a small rocky cleft of this inhospitable island.[13]

Due to the encounter with BYMS 72, much time was lost before the western force could continue. With the coast defences alerted, the flotilla began taking artillery fire while still some 11 kilometres from Leros. The convoy turned about under cover of smoke. After three attempts to reach Gurna Bay, Weissenborn withdrew. Further attempts in the course of the day resulted in heavy casualties for *II./Gren.Rgt.16* and increasing damage to their assault craft and escort vessels. Each time, the soldiers and seamen ran a gauntlet of deadly artillery fire. The noise alone was terrifying: shells roared through the air before exploding with a terrific crash and fragmenting into lethal steel splinters amid huge, hissing sheets of icy spray. An otherwise calm sea was churned into a boiling fury. Dipping and rolling through the troughs, vibrating and shuddering as the waves slammed against their hulls, the three flat-bottomed F-lighters pressed on, the occupants off-balance and fighting to control the awful rising bile of sea-sickness. Those crammed on to the two smaller *I-Boote* hardly fared better. Air support was requested, but even *Stukas* could not silence the guns. The situation was hopeless and eventually Weissenborn was forced to seek sanctuary at Kalymnos.

Shortly before 0645, *Kampfgruppe* Dörr turned back under heavy fire from shore. During a second attempt at 0930, the lead *MFP* received two direct hits which left at least eight men dead and up to forty-nine wounded. When the guns switched fire to the accompanying *Pi-La-Boot*, it, too, was forced to veer away. Unable to press on under such conditions, the force withdrew towards Pharmako.

It had been the intention of *Generalleutnant* Müller to land each group simultaneously and to seize control of central Leros before the defending forces could recover from their initial surprise. Instead, only part of the invasion force had been put ashore and not all at their designated area. With daylight, the shore batteries had been able to pick out targets so that casualties were mounting even before the land offensive had begun.

With troops prevented from landing on the southern coast, the proposed drop zone for the *Fallschirmjäger* could not be secured. *Kampfgruppe* Kühne, with approximately 430 men, was en route from mainland Greece when the air armada was met over Levitha by two Arado floatplanes and advised with red flares to abort the drop. The feelings of the paratroopers inside the aircraft can hardly be imagined. To sit in cramped discomfort, weighed down with parachute and equipment, awaiting the stomach-churning order to prepare to jump is one thing. To be told that the jump has been postponed is another: indescribable relief is mixed with the awful realisation that one will almost certainly have to repeat the whole process before long. Sure enough, no sooner had the Ju 52 transports landed than they were ordered to take off and return to the island.

At Appetici, the *Küstenjäger* had begun their ascent. The Germans remained unseen by observers on the summit until they neared their objective at which point they began to attract small-arms fire. The second-in-command at Battery Lago, *Sottotenente* Corrado Spagnolo, led the defence until he was mortally wounded later in the day. When the seriousness of the situation became evident, a Navy platoon under *Tenente* 'Ercole' Rocchi rushed to assist from nearby Pandeli Castle. Air support was requested and by 0930, two of the gun emplacements had been taken. The two remaining guns continued firing under the battery commander, *Capitano* Ernesto Nasti.

As the *Küstenjäger* were struggling up the steep slopes of Appetici, Lieutenant Ted Johnson of the Royal Irish Fusiliers was informed by his runner, Fusilier Roberts, that he was wanted at 'C' Company Headquarters. This was situated in a cave on the side of Meraviglia overlooking Pandeli Bay. There, Johnson was told by his company commander, Major Ben Barrington, that as part of the battalion reserve company, 13 Platoon was to spearhead a counter-attack and retake Appetici. This would have been a daunting prospect even for an experienced officer. Johnson had never known combat and his company was unrehearsed for such a role. Furthermore, no one had reconnoitred likely routes to Appetici or seen the ground that was to be fought over. The platoon moved out at about 0845. In an effort to avoid being spotted by the ever-present Ju 87s, Johnson cautiously led the way down past the outskirts of Leros town (Platanos) before ascending the lower south-western slope of Appetici. As prearranged, he was met by an Italian officer and, with Fusilier Roberts, escorted further up the slope in order to assess the situation. Little was achieved by the exercise, so Johnson called forward the rest of his men who made their way to the summit where they took up fire positions and awaited the arrival of the rest of the company. It was already 1000 and although they had been subjected to air attacks, the Faughs had still not contacted enemy ground forces. Major Barrington ordered the troops to push on towards

Battery Lago whose four gun emplacements were by then reported to be in German hands. Johnson recalled:

> My immediate task was to take the first and nearest emplacement and thereafter go for the next one if possible. While one of the other platoons went for ground on my left flank the third platoon was kept in reserve at this stage. After much un-aimed covering fire I found myself with one of my sections in possession of the first emplacement. Until this moment I had still not seen any of my opponents, nor could any of my men give me any accurate reports of sightings in spite of much hostile fire cracking past us. Suddenly my section commander, Lance Sergeant John Caldwell, who was beside me and who was trying to get a sight of a target, fell back. He was shot cleanly through the forehead and had died instantly. My immediate reaction was to push on out of that unhealthy gun emplacement and take John Caldwell's section further down the slope in the direction of the next gun emplacement with all weapons blazing.
>
> This second emplacement was not occupied by the enemy, nor did I see any of its former Italian gun crew. It was not a place to hang about in as it had already been well hit by dive bombing and I recall running and jumping over the boulder and scrub strewn ground in a frenzy of zigzag movements to cover another 30 yards or so of ground before diving into scrub and rocks where we reorganised and remained. The platoon on my left had a similar experience. Its platoon sergeant, Sergeant O'Connell, was badly wounded during this action and later died of his wounds. The action as a whole had the effect of taking back the summit area of Appetici and at least two gun positions.[14]

Lieutenant Johnson and his men stayed in the area for the rest of the day under constant *Stuka* attack, but without suffering further casualties. Among the rocks and boulders lower down, the *Küstenjäger* also remained under cover to avoid presenting themselves as targets of opportunity for British sharpshooters and as a precaution against their own bombs!

Five kilometres north-west of Appetici, there was fighting for much of the morning as 'D' Company of the Buffs attempted to repel *5. Kompanie* of *II./Gren.Rgt.65*. The heights overlooking the east side of Vagia Bay were defended by 8 Section led by Corporal Bertie Reed. In a determined effort by the Germans to break out of the confined beachhead, Corporal Reed was killed, following which 8 Section withdrew 500 metres south-west to Point 95. A kilometre further west, in the area of Point 56, the commander of 18 Platoon, Lieutenant Eric Ransley, prepared to enter the fray:

> Leaving 7 Section behind to continue covering Blefuti Bay, the rest of 18 Platoon was dispatched to della Palma [Vagia Bay] to restore the situation, making its way to the track junction just below Point 95 and meeting up with 8 Section where Private Lambert informed the Platoon Commander of the death of Corporal Reed and of the substantial numbers of the enemy.
>
> An initial probe over the crest of Point 95 met with fierce resistance from the enemy and Corporal [Ernest] Cowell was lost. Radio communications through 38 set to Company Headquarters were not working and indeed throughout the battle communications were exceedingly difficult. Following a message by runner to Company Headquarters, reinforcements and additional 2-inch mortar bombs arrived.
>
> Subsequently, in conjunction with mortaring the enemy in the area south of the beach, an attack was launched north and east of Point 58, at the same time holding the ground just west of Point 95. As the flanking attack went in and the section under Corporal White went forward from Point 95, a German officer appeared ...[15]

As he advanced, Ransley took in the scene: the enemy officer, all but deafened by mortar fire and, close by, the bloodied corpse of a young German soldier. Keeping his Thompson sub-machine-gun levelled, Ransley requested the officer's surrender. The exchange was witnessed by *Feldwebel* Wehrs:

> The British were positioned a short distance from us further uphill [on Clidi] and gave us a hard time. Sometimes, you could even see them as they handled their guns. They had trouble depressing the gun barrels to aim at us. The shells went whizzing past closely above our heads. But they succeeded with their mortars and light weapons. A runner a few metres from me was hit. 'Herr *Feldwebel*, I am dying,' he said to me with blood gushing from his mouth after each word – a truly extraordinary situation. Eventually, *Feldwebel* [Georg] Steinbach managed

with another comrade to climb onto the ledge on the right side and once there had to defend himself with his pistol and hand grenade against the Tommies, who ... all of a sudden were among us. 'Wehrs, now what?' *Leutnant* Drabant asked in his unmistakeable Silesian accent. 'I suppose this might be the end,' I replied, whereupon *Leutnant* Drabant said to the British [officer], 'You are surrounded by 2,000 Germans,' which was met with a ready response, 'Yes and behind them there are 10,000 English.'[16]

When viewed from a different perspective, the same event will often vary in its description. Ransley denied that such a conversation took place. A rumour among the British that there was a misunderstanding over who should be surrendering to whom is also refuted:

There was no argument between myself and the German officer (who understood English). My exact words were, 'You are completely surrounded and I must ask you to surrender', upon which he handed me his Luger [pistol]. I do, however, recall that in a later conversation with our IO [Lieutenant P. F.] Fielden, he said that during his interrogation the German officer said or suggested that someone had displayed a white flag. If so, this could only have been the Italian gunners holed up in their underground gun emplacement [*P.L. 899* west of Vagia Bay] and of which we would have been unaware.[17]

Wehrs thought that *Leutnant* Drabant was the only officer present among forty or so troops, although this figure is almost certainly an underestimation. Even near contemporary accounts cannot agree how many prisoners were taken by the Buffs, who were credited with having seized three officers and up to forty-five ORs to as many as seventy Germans. These men were escorted off the battlefield and later incarcerated in a tunnel used as a temporary holding area. Of his captors, Wehrs recalled:

They did not seem to be used to this kind of situation as they allowed us to throw into the sea behind us the bolts of our rifles, MPs and machine-guns, thus rendering our weapons useless. I still had my pistol but while on our way into a tunnel, I managed to get rid of it. Soon *Leutnant* Drabant became separated from us. Naturally, a Tommy was posted outside our tunnel. But these sentries did not feel comfortable at all, and one of them indicated to me: 'Tomorrow, maybe you will be on guard here, and I will be sitting in there,' pointing at the tunnel.[18]

Meanwhile, the remainder of the *Bataillon* and of *II./Lw.-Jäger-Rgt.22* were able to push inland from nearby Pasta di Sopra Point towards Point 234 on the Vedetta feature, from where Captain Olivey's men were engaged at about 1000 hours by sniper, mortar and machine-gun fire. In view of the strategic importance of Clidi, Brigadier Tilney decided to reinforce the position with the Fortress Reserve, 'C' Company of the King's Own, under Major W. P. T. Tilley, and all available jeeps were allocated for the move. When the troops arrived at Battery Ciano, Olivey discussed the situation with their commanding officer. It was agreed to hold one platoon in reserve and to use two platoons to dislodge the enemy; one was directed left and the other right to Point 192. The plan began to go wrong almost immediately, as Olivey recalled:

The platoon to the left hardly got forward at all before they were under fire and withdrew to the hill at the rear. The platoon on the right were much too far back and I asked if they could not go forward – this was ordered ... about half an hour later, I saw them about 1,000 yards to the right and quite 800 feet below us. They would never be on the neck in time and would come under the direct fire of the enemy when they started to climb up again. I offered to send my Sergeant down to show them the best way up, but Major M [sic] thought they would find it themselves. What happened to this party eventually, I do not know, but I know they never got round to the right. The platoon on the left was now brought over to the right and got forward as far as the trenches. Some mortar fire rather upset them and I found the whole lot streaming back to the hill in the rear. I pleaded with their officer, but to no effect.[19]

What happened to those sent to Point 192 is a mystery: presumably, all were killed or captured after running into the enemy. Certainly, at 1045 Fortress Headquarters had acknowledged the capture by enemy troops of 192, and of Points 217 and 188 on the Vedetta feature. Half an hour later, Clidi received a signal from Meraviglia to hold on at all costs. At about this time, a mortar bomb severed communications between the guns and Lieutenant Price, who was slightly wounded. With little hope of getting the message through in time, Olivey's wireless was used to relay a fire order via headquarters to the 25-pounders to place fifteen rounds on to the mortar position. As the situation deteriorated, the infantry was ordered to reconnoitre forward of Clidi. According to Olivey, 'No one wanted the job' so he took it on himself, returning to report enemy locations and troop movements.

By now, most of the Italian gunners on Clidi had fled and just No. 2 gun remained in action, manned only by *Sottotenente* Ferruccio Pizzigoni and an Italian OR. They were later joined by several British soldiers. Others were less than enthusiastic. Some of the British infantry, evidently affected by the harsh reality of battle, were content to remain in comparative safety behind Clidi. The Germans seemed to sense a quick victory. From a forward trench they could be clearly seen – and heard – as they called on their enemy to surrender:

> The commander of their detachment was standing in the open shouting 'Hi, Aussie'. Bennett got his Bren trained on him and we saw him drop. I left Bennett with his MG and promised to send another man to support him. I sent Oelofse. Not long afterwards, Bennett received a bullet in the flash eliminator of his gun. This sprayed him with bits of metal and [left him with] blood ... pouring from his face.[20]

Shortly after Rifleman Andy Bennett was sent to the dressing station, the LRDG suffered another casualty:

> Sergeant Calder-Potts was now with Ox [Lance Corporal Don Coventry] in the trench on the right and was able to engage the enemy on the hill opposite. The enemy soon spotted his position and had a sniper trained on him. Sergeant Calder-Potts received a splatter of rock in the face which necessitated his withdrawal for the time being.[21]

Eventually, a platoon of the King's Own was moved up to the forward trenches overlooking the German positions, but their presence merely diverted the attention of snipers and attacking aircraft. Pizzigoni, who seemed impervious to the danger, continued to harass the enemy, having temporarily exchanged his artillery piece for a machine-gun:

Second Lieutenant Petsigonne [sic] was fighting like a demon ... he was busy firing this gun completely in the open and with great courage. An enemy gun jammed it shortly afterward, however, and he returned to his No. 2 gun.[22]

Second Lieutenant R. F. White of 'A' (New Zealand) Squadron LRDG was in command of ten men at another OP near Battery San Giorgio on Mount Scumbarda. Although not directly affected by the fighting in the north, the area was nevertheless subjected to dive-bombing attacks. At about midday, White reported:

During the lull in the bombing on our end of the island I went with Private Gregory to see what the position at the AA battery was. Their barracks had been completely destroyed. The easternmost gun had had a direct hit, the barrel lying up against the gun pit. The rest of the guns had all been put out of action with punctured barrels or elevating and traversing gear destroyed, except for the gun on the north-west face, which only required stones and debris removing from it. Two MGs were also alright: the battery had had heavy casualties, some badly wounded had already been brought down to a cave near our post. We counted seven dead around their guns and shelters. Interviewed the Officer in Command of the battery who refused to fire the remaining gun, so I took him under escort across to the San Giorgio battery and through Gunner Morrison (Signaller) as German interpreter and Italian Corporal Mareo [sic], who showed considerable co-operation the whole time I was on the post, I got the Italian to understand they had to get the gun in action again. This they did until the afternoon of the 13th.[23]

On Point 112, just north of Gurna Bay, Captain Ashley Greenwood, liaison officer between the LRDG and Major Lord Jellicoe of the SBS, had joined Major Alan Redfern, LRDG, and three joint LRDG/SBS patrols comprising three officers and twenty-seven men. They were to operate as a mobile force on the orders of Brigadier Tilney, carrying out reconnaissance, anti-paratroop and other patrols. Shortly afterwards, Captain Alan Denniff, commander of 'Y' Patrol, was dispatched with four ORs to Partheni Bay to search for enemy activity. The remainder of the force watched and waited. These were experienced troops. They listened to the firing echoing around the hills north and east of their position, knowing it was only a matter of time before the battle reached them, too.

When it became clear that at least part of his battle-group had gained a foothold on Leros, Müller had decided to risk redeploying his paratroopers. At about 1430 the air armada with *Kampfgruppe* Kühne began its approach at wave-top height: some three dozen transports in line ahead escorted by Arado floatplanes, Ju 87s and Ju 88s. On the order, *'Fertigmachen!'* ('Get ready!') the twelve or so troops inside each noisy, lurching aircraft rose unsteadily to their feet. The nausea caused by a combination of air sickness and fear was ignored as each man went though his pre-jump routine. The Ju 52s climbed to a drop height of just 400–450 feet and as the leading machine reached the coastline of Gurna Bay there came the warning order: *'Fertig zum Absprung!'* ('Prepare to jump!'). Hooked up and ready to go, the first man of each stick positioned himself in the open doorway in the aircraft's port side, legs well apart, feet in the corners, hands gripping the vertical support rails on either side. His body was hunched slightly forward with his head outside the aircraft, the distorted features registering the tremendous force of the slipstream. Some, a few, relished the moment: little compares with the dreadful excitement of parachuting into battle. A klaxon sounded; the signal for the first man to leap into space: *'Raus!'* ('Out!'). Using the support rails as leverage, he flung himself through the exit, automatically assuming an X position in order to hollow his back against the slipstream. A moment later there was the familiar, reassuring jerk and sudden decrease in acceleration as the parachute canopy deployed. As the roar of the departing Ju 52s gradually faded, the paratroopers became aware of another, terrifying sound – the all too familiar whines and cracks of incoming small-arms fire.

Obergefreiter Walter Keller, a machine-gunner in 3. *Kompanie*, recalled:

I was third out of the plane, dropped my MG – it was secured to my belt with a rope – and suddenly felt something warm running down my right upper thigh. Later it transpired that my water bottle had been pierced by a 2 centimetre *Flak* shot. A second shot caused it to come loose from my *Brotbeutel* [haversack]. After the fighting, I found it again and took a photograph of it. All hell had broken loose. Shots were fired from every direction; a tremendous noise. I came down on the edge of a roof of a barracks building about five metres high, but instead of landing on the roof itself, I fell backwards onto the ground with my MG still lying on the roof. I pulled the rope and brought it down on to its flash suppressor and crushed it. The feed tray cover had also shifted: in short, the thing was no longer working. I looked for another in a weapons container, but in doing so encountered ten Tommies who were just as bewildered as I was and before one of them could shoot at me, I was gone again ...[24]

For the British on Leros their first intimation of the impending paratroop assault had been an ominous rumble rising to a roar like the sound of an approaching train through a tunnel which steadily grew louder and louder. At the same time a number of low-flying aircraft appeared to strafe and scatter anti-personnel bombs, raising the tree tops as they swept past. The slower transports followed. Men stared in awe at the fearsome spectacle and even when the sky began filling with parachutes some were slow to react. Others quickly recovered from their surprise. The LRDG and SBS immediately brought their machine-guns to bear from positions less than a thousand yards from the drop zone. Captain John Olivey recalled:

> Everyone seemed to be firing. I'm not sure the officers didn't fire their revolvers. I had a Bren which got rid of three mags in almost no time ... It was impossible to estimate the number of planes, but roughly, I should say [there were] 50 in all. Each troop carrier, about 30 in number, dropped about 10 men ... Many of the men dropped in the sea. Many never got up again but those that did very quickly disappeared from sight. It was a perfect day for the manoeuvre and it was excellently carried out. A few of the planes had to come back to drop odd men who obviously hadn't made it and how they avoided being struck by the plane behind was certainly a wonder I shall never forget. One must give the Germans top marks for that performance.[25]

The landing was also opposed by 'D' Company of the Faughs from Point 36, Germano and San Giovanni; by 'B' Company of the Queen's Own Royal West Kents, also at San Giovanni; and by the Buffs at lower Quirico. The paratroopers sustained losses of around ten per cent during and immediately after their descent, including the adjutant, *Oberleutnant* Lichy (who was killed on his 23rd birthday), *Unterarzt* Katersohn, medic, and the signals officer, *Leutnant* Schukraft. One of the transports was also lost together with three of its four-man crew when it crashed, probably as a result of ground fire.[26] An incredulous Marsland Gander described the scene immediately after the landing:

> The parachutists surely had all been massacred. We searched the hillside through glasses and could discern parachutes strung on telegraph lines and tree tops. Great optimism prevailed, for it seemed impossible that the survivors, however courageous, could arm and establish themselves before being fallen upon and exterminated by the troops whom we assumed would be in the neighbourhood. This was one of the occasions when all decent feelings of humanity are in most men swamped by the instinct of self-preservation. We thought of those recklessly brave parachutists as vermin to be wiped out ruthlessly, instantly. I still fail to understand why it was not done, before they had time to reach their containers and equip themselves. Nor can I fully understand why such a large proportion escaped the fusillade of fire poured upon them as they descended.[27]

Major Pat McSwiney, commanding 3rd LAA Battery, also recalled:

One of these paratroopers landed above our Battery HQ dugout and started to slide down the hill towards us with his parachute still attached, but his submachine gun moving in our direction. The Battery Sergeant Major and I, both armed with revolvers, had a pot shot at him before he could steady himself to retaliate. Neither of us were good marksmen, and the paratrooper was later removed to the casualty clearing station in Meraviglia, sufficiently wounded in both the leg and the shoulder not to bother us further.[28]

The paratroopers were virtually powerless to defend themselves during their descent but once free of their parachute harnesses they quickly reverted to their role as shock troops. Due to an oversight, the radio which was to have provided communications with headquarters was not dropped. It was a serious blunder, but these were seasoned troops, with combat experience on many fronts. The battalion had already taken part in airborne operations in the Netherlands, Corinth and Crete, and had fought in Poland, Russia and North Africa. Officers, platoon and section leaders rapidly assessed the situation, made for the nearest cover and pushed towards their objectives. *Hauptmann* Martin Kühne explained:

> I had chosen this [drop zone] myself as it was most appropriate to achieve our objectives which were to split the north of the island from the south and, based on thorough air reconnaissance which provided a detailed description of the rugged terrain, it appeared most suitable for the jump. In contrast to previous missions, I was of the opinion that in order for the *Truppe* to re-group – the most dangerous time immediately after the drop – the existence of cover should be the most decisive factor when choosing the drop zone. Jump injuries had to be taken into account. Furthermore, every para carried hand-held weapons to increase their battle preparedness once they had reached the ground.[29]

On Point 112, just a few hundred metres from the drop zone, Major Redfern and his men also joined in the firing as the paratroopers descended. When, after about ten minutes, no orders were forthcoming from Fortress Headquarters, the officer decided to deal with the situation personally. 'T2' Patrol, with Second Lieutenant M. W. Cross and seven ORs, was ordered to remain on Point 112; 'Y' Patrol was tasked with moving up on the paratroopers from the north side of Point 64 (Germano), which bordered the drop zone, while Redfern led Captain Charles Saxton's 'T1' Patrol into a valley on the north-east side of Germano. Machine-guns manned by SBS were to be placed on top and south of the feature.

The hastily organised mission was a disaster. Although 'Y' Patrol managed to move into position and get their machine-guns into action, the SBS were unable to get their weapons to the top of the hill. On the north-east slope, Major Redfern's party ran into machine-gun and mortar fire. Redfern was shot and killed instantly and the remainder of the group forced to withdraw. Neither did the rest of the LRDG meet with any success and they, too, were obliged to pull back.

Teenager Dimitris Tsaloumas lived between San Quirico and Alinda Bay. He had watched in amazement as paratroopers landed under intense fire near his home. Some did not get up, but remained motionless beneath their silken canopies. Indeed, it seemed to Dimitris that few had survived until later that afternoon, when one, then another seemingly came to life and, taking advantage of a lull in the firing, raced towards cover.

After gathering all available *Fallschirmjäger*, Kühne soon attained his primary objectives. Assisted by *Stukas*, *1. Kompanie* under *Oberleutnant* Haase severed all roads and lines of communication to the north; *2.* and *4. Kompanien*, led by *Oberleutnants* Fellner and Möller-Astheimer respectively, took Rachi at the first attempt, while *3. Kompanie* established a road block between Platanos and Partheni about a kilometre west of Alinda Bay and reconnoitred north of the island. On Germano only 17 Platoon of the Faughs continued to hold out, with Sergeant O'Connell in command following the loss of the OC, Captain Bill Robinson.[30] Brigadier Tilney was virtually powerless to react:

> There is no doubt that the selection to land [airborne] troops in this area was not only a bold move, but took the defence by surprise since it was not one which had been considered suitable for such an operation. The selection of this improbable and rather hazardous dropping ground by the enemy coupled with the immobility of the defence rendered an immediate counter-attack impossible. Even if the Reserve Company had not already been committed, it is doubtful whether it could have materially affected the issue, since by the time it would have arrived in the dropping area the enemy would still have had time to re-organise and the company would have been heavily outnumbered.[31]

At about four o'clock in the afternoon, Marsland Gander made his way to the eastern exit of the headquarters tunnel where he witnessed a disconcerting sight:

> I encountered an intelligence officer with a great armful of papers which he proceeded to dump on the hillside, drench in paraffin and set a match to ... I asked what the idea was. 'Oh, we're just burning secret documents,' he said casually. 'Just a precaution, you know, code books and all that.' The fire crackled merrily as others began to make their contributions to the pyre.[32]

After the parachute drop, those on and around Clidi experienced a curious lull in the fighting, although ever-vigilant snipers were quick to deal with anyone careless enough to show themselves. Among the casualties at this time was the South African, Rifleman Louis Oelofse, who was shot in the head and killed outright. The situation was made worse when wireless communications between Clidi and Meraviglia broke down altogether.

On Vedetta, 7./Lw.-Jäger-Rgt.22 with part of 6. Kompanie attached had received orders to join an attack on Clidi and moved south-west, over the ridge between Points 234 and 264 and across to 228. By 1500, they were in an open valley with their objective towering above. At about this time Sottotenente Pizzigoni went missing after having taken a machine-gun and setting off in search of targets. Italian sources maintain that he was taken prisoner and shot when he refused to conceal his identity from his captors – one of a number of Italian officers who were executed by the Germans on Leros. Subsequently, Olivey recommended Pizzigoni for an award in recognition of his outstanding performance, although it is doubtful whether this unusual gesture was approved by General Headquarters (see Appendix D). His own countrymen acknowledged Pizzigoni with a posthumous award of Italy's highest wartime decoration for bravery, the Medaglia d'Oro al Valor militare (Gold Medal for Military Valour).

In the afternoon, Olivey risked enemy fire to inspect his area and found Lieutenant I. L. Brown and a platoon of infantry pinned down in a trench to the south-east; another trench had been virtually buried by the bombing, while No. 3 gun was covered by the enemy on an adjacent hill and no longer accessible. On returning to his position, Olivey called to Brown but there was no reply. He and his men had disappeared. After taking the forward trench and killing or capturing its occupants, the enemy began to move up on Olivey's left flank. Olivey hurried across to the position held by 'Major M' who agreed to send a platoon to counter-attack:

> We gave covering fire as best we could from the right flank. The infantry could not get forward, however, as every time they moved, they were met by grenades and mortar fire. Major M said he would take them forward himself. It was now about dusk and the enemy were on No. 3 gun position and below No. 1. We could hear the orders of the forward officer instructing the mortar how and when to fire. The bombs would drop most accurately at the feet of our infantry. The infantry made a charge but it was impossible to get to the Jerries' position over such rough ground. Major M was wounded in the neck

and put out of action and the infantry withdrew to their hill behind.

It now became a fight between LRDG and the Jerry. I had a Bren gun with which I could sweep over our left flank and I was able to cause great havoc in a party of the enemy who had moved across to No. 4 gun. I took very careful aim and knocked out their leader as he crossed the wall. This made the enemy withdraw from this flank. They had also occupied my own trench behind No. 1 gun and, using grenades, I was able to drive them out of this. They took up a position on the far and almost sheer slope of No. 3 gun emplacement and from here, they would make sallies forward, pelting us with grenades.[33]

The Germans had found several boxes of British grenades. Olivey and his men, meanwhile, were reduced to using inferior Italian grenades which did little damage. By 1610, enemy troops were on Point 278, just north-east of the summit of Clidi.

I was using my Bren like a Tommy gun and a German soldier behind No. 1 gun was firing back at me. It was almost dark and neither of us could see our sights. We would both bob up to get a better view, fire a burst at each other and [get] down again. His shots were going a bit too high, although one struck the stones in front of me, giving me a gash on the cheek and mouth. We were fast running out of grenades and our position was most insecure, as any troops coming round to the right could now very easily get us.[34]

With the enemy closing in, Olivey's group was joined by Signalman James Bremner.

He was only just in time as a Jerry must have worked his way up to the fort [command post] and fired in at the window. Bullets came out through the other window and completely destroyed the W/T set. I dropped a grenade over the other side and the Jerry ran and fell as he ran.[35]

Olivey had been instructed to defend the battery on Clidi and, in the event of it being overrun, to destroy the guns. He ordered his men to withdraw to No. 2 gun where Rifleman van Heerden was waiting to blow up the position.

We lined up on the steep side of the rear of No. 2 gun and waited for the enemy to appear, when we would give him the last of our grenades. I told everyone to keep well behind the gun emplacement as they were then safe from grenades. Van Heerden was sitting on the gun. A grenade came over and exploded on top of the emplacement and Sergeant Calder-Potts, who had not got behind the emplacement, got the full force of the explosion in his stomach. I ordered two chaps to help him back and we gave the Jerries our last grenades – at the same time, van Heerden pulled the switch. This gave us 30 seconds to get away. We made back towards the hill to the west. The 30 seconds seemed like an hour and I almost thought that the charge had failed, but suddenly, with a tremendous explosion which I knew would signal the fall of the hill to Headquarters, the gun blew up.[36]

II. *Zug* of 7./*Lw.-Jäger-Rgt.22* had taken the height, for the loss of its commander, *Oberfeldwebel* Schröder. In carrying out a flanking attack, 6. *Kompanie* also lost its commander, *Oberleutnant* Frenzel, while that of 7. *Kompanie*, *Oberleutnant* Böttcher, was severely wounded just before reaching the summit. Reinforcements arrived an hour later, and mopping-up operations continued until about 2000 hours. During the night, the northern face was secured by the remainder of 7. *Kompanie*, while the *Pionierzug* of II./*Gren.Rgt.65* captured the opposite slope. *Kampfgruppe* von Saldern had achieved its objectives and now held the high ground stretching from Point 264 (Vedetta) through Points 228 and 320 (Clidi) to within 500 metres of the coast at Santa Madonna (Alinda Bay). With Kühne's paratroopers in control of most of the key points south of Clidi, the Germans had effectively divided the island in two.

Earlier, Brigadier Tilney had moved three companies of the King's Own from the low ground to support the gun positions on Scumbarda and east of Serocampo Bay. When it became apparent that the enemy's main effort was being concentrated in the centre of the island between Clidi and Appetici, the King's Own was redeployed mainly in the Meraviglia area. Another company was transferred from the north shore of Lakki to positions covering Point 248 (Patella). 'C' Company of the Faughs was also recalled by the brigadier from their hard-won positions on Appetici, returning without their company 2 i/c, Lieutenant Hugh Gore-Booth, who had gone missing that afternoon during a patrol on the east face. The withdrawal of 'C' Company left only the Italians to defend the feature, prompting an anxious request for Tilney to send back one platoon. This was agreed to, although the order seems to have been passed directly to 15 Platoon, bypassing the normal chain of command and leaving Lieutenant Colonel French, and everyone else, in confused ignorance. Tilney's failure to observe standard military procedure would prevail throughout the battle, with predictable results.

At 1800 hours, LRDG call sign 'Stupendous' sent an unofficial situation report making no effort to disguise the anger and frustration felt by many on Leros:

Lack of RAF support absolutely pitiful. Ships sat around here all day and Stukas just laughed at us ...[37]

That evening, Lieutenant Colonel French was tasked with leading a night attack to throw the enemy off Rachi. Tilney maintained that the attacking forces were to comprise two companies (less one platoon) of the Faughs and two companies of the King's Own. Other sources mention only 'C' Company of the Faughs and HQ Company of the King's Own. Lieutenant Clifford Clark, then 2 i/c of 'B' Company of the Royal West Kents, also noted at the time that he took charge of his old 10 Platoon in order to form a composite spearhead company with two platoons of the Faughs (evidently 13 and 14 Platoons) which was to have preceded a company (of four platoons) of the King's Own.

Due mainly to the delayed arrival of the King's Own, the attack, originally timed to begin at 2300 hours, had to be postponed, though apparently not before 'C' Company of the Buffs had expended 3,500 rounds in a wasted effort to provide machine-gun support. In the early hours of the 13th, Tilney cancelled the operation altogether:

... due to developments on Appetici and to the fact that one of the attacking companies had proceeded to the wrong RV and had got lost in the darkness. The failure to put in this attack undoubtedly gave the enemy an unexpected opportunity to strengthen what was, initially at all events, a somewhat shaky hold on the narrow neck in the centre of the island.[38]

Although not stated as such in the report, the company referred to was 'C' Company of the Faughs. Between 2300 and midnight, Fortress Headquarters received word that 15 Platoon on the eastern escarpment of Appetici was being attacked and required reinforcements. Tilney therefore ordered the remainder of 'C' Company to assist, while a further platoon was sent to help defend Pandeli Castle.[39] However, the move of the platoons to Appetici was countermanded in a message from Fortress Headquarters without the brigadier's knowledge and it was not until 0400 on the 13th that they finally moved out. A different version of events is provided by Lieutenant Johnson. On returning to Meraviglia, 13 Platoon had been resupplied and provided with a hot meal. After waiting in vain for further orders, the men settled down to sleep. During the night Johnson was woken and instructed to make his way to a prearranged rendezvous on a track used by troops moving towards Platanos and Appetici. He was joined by the commander of 14 Platoon, Second Lieutenant G. M. Riordan:

> Sergeant Major Conners suddenly appeared to say that 15 Platoon had already gone back to Appetici and that we, that is 13 and 14 Platoons, were to wait at our present RV for the Company Commander. How it was that the CSM came to give us such an order remains a mystery. It was wrong anyway and he must have known at that stage that Ben Barrington was either already back on Appetici with 15 Platoon or was perhaps en route for that destination even as he spoke. We waited in vain for about one hour. This uncertain grip worried me and I was beginning to realise that I was on my own in this battle. I contacted Battalion HQ by line from Stony Force [an outpost approximately 500 metres from 'C' Company's defensive position]. When I spoke to Maurice French he told me to join up with 15 Platoon on Appetici. This we duly did after a hard slog across the valley and up the rocky face once again.[40]

Just before the attack on Rachi was cancelled, Lieutenant Clark had also arranged to meet Barrington:

> I reported with my Platoon at the RV at 0200 and met the Major, whose other two Platoons had so far not turned up. We waited a bit and then went in search of them. After frantic enquiries and phone calls, the

> Major eventually made the tragic discovery that his two Platoons had gone to a wrong RV, about two miles away and the other side of the hill, and were out of touch. I have never seen a man quite so worried, as it was then 0230 and half an hour to Zero! Eventually he gave me the thankless task of reporting the position to the Colonel while he went in search of his men.[41]

It is virtually impossible to determine precisely what went wrong that night, but if the timings noted by Clark are correct, the implications are serious indeed.[42] It seems inconceivable that Tilney was under the misapprehension that he had at his disposal one more company of the Faughs than was actually available, and yet it does appear that 13 and 14 Platoons of 'C' Company were allocated two simultaneous tasks: to join the counterattack against the paratroopers on Rachi, and to reinforce 15 Platoon on Appetici. It was dawn when Lieutenant Johnson arrived at Appetici where he met Major Barrington who had presumably returned to the feature in search of his 'missing' companies.

> He asked me where the devil I thought I'd been all night. Well, where the hell did he think I was?[43]

At dusk, the *Faulknor*, *Beaufort* and *Pindos* left Alakishli Bay and swept the Leros-Kalymnos area to prevent the arrival by sea of further enemy reinforcements. Between 2210 and 2218 the destroyers responded to a request by the army by shelling enemy positions on Mount Clidi. A total of fifty-seven rounds of 4.7-inch and 4-inch HE were fired following which the force carried out an uneventful search for enemy vessels at Levitha before returning to the safety of Turkish waters. After lying-up during daylight hours in the Gulf of Mandelyah, the torpedo boats which had earlier departed Leros also put to sea. MTB 307 developed engine trouble and 263 struck a rock and damaged two propellers, leaving just 315 and 266 to continue their patrol.

Throughout the day, the *Luftwaffe* had maintained a menacing presence, with Ju 87 and Ju 88 dive-bombers on call by the assault troops. That night, German aircraft delivered ammunition supplies to the *Küstenjäger* holding out on Appetici and dropped a radio set to Kühne's paratroopers, only for it to be damaged and rendered unworkable!

Beaufighters of 46 and 227 Squadrons were prevented by Messerschmitt Bf 109s from approaching Leros, but to the west, later in the day, eight Beaufighters of 47 and 603 Squadrons and two B-25 Mitchells of the USAAF 310th Bombardment Group struck at a convoy reported as comprising two merchantmen and five escort vessels. Two escorting Arado floatplanes were claimed as damaged, at a cost of one Beaufighter and its crew.[44] Afterwards, the convoy entered Suda Bay whereupon fire broke out on the *Pierre Luigi* which resulted in the loss of the steamer. As the original crew had deserted shortly before the vessel's last voyage, sabotage was strongly suspected.

CHAPTER 9

Day 2 Saturday, 13 November 1943

ON FRIDAY NIGHT, COMMANDER S. A. Buss, 5th Destroyer Flotilla, arrived in the Aegean in HMS *Dulverton*, with *Echo* and *Belvoir* in attendance. After being detected and shadowed by German aircraft, the unit was attacked with glider bombs and at about 0145 on the 13th *Dulverton* was hit. There was little warning as the glider bomb approached, only a sinister sound of rushing air immediately before the projectile slammed into the ship, blowing off her bows. *Dulverton* caught fire but somehow remained afloat. With aircraft still overhead, *Echo* and *Belvoir* circled the scene before they risked stopping for survivors. The rescuers were guided by the harrowing screams of terrified, severely injured men, many of whom could be seen in the eerie light of the spreading flames. Others were located only by the tiny red emergency lamp on their life-jackets. From time to time, *Belvoir*'s guns added to the pandemonium as enemy aircraft were engaged. However, no more bombs fell during the rescue operation. For Midshipman I. N. D. Rankin on *Belvoir*, the sights and sounds were all too much and he plunged into the cold sea to assist the injured. By 0320, *Dulverton* was ablaze from end to end and *Belvoir* was ordered to sink her by torpedo. At 0333, the stricken ship disappeared beneath the waves and the depleted division departed for the Gulf of Kos, the *Echo* leaving behind her Carley floats with the *Dulverton*'s whaler for any survivors who might have been missed. Between them, the destroyers had saved six officers and at least 103 ratings[1]; Commander Buss was not among them. Neither was Midshipman Rankin.

During their first night on Leros, German paratroopers concentrated on securing the Alinda Bay area. *Obergefreiter* Walter Keller was lucky to escape unscathed during a patrol along the coast road in the early hours of the 13th. On reaching the half-open door of a house, he peered inside and was challenged in Italian: '*Inglese?*' 'No, no', he replied, '*Tedesco.*' Without further ado, a hand grenade was hurled from inside the building. Fortunately for the patrol, it fell short and exploded behind the door. Keller recalled:

> Behind us at the window was a fixed *sMG* – a heavy machine-gun – and he immediately started firing and the guy behind me, his name was [*Obergefreiter* Hermann] Horch, from Redbrücken on the Main, I'll never forget, they blew away his entire head. That was the end of him ...
>
> [*Obergefreiter* Helmut] Dassler ... said, 'Come on, we'll go up on the roof', so I held my hands open, he stepped into them and, like children, we clambered on to the roof, where he said, 'I still have a *Sprengbüchse.*' This was basically a tin with two kilograms of explosive in it; you fix a detonator and a fuse and then it blows up nicely. So we threw this through a ventilation shaft or maybe a chimney, and it exploded. Of course, most of those inside were wounded; I don't know how many were killed. Anyway, the rest came out. One of them was an officer and our *Gruppenführer*, [*Oberjäger* Franz] Prokov, said 'Man, that's an officer, we will have to hand him in.' Then, the Italian – I don't know, maybe he understood a little German – immediately started to whimper and said, '*Bambini*' and outlined a woman's body with his hands and repeated '*Bambini*'. He had photos and showed them to us. 'Man, what good will it do if he gets shot? It's not like it will do us any good.' So, we told him to put on an ordinary soldier's uniform.[2]

The prisoner was no doubt aware of the fate awaiting Italian officers who resisted the Germans. Hardly daring to believe his good fortune, he hurriedly changed out of his own distinctive uniform. As a token of appreciation, he handed over his watch, which Keller gratefully accepted. The prisoners were passed back and the paratroopers resumed their patrol.

Before dawn, *Kampfgruppe* Aschoff with *II./Gren.Rgt.16* attempted another landing, this time on the north coast. Initially, the attention of the shore defences on Leros was diverted when the patrolling MTBs *315* and *266* were mistakenly illuminated and fired on. The torpedo boats were dissuaded from remaining in the area and therefore failed to intercept the landing flotilla. Subsequently, the searchlights and batteries were turned on the convoy. Casualties began to mount but this did not prevent many of *II./Gren.Rgt.16* from landing at daybreak near Pasta di Sopra Point. One landing craft was disabled and drifted with a damaged rudder close to Santa Madonne in Alinda Bay where she was hit again by Bofors and anti-tank guns from the southern shore and set on fire. The flames spread, detonating the ammunition on board and causing further casualties, while those who could leapt overboard and struggled to reach the coast 200 metres away. The remnants of the battalion gathered on the eastern slope of Vedetta until ordered by *Major* von Saldern to advance via Val Camere (south of Clidi) towards Rachi to link up with the *Fallschirmjäger*. As they descended the southern face of Point 192, some of the troops were unsuccessfully engaged by British 25-pounders from the area of San Giovanni. Another, more accurate, barrage scattered those already in the built-up area below the height. Shells also fell among small groups as they advanced towards Villa Belleni.

Following the failure of *Kampfgruppe* Dörr to reach Vagia Bay the previous day, *III./Gren.Rgt.440* also benefited from the diversion resulting from the presence of the British MTBs before coming under heavy artillery fire while trying to land at Appetici. Only *9. Kompanie* succeeded in getting ashore and at 0630 joined up with the *Küstenjäger* on the eastern slope. About thirty men of *10.* and *11. Kompanien* also landed north of Grifo Bay where they were incorporated into *II./Gren.Rgt.16*. Having lost one engine and prevented by rough seas from reaching shore, the remaining landing craft returned to Kalymnos, shipping water and with the occupants bailing furiously with their steel helmets in order to stay afloat.

Unfavourable weather conditions also delayed a proposed pre-dawn parachute assault until 0645 when *15./4.Rgt. Brandenburg* and about forty men of *I./Fallschirmjäger-Rgt.2* were dropped west of Rachi. As opposed to the previous day, the Ju 52s arrived over the island individually so that each in turn became the focus of attention for AA gunners. Consequently, the paratroopers suffered heavy losses. At least one stick was dropped at such a low altitude that none of the parachutes opened in time. Others were blown towards Point 81, on the lower south-eastern slopes of Quirico. Marsland Gander was again one of the many spectators:

Our machine guns chattered away furiously. Bofors guns joined in, and one of the slow troop carriers, hit fair and square, went flaming down into Alinda Bay, a horrifying spectacle, with one solitary parachute visible dragging behind it, the doll-like figure still attached. Another Ju flying lower and lower in distress dropped all its parachutists into the water where the silken chutes lingered for a short time like water lilies. Once again, however, it seems certain that a large number of the paratroopers did land safely, and went to reinforce their comrades.[3]

Ground fire accounted for at least two Ju 52s of *II./T.G.4*. One aircraft (*Werknummer* 640187) had just dropped its paratroopers when it was shot down into the sea; all the crew were rescued. *Unteroffizier* Andreas Hutter was the air-gunner on board the other aircraft (6799/G6+FP). For Hutter, who had also flown in the previous day's missions, this was his sixty-fourth operational sortie:

Flight control told us that the intended drop-off point (past Alinda Bay) had already been taken by German soldiers. Therefore we flew over Alinda Bay. In doing so, the first plane was hit and went down burning into the sea. Our machine was shot at too and badly damaged and as a result the radio message ordering the paratroopers to go was not released so they didn't jump. Due to heavy damage, our machine had to make an emergency landing in the sea about two kilometres from the coast at Palma [Vagia] Bay.

The twelve paratroopers were still in the plane and unfortunately had no life jackets as they were wearing their parachutes. The plane sank very quickly. Out of five crew, four managed to get out together with several paratroopers. One crew member died while still in the plane. We lost each other due to heavy seas ...

I tried to inflate the rubber dinghy but couldn't as it had been completely riddled with bullets and therefore I was unable to help the paratroopers. I had to save myself by swimming for about two to three hours (although I had a life jacket I was also wearing full uniform and shoes!) and only just managed to reach the coast where Italian soldiers captured me and handed me over to the English.[4]

The pilot, *Feldwebel* Günther Voigt, the observer, *Unteroffizier* Max Ehrig and wireless operator, *Unteroffizier* Viktor Langos, all survived to be rescued by their own side. The flight engineer, *Unteroffizier* Friedrich Meyendicks, was fatally wounded and remained inside the aircraft. It is not known how many paratroopers managed to escape. Hutter's parents in Austria were advised that their son was missing in action (see Appendix E); they did not learn that he was still alive until much later. According to Marsland Gander, the *Luftwaffe* suffered a further loss:

> One seaplane came boldly down into Alinda Bay and attempted to alight, as if the island were already in German hands. It met such a torrent of fire that it sank immediately.[5]

On Appetici, a concerted effort by the *Küstenjäger* and *9./Gren.Rgt.440* saw all four guns of the battery and a number of British and Italians captured at 1100. Lieutenant Ted Johnson, on the north-west slope of the summit, was informed of the situation and soon afterwards experienced substantial rifle and machine-gun fire:

> Eventually word came to abandon the feature. My first intimation that all was not under control was when I saw men running down through the trees from the summit towards me, shouting that they were being closely followed by the enemy ... I got the impression that they were running for their lives and in doing so were causing panic to those of us whom they passed. It became obvious that my company HQ and 15 Platoon had been driven off the summit and that this was the reason that I too was to abandon the hillside. This was done in some confusion and was certainly not a planned and disciplined withdrawal. Sergeant Fitzgerald, my platoon sergeant, and I gathered our platoon together again at the bottom of Appetici on the edge of Leros village [Platanos] and once again made our way back to our old positions above Pandeli bay, reorganised into a company of two platoons and waited for our next assignment.[6]

Lieutenant A. Woods, commander of 15 Platoon, and Johnson's runner, Fusilier Roberts, were taken prisoner and Lieutenant Armstrong, a South African in command of 14 Platoon, was wounded and later evacuated to

Egypt. Earlier, Johnson's platoon had also lost Fusilier James McMaster, as recalled by former Lance Corporal, Walter Pancott:

> My sergeant [John Caldwell] was shot by a sniper; that left me and my gunner [McMaster] in the sangar. A mortar bomb came over, landed at his feet and blew him to bits. I got shrapnel in the leg.

> Eventually, German soldiers arrived at the position.

> I had nowhere to hide or go, so I rubbed blood on my face and head and played dead ... the gunner was a terrible sight. I heard one German say, '*Drei Mann kaput*' I was glad when I heard them going away. My leg was getting very sore, so I had to stay put.[7]

The loss of Appetici caused considerable difficulties for 'B' Company of the Faughs, whose area at Pandeli, south of the feature, was now over-looked and dominated by the enemy. There were a number of casualties from mortar fire and communications were frequently disrupted due to a damaged wireless set and breaks in the land line.

At 1220, *P.L. 899* at Blefuti Bay came under machine-gun fire, causing casualties and prompting a call for assistance. The position was reinforced later in the afternoon by Italian marines, who used automatic weapons and the 76mm battery guns against the Germans on Vedetta and Clidi.

At 1315, *7./Gren.Rgt.16*, in conjunction with *6./Gren.Rgt.16*, moved against Point 111, overlooking Val Camere. *6. Kompanie* cleared the south side of the feature, following which both *Kompanien* turned south. Along the way, there was much close-quarter fighting as pockets of resistance were encountered in gardens along the waterfront. Shortly before 1500, *3. Zug* met up with the *Fallschirmjäger* at San Nicola, and the latter was placed under the command of *II./Gren.Rgt.16*. During the afternoon there were further clashes along the southern shore of Alinda between British troops and elements of both *II./Gren.Rgt.16* and *III./Gren.Rgt.440*.

There was also much activity in the vicinity of Point 320. According to the after-action report of *II./Lw.-Jäger-Rgt.22*, at dawn, firing alerted the battalion's *7. Kompanie* atop the height to a British breakthrough south of their position in the area occupied by the *Pionierzug* of *II./Gren.Rgt.65*:

The enemy was overwhelmed in close combat, the scene cleared and the position was held.[8]

Between 0730 and 0800 the area was again shelled as British troops attempted another assault. Once more, they were beaten back with grenades and small-arms fire. 7. *Kompanie* on Point 320 was relieved by the *Pioniere* later that morning. In the afternoon, *Hauptmann* Gawlich and fifty-two men of II./*Lw.-Jäger-Rgt.*22 took over with orders to hold out under all circumstances. British reports fail to clarify events but at some point, troops of 'HQ' Company of the Buffs were sent to Point 184 (Quirico), just south of Clidi. Certainly, Quirico fell to the enemy during the day, prompting an unsuccessful attempt by 'C' Company of the Buffs to recapture the feature that evening. Lieutenant Geoffrey Hart, then in command of both 13 and 15 Platoons, recalled:

Late in the day, I was ordered to prepare my platoon and 15 platoon for a night attack soon after dark on Quirico, which was about 1,000 yards forward [east] of 'C' Company. We had no opportunity for a daylight reconnaissance and no information as to enemy strength, but I was told parachutists had established themselves on the feature; this was a high, steep hill.

The attack was more like a fighting patrol. First: find out what was up there and then go in. We advanced to the near summit, found barbed wire which I and my sergeant [Nolan] cut and made a gap. We located one slit trench and the area of another. Since we had planned to go in from our right (the German left flank) and sweep across the position, we silenced the first slit trench and were watching out for the one 100–150 yards half-left. We had not identified a third on our right, and were subjected to considerable machine gun fire from this direction. Possibly, we had not gone far enough right although I think we were probably unaware how far Quirico stretched back to the southeast, as the Germans who shot us up were more to the rear rather than to the right. Both I and my sergeant were hit and I rolled back down the hill, fortunately in cover from gunfire. We were the only casualties. Sergeant Nolan was not seriously wounded and stayed with the platoon for a while. Basically, I took no further part as I was wounded in the thigh and leg.

After rolling and crawling down the hill, I reached the road and found the CO's driver who took me in a vehicle to Battalion Headquarters. I reported as much as I could about the German position and suggested that another officer be sent up as the attack was, in my view, quite a possible venture. The CO, I learned afterwards, preferred to wait until daylight and put the whole of 'C' Company into the attack with other supporting fire.[9]

At the same time and slightly further south, Captain Ashley Greenwood took an SBS patrol to recover two jeeps and stores from a track just west of Germano, while Captain Charles Saxton led 'T1' Patrol (LRDG) to clear a nearby house. Both achieved their aim, with Saxton's party finding one German whom they took prisoner.

At the end of day two, German forces held Appetici and had established a pocket around Alinda from the coast at Vedetta, south-west past Clidi to Quirico and south-east to Germano, Rachi and towards Krithoni. However, an attempt by the enemy during the afternoon to take Pandeli Castle had failed in the face of artillery, mortar and machine-gun fire. Neither had *Kampfgruppe* von Saldern linked up with the *Küstenjäger* and *9./Gren.Rgt.440* at Appetici which was crucial if Alinda Bay was to be secured for the landing of heavy weapons. Like the British, the Germans were also experiencing serious difficulties maintaining wireless contact.

In the north, British troops were still holding out in the Clidi area. Lieutenant Colonel D. P. Iggulden was ordered by Brigadier Tilney to stabilise the situation that night, and to be prepared to move south the following day to secure the northern slopes of Rachi. In fact, Iggulden had already made up his own mind to advance on Clidi and since communication problems prevented him from maintaining contact with the brigadier, intended to carry out his plan at dawn on the 14th. At Germano, 17 Platoon of the Faughs remained in position until about 2000, when Sergeant O'Connell withdrew under orders from Battalion Headquarters. The enemy chose this moment to attack, forcing the platoon to leave behind their wounded. Near by, the commander of 16 Platoon, Lieutenant Prior, had been injured and replaced by Lieutenant S. A. (Arthur) Stokes, a South African on secondment to the British Army and attached to 'HQ' Company of the Faughs.

During the afternoon, Stokes had led an attack in which an estimated twenty Germans were killed and wounded. Among the casualties was an officer carrying a case containing plans of attack including aerial photographs. Earlier in the day, the LRDG in the area of Point 256 (Marcello) had also acquired maps, an aerial photo and details of personnel of *5./Gren.Rgt.65.*[10]

For Brigadier Tilney the loss of Appetici represented as much of a threat to Meraviglia as did the German occupation of Rachi. In the morning, he had therefore issued instructions for Lieutenant Colonel French and Lieutenant Colonel S. A. F. S. Egerton, commanding the King's Own, to prepare for another night attack on Appetici. As he was familiar with the terrain, the CO of the Faughs was asked to co-ordinate the plan. According to Tilney, three companies of the King's Own, each with a guide from the Faughs, were to take part in the attack. 'A' and 'D' Companies were to approach under cover of darkness and clear the feature shortly after moonrise. 'HQ' Company was to follow up, organise and hold the position. 'A' and 'D' Companies would then withdraw to 'the Anchor' so as to be available for further offensive operations towards Rachi. When French announced his intention to lead the attack, Tilney was astonished:

> Colonel French stated that it was on account of his knowledge and Colonel Egerton's ignorance of the ground. Since there was complete command from [Meraviglia] of the ground over which the approach march and attack were to be made and Colonel Egerton had had at least two hours in which to study and discuss it with Colonel French, it seemed surprising that Colonel Egerton had not himself resisted this unusual procedure. The latter had not got into touch with me, nor could he be found either at his HQ or with his company commanders at the RV with Colonel French for orders. Consequently, I was forced to accept Colonel French's leadership of Colonel Egerton's battalion for the attack. I therefore approved Colonel French's plan ...[11]

Lieutenant R. A. (Austin) Ardill, one of only three Royal Irish Fusiliers known to have been involved in the operation, had previously commanded the battalion Anti-Tank Platoon on Appetici. He was asked by his CO to provide a brief plan of attack based on his knowledge of the area. Later, he was again summoned to Battalion Headquarters where he was required to repeat his orders at an 'O' Group:

The rendezvous was at 2300 hours ... I went over the plan and refreshed the various Company Commanders with their orders, objectives and rendezvous. At 11 o'clock we moved off. At the last minute, and much to my surprise, Colonel French said to me, 'I will come with you, but you are in command.' The simple plan was a company north, a company south and my company in the centre, with a pincer movement on the [gun] emplacements.[12]

According to some accounts, 'B' and 'C' Companies of the Faughs were to have been attached to the King's Own for the operation, but 'B' Company could not be extracted from Pandeli and was instead replaced by 'D' Company of the King's Own, while 'C' Company was withdrawn in response to reports of a German attack on Meraviglia from Rachi Ridge. In fact, 'C' Company was neither given a warning order for the move to Appetici nor informed about the suspected enemy assault and spent an uninterrupted night in its own defensive positions. Tilney later stated that he tried to recall part of the attacking force. Certainly, 'HQ' Company of the King's Own was redeployed leaving just 'A' and 'D' Companies to continue. The brigadier's instructions were delivered by the LRDG intelligence officer, Second Lieutenant Pav Pavlides:

At approximately 2200 hours enemy parachutists on Rachi attacked main Fortress HQ position (Mt Meraviglia) from north-west using 3 inch mortar. Attack developed and seemed sufficiently threatening to the Fortress Commander to warrant alteration of plans. IO 'A' Squadron LRDG with a runner was dispatched to Colonel French ordering him to call off attack on Appetici and to hasten back to area 'Charing Cross' in order to launch from there a counter-attack northwards. Colonel French was contacted at the head of the attacking column, about 150 feet below the summit of Appetici. Colonel French decided that having reached that far unobserved he had achieved the element of surprise for an attack but could not hope to turn the whole force back without being fired on from above, so decided to send back 'HQ' Company, which was low down, and continue the attack with the rest, hastening back as soon as he had mopped the enemy up ...[13]

In the event, Fortress Headquarters was not attacked, but during the night a *Kompanie* of *I./Fallschirmjäger-Rgt.2*, reinforced by troops of *II./Gren.Rgt.16*, was ordered to take Point 101, on the western edge of the Meraviglia feature, which may account for the panic within the British camp.[14] At 0327 and 0429 hours on the 14th, the Germans intercepted two identical plain language transmissions:

> All radio messages destroyed. No code. Everything destroyed. Radio station continues working.[15]

The source of the signal was almost certainly Naval Headquarters on Meraviglia whose staff had overreacted in the belief that they were about to be overrun. Thereafter, the signals officer, Lieutenant Alan Phipps, had to rely on an already congested Army network for communications.

Allied aircrew continued to suffer losses in the day. The less manoeuvrable Beaufighters and Mitchells were outclassed by patrolling Messerschmitt Bf 109s and their ineffectual presence went virtually unnoticed by those on the ground.[16] With the island beyond the range of Allied single-engine fighters, it meant that none could be employed in an infantry support role, or to escort bombers on daylight missions, while night bombing was impractical due to the size of Leros and the proximity of friendly and enemy forces. Although an effort was being made to reduce the scale of German air attack, with Allied bombers carrying out night raids against airfields in Rhodes and Kos, deteriorating weather conditions had prevented Mediterranean Air Command from mounting large-scale operations over Greece, where the majority of enemy bombers operating against Leros were based. On the 13th, winds rising to gale force also disrupted German air cover and delayed the arrival of further troops on both sides, including British reinforcements from Samos requested by Brigadier Tilney. Just 'A' Company of the Royal West Kents embarked on MMS *103*, but valuable time was lost when another island was wrongly identified as Leros. When the mistake was realised it was too late to continue with the risk of interception during daylight. Accordingly, the ship's captain was forced to lie up in Turkish waters until another attempt could be made the following night.

CHAPTER 10

Day 3 Sunday, 14 November 1943

DURING THE NIGHT OF 13–14 November, HM ships *Faulknor*, *Beaufort* and *Pindos*, now critically short of fuel, were able to depart following the arrival in the area of *Echo* and *Belvoir*. The latter unit arrived off Alinda Bay at 0035 on the 14th to provide fire support for the proposed British assault on Appetici. At 0045, HMS *Echo* commenced bombardment of the feature. *Belvoir* opened fire shortly afterwards. Within ten minutes, ninety-eight rounds were expended following which both vessels departed. The ground attack went in one and a half hours later, at approximately 0230. It was an especially dark and windy night, which benefited and, to a degree, hindered the attackers. The enemy might not have been able to see or hear their approach, but conditions were hardly ideal for the King's Own. Because of the featureless terrain it can be difficult even in daylight to determine exactly where one is on Appetici's slopes. In common with much of the island, the landscape is extremely rugged, rocky and covered with Greek spiny spurge, a dense, thorny, netlike plant which snares the unwary in a clinging embrace. Negotiating this natural obstacle can be a slow, frustrating and painful experience. It is worst when the weather deteriorates, as it did on the night of 13–14 November when the exposed slopes are battered by a thunderous wind which leaves one feeling disorientated and sapped of energy. Lieutenant Colonel Maurice French and his force had all of this to contend with and more: the men were unfamiliar with the area, tired after two days of activity and hardly enthusiastic about attacking a resolute enemy. The preliminary naval bombardment was also just as harrowing for friendly forces, as Lieutenant Austin Ardill recalled:

Having survived the Naval attack, my company got into position for the final assault. To the absolute amazement of my King's Own, I ordered 'fix bayonets'. I actually had to explain why and what bayonets were for, apart from opening cans of Bully Beef. We did then 'fix bayonets' and I led the central attack on the gun emplacements. We took our objective with not too much difficulty ... The Germans counter-attacked from where the northern King's Own Company should have been with heavy machine gun and rifle fire. Colonel French, who had been reasonably close by me all the way, was firing from the shoulder when he was caught in the heavy fire and fell mortally wounded. I was hit but not seriously wounded in a conflict which turned out to be almost a solo effort. We were eventually obliged to disengage, not having any support for mopping up. The King's Own had disappeared. I had only my batman. As we made our way back we picked up some King's Own troops in disarray. They didn't know me and I was not very interested in them. Their Officers had disappeared. Their two [sic] Companies which were supposed to have formed the pincer movement had vanished, failed in their mission and didn't re-appear.[1]

Although two platoons of 'A' Company had disappeared during the night, having no doubt lost their way in the dark, part of the King's Own succeeded in reaching Battery Lago. At dawn the *Kommandeur* of *9./Gren. Rgt.440* led a counter-attack, pushing back the British. At least one officer of the King's Own and seventy or so ORs remustered after the attack. Fifty-five British and forty-five Italians were taken prisoner. The death of Lieutenant Colonel French was a devastating blow and not just for his own battalion. Brigadier Robert Tilney later wrote:

When we lost Maurice we lost the battle. That sounds, maybe, something rather big to say, but I think it would be confirmed by the majority of my command at the time. I recommended him for a posthumous 'Mention in Despatches' which is the utmost one can do for one who died in circumstances when the award of a Victoria Cross is only forgone for lack of positive evidence to support it – I believe he probably earned it.[2]

In war, it is not uncommon for men to have a presentiment of their own death, and it is evident from a letter to his family before the battle that

Lieutenant Colonel French had a sense of foreboding (see Appendix F). The battalion adjutant, Captain H. W. Dougall, also noticed the change in his commanding officer:

> Before going out on the operation we persuaded him to rest and he slept for about 40 minutes – the first sleep for 48 hours. When leaving Battalion HQ he looked at me and said 'Goodbye, Dougie.' This worried me for our usual greeting when he was going anywhere was 'Well, *Faugh a Ballagh*.' I do believe he knew something would happen.[3]

At 0600 on Sunday morning, *Kampfgruppe* von Saldern prepared to push from Rachi towards Meraviglia with 2. and 4. *Kompanien* of the *Fallschirmjäger* reinforced by two *Züge* of *II./Gren.Rgt.16*. Troops from *II./Gren.Rgt.65* were also deployed along the coast road of Alinda Bay while the larger part of *II./Gren.Rgt.16* was tasked with securing a line from Point 22, on the road between Quirico and Germano, through Germano and Rachi. *II./Lw.-Jäger-Rgt.22* with elements of *III./Gren.Rgt. 440* and *6./Gren.Rgt.65* was to establish a line from Mount Vedetta through Clidi, Quirico and the area south. The paratroopers were covered during their assault by a captured Italian anti-aircraft gun (almost certainly *P.L. 211* on Rachi) and by 0700 had reached Points 108 and 113 north and west of Meraviglia's summit. Two *Kompanien* of *II./Gren.Rgt.65* also advanced east and established a line from Santa Marina on the coast to Point 108.

Further moves by the Germans were thwarted when they were forced to call off their offensive and redeploy in response to a simultaneous effort by the British to recover lost ground with the intention of destroying the enemy in the Rachi area and containing his forces on Appetici. Even as the *Fallschirmjäger* battled their way along the western slopes of Meraviglia, Lieutenant Colonel D. P. Iggulden's attack against *Hauptmann* Gawlich's force on Clidi was already under way. Led by Major Ernest Hole, and supported by artillery and mortars, 'B' Company of the Buffs advanced east from Point 252 and by 0725 had taken the height and with it some forty prisoners.

For their part, the LRDG were tasked initially with clearing a cave just east of Point 320. Captain John Olivey ordered three of his men to keep the occupants busy while he attempted to flush them out with grenades:

It didn't quite work out like that as a Jerry with a sub-machine gun engaged me while another engaged them. Still, I was able to see where he was and reach him with grenades. I prepared four and had them ready. Next time Jerry came out I dropped a grenade at his feet. It exploded after the correct time. I dropped another with the same results. This brought cries of *'Kamerad'*. I dropped another. This now set up a shout. I dropped another, this time with the pin in so it would not explode, gave them time to all begin shouting again and dropped myself in front of them. They all put up their hands and looked surprised as I picked up the grenade. We had captured 15 Germans in this cave and we trooped them all up to the top. Some of them were badly wounded and all were badly shaken. It was a good bit of work and we felt pleased with ourselves.[4]

Olivey's patrol was then divided into three-man teams to guide the Buffs in their sweep of the area. During this stage of the operation the British took a number of casualties, including Major Ernest Hole, who was killed. By this time, Olivey had decided to return to Point 320 where the patrol was reinforced by several men from Second Lieutenant M. W. Cross's 'T2' Patrol which, together with Captain Alan Denniff's 'Y' Patrol and Captain Charles Saxton's 'T1' Patrol, was now operating under the command of the Buffs:

I contented myself in now defending the fort and visited my old office again. Everything had been turned upside down. My photos and frames had gone – everything of any value had been taken. The place was full of dust, grenades and dead – some Jerry had spilt a tin of fish over my bed and it stank of rotten oil. I put on two of my men to clean the dead out and clean the place up a bit.[5]

It was originally intended for 'B' Company of the Buffs to continue down to the north shore of Alinda and link up with the battalion's 'C' Company pushing east via Quirico. Instead, 'B' Company would spend the day trying to dislodge the enemy from the high ground, for as soon as Clidi was overrun, *II./Lw.-Jäger-Rgt.22* was ordered to retake the height. An assault troop was formed with eighteen men (mainly wireless operators, clerks and kitchen personnel) under the command of *Oberleutnant* Kleinert and at

1100 launched an attack from Mount Vedetta, south past Point 228 and towards Point 278. While passing a trench line south-east of 228, one man was badly wounded by sniper fire from the dominating massif of Point 320; the rest of the force immediately went to ground. Soon after, they were joined by another *Stosstrupp* led by *Leutnant* Klein who agreed to try to reach Clidi from the south. No sooner had Klein's men moved out, however, than they were engaged from the southern slopes of 228. Kleinert's force responded by providing cover fire, which, in turn, attracted the attention of a machine-gunner who accounted for three men killed and four wounded. The survivors withdrew from the exposed valley and ascended the rocky slopes leading to the razor-edged Point 278.

After regrouping, *Leutnant* Klein's *Zug* together with a ten-man *Stoss-reserve* launched an assault on 228, pushing the British into a nearby ravine south-west of the height. One British officer and four ORs were killed and several Germans were wounded, three of them seriously, including Klein. The British on 320 responded by pounding the feature with mortar and machine-gun fire, forcing the Germans to seek cover on a hill behind 228. Although the enemy failed to recapture Point 320, neither did the Buffs manage to advance past Point 192 and eventually they fell back on Olivey's position, which was to remain in Allied hands for the duration of the battle.

Nearby, 'C' Company of the Buffs under Major Vincent 'Pistol' Bourne had, by midday, taken Quirico and a number of prisoners (accounts vary from 'over thirty' to as many as seventy).[6] The company proceeded east to Alinda Bay before changing direction towards Villa Belleni and, after skirmishing through the gardens and houses on the west side of Alinda, penetrated the line held by *1. Zug* of *7./Gren.Rgt.16*. Bourne recalled:

When we reached the coast we turned south. We encountered small pockets of Germans and took a few prisoners. It was at this time that 15 Platoon commanded by Lieutenant Gore was fired on by Germans from inside the hospital at Alinda Bay [Villa Belleni]. Lieutenant Gore asked me what he should do. I told him that he must silence them and told him to fire one round from his PIAT at the building. This was done and enabled us to clear the Germans out. The Doctors naturally objected strongly. We gathered more prisoners and I had their arms collected and thrown into the sea.[7]

Prevented by communication problems from requesting close artillery support, the Buffs were unable to exploit the situation, and in the face of determined resistance the advance inevitably faltered.

In the morning, Brigadier Tilney had briefed the commanding officers of the King's Own and the Faughs – the latter now led by Major Bill Shephard – for an attack on Rachi. Details of the plan vary depending on the source, but essentially called for 'B' and 'C' Companies of the Faughs assisted by 'B' and 'HQ' Companies of the King's Own to clear the ridge north-west to Point 100, while 'B' Company of the Royal West Kents with 16 Platoon of the Faughs attached advanced west past the feature to Germano. Once Rachi was clear, the fortress commander proposed personally to co-ordinate its organisation. Tilney recorded that the attack commenced at 0930 with 'C' Company of the Faughs as spearhead making good headway and taking a number of prisoners. The battalion's 'B' Company and the Royal West Kents were therefore ordered to advance along either side of Rachi, while the brigadier went forward with an artillery OP party to the southern end of the ridge. However, the two King's Own companies were delayed by enemy pockets overlooked by 'C' Company in the haste to move forward. The focal point of resistance was a small knoll between Rachi and Meraviglia known as 'Searchlight Hill' (Point 97). When he went ahead to reconnoitre, Tilney became caught up in the battle and one of the King's Own company commanders who accompanied him was shot dead. The other company commander was also killed during the fighting which ended that evening with the feature in British hands. An effort to take the adjacent Point 109 failed when it met with a counter-attack by paratroopers together with headquarters staff and 8. *Kompanie* of II./*Gren.Rgt.16*.

Lieutenant Clifford Clark, who observed proceedings from his vantage point on San Giovanni, noted that the operation involved a company of the Faughs together with a company of the King's Own, and the majority of 'B' Company of the Royal West Kents under Captain E. P. (Percy) Flood, who was directed to attack north and link up with the Buffs:

Percy collected the Company and moved down the hill. He left me behind with the six Vickers and the spare Bren LMG in each section, nine in all (we had two Brens per section for defence), to cover the attack of the RIrF Company and King's Own Company along the ridge and also, if necessary, our own Company. I was feeling particularly bloody, but helped myself a bit by manning one of the Vickers and belting anything I could see. We got some grand shoots.

The two Company attack along the ridge was fierce going, the parachutists time and again directing the bombers overhead on to the attacking troops, using their dive bombers as artillery. They used a system of coloured Verey lights and coloured smoke. Eventually the ridge was cleared, except for a few men holding out in a ruined building on the top. We mortared it heavily, and I put a thousand rounds into it, but they clung on. They were tough babies! We let up on it for a bit, and I saw a few of our chaps crawling up to within a few yards of the building. Jerry had seen them, however, and a couple stood up and threw grenades into the middle of our chaps. They must have been hit, as when the smoke had cleared they remained motionless. I couldn't help them at all, they were too near ...

Percy and the Company got into the valley and halfway across before they came under fire, but they were in good cover and only a couple were wounded. I was in touch with him by wireless the whole time, and he reported back fully, including names of casualties. Percy was slightly wounded in the leg, but not enough to put him out.[8]

Lieutenant Ted Johnson recalled that 'B' and 'C' Companies of the Faughs were detailed to advance from 'Charing Cross' along the low ground west of Rachi. 'B' Company had a separate objective to that of 'C' Company, whose task was to occupy a former position of 'D' Company at the western end of the ridge. H-Hour was originally set for 0800 but put back to allow company orders to be held. In the interim, the Faughs were spotted and bombed by Ju 87 *Stukas*, albeit without incurring casualties. At last, the order came to move out:

We advanced down the road at a steady double to the Italian barracks on the corner. As prearranged, 'B' Company then swing out to the right flank and I brought my Platoon on to the left flank. There was the hell of a noise going on and people seemed to be shouting from all angles. The pace was pretty fast but I was determined to get on down the road.

We were being given good support by MGs and Bofors firing at ground targets. The shots seemed to be passing just over our heads, but I don't suppose they were really anywhere near us. By now we were half way down the road with our men rather badly strung out. There were only about six men up to the fore so we checked the pace, gathered up a few extra men and made a final push on to 16 Platoon 'D' Company's old positions just below Point 100. We occupied the positions and waited for Barrington to follow us up with the rest of the Company. My force was now numbering about seven [including] Sergeant Fitzgerald, Sergeant Wallace, Fusilier Long [and] Corporal Neill ...'

For Corporal Vic 'Taffy' Kenchington, a stretcher bearer in the Faughs, this was his first infantry assault:

I was feeling very nervous and shaky and wished I was somewhere else, as suspense and fear of the unexpected took hold. The troops in front of us went forward at a steady trot, with weapons at the high port. We could hear the 'swish-swish' of the German mortars and the buzzing of spandau bullets coming our way. Red Verey lights from the German positions signalled the *Stukas* to come in with 50 kilogram bombs and MGs. A bomb landed about three yards from me – we had taken cover behind a small wall – and I felt a bang on my back and I really thought that I had been hit, but the bomb fin had hit the wall above me and then landed on my back so I just got a singed shirt and bruising. The *Stukas* were lined up just like a 'taxi-rank', awaiting the Verey lights and down they would come.

Soon, we got the call: 'Stretcher bearers!' We ran forward to our first wounded, passing men in statuesque postures who we knew would never get up again. They had that greyish white, or pale blue-green tinge with blood seeping from nose or ears, although we could see no real wound. They had been killed by blast. We reached our first wounded man. He was from the Buffs [sic] and had a very bad scalp wound. It took a shell dressing to cover it. I gave him a shot of morphine as he was babbling a lot of gibberish and was relieved to get him back to the RAP, as he had lost control of his bowels.

Soon, we were off again, treating the badly injured first and then bringing the walking wounded back with us, including Germans and the odd Italian. We had to treat the really badly injured with extra care. Some were calling for their mothers and were in a pitiful state.[10]

When the intentions of the Faughs were realised, *Hauptmann* Philipp Aschoff had ordered *3. Zug* of *7./Gren.Rgt.16* to secure the western side of Rachi. Lieutenant Johnson and his party could advance no further:

> When Barrington finally joined us, I told him that the top of Point 100 was held strongly by MGs and in view of our small numbers he asked OC 1 King's Own to send a platoon to attack. In the meantime he brought a 3-inch mortar detachment down to our position and throughout the day it mortared under great difficulties, with Fitzgerald and Wallace as spotters. When 1 King's Own came down the road and were preparing for their attack, they were heavily sniped and as chaps approached one corner of the feature in particular they fell in their tracks. The road was now well covered by the enemy and although Wallace, Fitzgerald and myself crawled up as near as possible to the enemy to try and pick one or two off, we were shot at by another position further round Rachi and had to retire. I don't quite know how one particular burst missed my foot.
>
> Barrington then sent me to contact OC 1 King's Own and find out his plan for the capture of this feature. I was away for about two hours, having to take a fairly roundabout route to avoid the road area. OC 1 King's Own held his 'O' Group on the west slope of Searchlight Hill and decided to attack Point 100 using two platoons at dusk. Our small force was to be ignored except for what supporting fire we could give by our observation. It was at the 'O' Group that somebody [Lieutenant Robert King of the King's Own] gave me half a tin of cold M&V [stew] and I thought it was the most wonderful thing I'd tasted for ages. I got back to our little force about half an hour before the attack was due to go in. We gave the feature all we'd got and a damn good mortar barrage of smoke and HE. We couldn't see the attack go in or for that matter hear it but soon after zero hour we withdrew back to our Company area as from OC 1 King's Own orders we were being ignored except for supporting fire.[11]

Elsewhere on the feature, 'B' Company of the Faughs made good progress until being slowed by close-quarter fighting and by late afternoon both it and 'C' Company had returned to their original positions. 'B' Company, in particular, suffered heavily, with at least three men killed and several wounded, including the OC, Captain C. R. Mason, who was temporarily replaced by Lieutenant T. West. Major Ben Barrington was also wounded and command of 'C' Company now passed to Lieutenant Johnson.

At dawn, 'D' Company of the Buffs under Major E. W. Tassell had advanced southwards, meeting fierce resistance at Germano, which held out until shortly before midday. Soon after, 'D' Company was able to marry up with 'B' Company of the Royal West Kents, which was then placed under Lieutenant Colonel Iggulden's command. Subsequently, both companies were directed to nearby San Nicola, with 'D' Company on the right, and 'B' Company on the left. Once again, the Buffs were disadvantaged by not having close artillery support. Progress was slow, the troops being prevented even from penetrating the village outskirts by an enemy who had made a strongpoint of every house in the area. Both companies, as well as 'C' Company of the Buffs, were relieved in the evening by LRDG patrols. In the meantime, Lieutenant Arthur Stokes and the remnants of his platoon had been sent by Captain Flood of the Royal West Kents to reinforce Lieutenant Clifford Clark on San Giovanni.

German air support had intensified dramatically on the 14th, with *Stukas* always on call. The constant presence of the *Luftwaffe* and the often intense bombing was a permanent feature of the battle. The indescribably mind-numbing din of exploding bombs, artillery, mortar and small-arms fire that could wreak havoc with a man's senses left many feeling drained and lacking the will to fight. By day three, troops on both sides were under a tremendous strain: tired, often hungry and thirsty, but ever alert to the telltale whistle of a falling bomb or the roaring 'whoosh' of another incoming round moments before it detonated with a sound like a huge door slamming shut. Sometimes, depending on a projectile's trajectory, there was no warning whatsoever: just an ear-splitting bang, a hot blast of displaced air and a deadly unseen spray of red-hot shrapnel, followed by a hail of stones and debris and choking dust. For some, the constant stress was unbearable, as Clark came to realise:

For a couple of days we had been taking pot shots at a man who we could see on a rock in the middle of the bay. We thought it was a parachutist who had been stopped short in the bay on the first day. Eventually, after two days and nights of what must have been terrible conditions, he swam in to shore and I sent a couple of men to pull him in. Imagine our astonishment when we found it was [a] Private from our Company who had left his post on the first day of the invasion and disappeared. We slated him good and proper, although we did give him clothes and food, and put him in a slit trench. I wasn't at all surprised when I heard he had disappeared again, and that was the last we saw of him.[12]

Dusk brought a temporary respite from the *Stuka* attacks and a lessening of the shelling that prevailed during daylight hours, but there was still intermittent gunfire as nervous sentries imagined seeing movement in every shadow. Whether from bravado or to reassure themselves, many Germans were especially vocal at night. It was a strange, almost surreal, experience for the British listening in their own defensive positions. In between sentry duty, soldiers on both sides huddled beneath greatcoats and blankets and tried to catch up on lost sleep. For others, there was little rest. After the day's attacks, the grim work of medical orderlies such as Taffy Kenchington continued:

> We were called on to dig shallow graves for anyone who had died at the RAP, or maybe find the Jeep to take some of the wounded to the ADS [Advanced Dressing Station] at Porto Lago [Lakki] and, when they had been patched up, maybe a chance to get them taken off the island by MTB, sub' or ML. This had to be done before dawn when the dreaded *Stuka* would be up looking for just such a target.[13]

After dark, a strong patrol of 'HQ' Company of the Buffs moved into position on Point 111, extending the British line which stretched west to Clidi and south through Quirico to Germano. The enemy was still contained on Appetici, and the ground from Meraviglia west to Searchlight Hill was still in Allied hands. To avoid being cut off by a strong British presence on Point 101, *Major* von Saldern pulled back his troops from the north-west slopes of Meraviglia and the line extending from Point 108 to Santa Marina, to a line from Rachi, north to the coast near Patriarcato. A

Kompanie was also deployed just north of San Quaranta on the west shore of Alinda Bay. *Kampfgruppe* Müller had suffered substantial losses and had failed to secure a number of key features. Neither were there sufficient troops to maintain contact between those in the Vedetta–Grifo Bay area and west Alinda Bay, leaving a dangerous breach which had to be covered throughout the night by reconnaissance patrols. If ever there was a time when Brigadier Tilney might have reversed the situation on Leros, it was now. Unfortunately, he was unaware of the German plight and with his own forces having also suffered during the day's fighting was unable to follow up on their successes:

> It was felt that the initiative could be better retained by attacking the enemy on two sides and attempting his elimination on the morrow. If that failed, a mainly defensive policy might have to be resorted to.[14]

Müller knew that his *Kampfgruppe* could not hope to continue without heavy weapons, but landing conditions were impossible. The best that could be achieved was to keep the troops resupplied with ammunition through continuous air-drops. Late on Sunday afternoon, he issued a revised battle plan: the beachhead at Mount Vedetta–Grifo Bay was to be held until ordered and that at Alinda Bay until 1400 hours on the 15th. The *Luftwaffe* would then support a major push via Meraviglia to Pandeli Bay with the intention of establishing a new beachhead from Pandeli Castle through Meraviglia, south to Points 132 and 79, and east to Point 102 (Mount Vigla). Sufficient forces were to remain on Rachi to prevent Allied movement between Alinda and Gurna Bays. Furthermore, *Hauptmann* Dörr with troops remaining from *III./Gren.Rgt.440*, *II./Gren.Rgt.65* and *6./Lw.-Jäger-Rgt.22* was to land in the evening of the 14th east of Appetici and take command of the units already there, preparatory to seizing Pandeli Castle and linking up with *Kampfgruppe* von Saldern.

In the afternoon, *Penn*, *Aldenham* and *Blencathra* steamed towards Leros with instructions to bombard enemy shipping at Alinda, each carrying a deck cargo of ammunition for the island. However, on being advised that the situation in Leros had deteriorated and due to his concern about the possibility of heavy air attacks, Lieutenant Commander J. H. Swain on board *Penn* ordered the cargoes jettisoned. At approximately 1730, the destroyers arrived at Alinda Bay and soon after, commenced firing on three enemy caiques before responding to a request from the island to engage German defensive positions. From onshore, a captured gun was turned against *Penn* in an attempt to prevent her searchlight from being used to illuminate targets. The response was an immediate burst of 20mm cannon fire. The bombardment continued for about fifteen minutes during which the hospital at Villa Belleni was hit, resulting in the deaths of several patients. While withdrawing from Rachi, Lieutenant Ted Johnson and his party were caught in the open, fortunately without incurring casualties. In the area of San Quaranta, 'C' Company of the Buffs also had to seek cover. In this instance, there were casualties and the disruption was such that Major Pistol Bourne considered it impracticable to press on:

> After it was all over, it was necessary to collect the Company together again. I was unable to make wireless contact with Battalion HQ and as it was now dark, I took the decision to reform on higher ground rather than stay in a less defensive area.[15]

Accordingly, the Buffs pulled back to Point 81, south-east of Quirico. On completion of the fire mission, the destroyers withdrew north-east of the island and *Aldenham* was detached to bombard Gurna Bay. As the destroyers departed, *Blencathra* reported 'extinguishing' a searchlight – presumably that reported by the LRDG on Marcello as having been damaged at their location! Shortly afterwards, *Penn* and *Blencathra* steamed to within a mile or so of Leros in order to shell additional shore targets, before proceeding north-east at 1923. Meanwhile, the *Aldenham*'s fire mission was cancelled, allowing her to rejoin the force. At 2115, *Hauptmann* Dörr and his command were ferried from Kalymnos and deployed below Appetici. During the operation there were several casualties possibly as a result of accurate shooting by coastal guns. While withdrawing, the flotilla was engaged by at least one of the British warships before the latter were attacked by Do 217s of *K.G.100* armed with glider bombs, two of which narrowly missed the *Aldenham*. The destroyers succeeded in returning to Turkish waters at midnight and arrived at Kulluk at dawn on the 15th.

Tilney's requested reinforcements were also on the way. After departing from Port Vathi the previous night, MMS *103* with 'A' Company of the Royal West Kents reached Lakki at 2240. The troops disembarked and moved to a nearby assembly area, while the company commander,

Major Robert Butler, proceeded to Fortress Headquarters for orders. The minesweeper remained long enough to take on board wounded before she again put to sea.

In the course of the day in the Leros area, a Heinkel He 111 was shot down during an offensive sweep by Beaufighters of 46 and 227 Squadrons. Two Beaufighters failed to return. According to *Luftwaffe* records, a Ju 52 was also lost to anti-aircraft fire. Further south, Baltimores attacked shipping in Suda Bay, Crete, without visible result, and seven out of sixteen Hurricanes were reported missing during sweeps over the island.[16]

At Leros, a night supply drop was carried out just north of Serocampo Bay, the sight of so many parachutes causing panic among the Italians in the sector held by Second Lieutenant R. F. White's LRDG. The former were convinced that they were about to be overwhelmed by German paratroopers, and reacted accordingly when they heard an unfamiliar voice from the rocks below: '*Inglese* officer – don't shoot!' The Italians promptly opened fire and it was with some difficulty that White made them stop, enabling him to call on the man to identify himself. There was no reply, which provoked another burst of firing from the jittery Italians. Once more, White brought them under control and this time was able to persuade the subject of all their attention to approach their position. From out of the darkness emerged an exhausted and shaken subaltern of 'A' Company, the King's Own. He told White that his company commander, Captain Cecil Blyth, had been killed that morning at Appetici and that he was under orders to evacuate Leros with a party of forty or so others. When informed, Brigade Headquarters had other ideas: the officer was ordered to return to action with his men and any other stragglers encountered along the way. Clearly, at least some of the island garrison were already convinced that they were fighting a losing battle.[17]

CHAPTER 11

Day 4 Monday, 15 November 1943

AT ABOUT 0200 HOURS ON MONDAY, Allied aircraft mistakenly delivered an ammunition resupply to the Germans on the neighbouring island of Kalymnos – thirty-six crates of machine-gun ammunition being located in and around Kalymnos town by daybreak.

During the night at Samos, several tons of ammunition and stores were loaded on board *Echo* and *Belvoir* and the majority of the remainder of the Royal West Kents embarked for passage to Leros. The destroyers were continuously shadowed and bombed by the *Luftwaffe*, although this did not prevent HMS *Echo* from landing her troops at Lakki in the early hours of the 15th. However, the slower *Belvoir* had to be rerouted to Turkish waters where she later transferred her troops to small craft for onward passage under cover of darkness.[1] At 0445, the *Echo* got under way to meet *Belvoir* for their return journey, having embarked the news correspondent, Marsland Gander, and his conducting officer, Captain David Crichton. Their photographer, Sergeant Wood, had orders to stay on the island.

Meanwhile, at 2240 on the 14th, MTBs *315*, *307* and *266* had slipped to carry out an inshore sweep around Leros. Soon after, a leak forced *307* to divert to Turkish waters, leaving just two boats to continue the patrol. An unidentified destroyer was spotted north of Leros, but disappeared before either boat could investigate further. Nearly two hours later, at 0455, the MTBs were illuminated by searchlights and engaged by shore batteries which necessitated a rapid departure from the immediate area. On board MTB *315* the senior officer, Lieutenant Commander C. P. Evensen, decided to search for the destroyer sighted earlier. Shortly afterwards, when just north of Alinda Bay, two 'R-boats' were reported just offshore and some 3,000 yards away, hurriedly proceeding south behind a heavy smoke screen. As the MTBs closed, searchlights on Leros snapped on to reveal about a dozen vessels heading towards the coast. Evensen reported:

> We found ourselves within 100 yards of a small craft very similar to our LCM, obviously full of troops as their heads were easily discernable against the searchlights. Action was immediately joined; closing the range to about 50 yards both MTBs opened a very heavy fire with .5 inch and 20mm guns.[2]

Those unfamiliar with such weapons cannot possibly imagine the carnage they can cause. The .5 inch and 20mm are rounds with a maximum diameter of half an inch and 20 millimetres respectively. Standard, or ball, ammunition consists of a copper-jacketed lead bullet, but it is usual to mix ball with other cartridge types such as tracer (phosphorus), high-explosive (HE) and armour piercing (AP). The composition of belt-fed ammunition varies but might typically consist of three or four rounds of ball followed by one of tracer and, perhaps, another of HE and/or AP. Automatic weapons, such as the .5-inch machine-gun, and 20mm cannon are capable of firing several hundred rounds per minute, although it is usual for a gunner to fire short bursts in order to maintain accuracy and conserve ammunition. But even three or four rounds can wreak havoc, and will easily punch through the thin metal skin of a landing craft. The effect on a human being is indescribable. The combined firepower of two MTBs would have been devastating and truly terrifying.

> At that range it was impossible to miss, and though the target took every kind of avoiding action we stayed with her until she was stopped and well on fire in at least six different places, and we had expended 2,000 rounds of our ammunition into her. Whilst this was going on we were engaged by, probably, an R-boat at extreme range; neither of the boats being hit. We next observed a large barge, power driven and apparently made of wood. At the same time we saw, in the searchlights, a destroyer which we presumed to be the same enemy destroyer we had seen earlier and apparently covering the landing. I gave the order to MTB 315 to prepare an attack with torpedoes, and detailed MTB

266 to attack the barge we had just located with depth charges, after which she was to follow us in and attack the destroyer. Fortunately, the destroyer suddenly challenged us and it transpired to be HMS *Echo*. Meanwhile, MTB 266 carried out a perfect depth charge attack on the barge, which apparently disintegrated. The *Echo*, coming through the position a few minutes later, reported hundreds of men in the water screaming for help.[3]

Marsland Gander was presented with a unique opportunity to record the event:

Despite the menace of coming light, the Captain [Lieutenant Commander R. H. C. Wyld, RN] had decided to make a last sweep round the island. We careered through the hoarse, surging sea, whipped by a fresh wind, at exhilarating speed. Then, as we rounded Point Bianca, jinking this way and that, we saw the Italian searchlight from the old castle groping over the water. Streams of red tracer came from the Germans waiting and crouching on the beaches and hillsides, but still the light was not extinguished. Presently it gripped something and halted. The *Echo*, too, like a beast before the kill, checked momentarily, and I felt the sinews stiffening. It was a German F-lighter, rather similar to one of our own tank landing craft, lying there motionless, perhaps preparing to unload. The *Echo*, vibrating now with all the full power of her engines, swerved and heeled violently towards the enemy. She closed to four thousand yards and her guns hammered till my eardrums seemed ready to crack.

The F-lighter, which I could see through glasses, was crammed with vehicles and guns. She was taken so completely by surprise that she never attempted to return our fire, perhaps her guns were silenced by the first salvoes. Now we were flinging over scores of 4.7 inch shells that erupted all round her in the water till she was lost to sight in smoke and spray. Some of our 'bricks' were plunging into the hull causing great spouts of flame, and then after a short, sharp action lasting at most only five or ten minutes we left her blazing furiously and drifting helplessly ...

As we continued to zigzag round the island one of the bridge lookouts called 'Craft bearing green four five, sir'. Straining in the half light

I could just detect three dim shapes. We challenged with a signalling lamp, and back came the code reply. They were two of our own motor torpedo boats about to attack another German landing craft. This time we held to our course, and let the MTBs get on with the job. There was a gigantic underwater explosion as one of the little attackers dropped a depth charge under the stern of the enemy craft. But we were not stopping now for anything.[4]

The torpedo boats withdrew, leaving two small craft close to shore and under heavy fire from coastal batteries. Their victims were, in fact, landing craft departing with German wounded and British prisoners. When the *MFP* attacked by HMS *Echo* returned from just north-east of Pasta di Sopra Point, the burning vessel was met by *Infanterieboot I-O-94*. But the ordeal of those on board was far from over. The flames spread to a cargo of mortar bombs which began to detonate in the intense heat. Nevertheless, the *I-Boot* managed to rescue thirteen seriously injured. There was a series of explosions as depth charges detonated on the landing craft before she started drifting, again came under fire and, according to the skipper of *I-O-94*, was sunk.

Observers on Leros reported a landing craft foundering in the same area soon after midday. The unidentified vessel somehow reached the coast and was found by a detachment of *6./Gren.Rgt.16*. The two men were guarding the *Kompanie* stockpile of ammunition and provisions on the west side of Pasta di Sopra Point when they were alerted by the sound of an approaching engine, as recalled by *Oberfeldwebel* Walter Lünsmann:

I thought: 'Now they've got us!' But then the coastal artillery started firing. This meant that it could only be a German ship. We went over the hill to see what had happened. The coastal artillery stopped firing. A *Fährprahm* was beached, with its doors open. I went on board and instructed the people there, some of whom were wrapped in blankets, to disembark. The first two did not understand German; presumably, they were English. The next ones refused or, perhaps, were unable to move. We carried the men off the boat in our ground sheets.

The laborious rescue operation continued into the afternoon:

We had got off eight men. I went back on board to look for the boatswain and machinist as somebody must have steered the boat.

Suddenly, the boat shifted and I only just managed to jump ashore. The boat reared steeply and disappeared beneath the sea. How many more men were still on board, I don't know.[5]

During the night, Brigadier Tilney had revealed his intentions for the 15th: to annihilate enemy forces in the Rachi–San Quaranta area, and thereafter to concentrate the defence around Meraviglia. The final plan would not be decided until much later in the day but essentially called for a two-phase attack involving the newly arrived 'A' and 'C' Companies of the Queen's Own Royal West Kents (the latter having disembarked shortly before dawn): firstly, 'A' Company was to pass through the King's Own on Searchlight Hill, with the unenviable task of securing Rachi Ridge from the centre to the northern limits of Point 100. The King's Own were to follow up and occupy the ridge from the centre back to Searchlight Hill. On successful completion of the first phase, 'D' Company of the Buffs with 'B' Company of the Royal West Kents were to advance southwards to San Quaranta and San Nicola and drive the enemy towards 'C' Company of the Royal West Kents. The latter was to proceed north-west on a one-company front, with its right flank on the coast road and its left on the eastern slopes of Rachi, and secure Santa Marina and Point 36.

At about 0630, Lieutenant Colonel Ben Tarleton, commanding the Royal West Kents, arrived by jeep at Fortress Headquarters with his 'R' Group and a liaison officer for a briefing by Tilney. Tarleton could hardly have approved of his men being sent into the fray so soon after their arrival, or to learn that during the attack 'A' Company would be directed by the brigadier from his vantage point atop Meraviglia. He would have been even less impressed had he known about the previous day's failed attempt to secure Point 100. Neither was he told that because of the already overloaded wireless net, communication between Fortress Headquarters and 'A' Company was to be by runner. After discussing with Tilney the role of 'C' Company, Tarleton returned to his men at the Anchor to brief Major Mike Read, OC 'C' Company. He was accompanied by Colonel Guy Prendergast, second-in-command of Raiding Forces Aegean,[6] who pointed out key features along the way.

When Major Robert Butler rejoined his men he issued a warning order for the company attack and then accompanied the first platoon aboard the only available lorry to the Forming Up Point (FUP) just west of Charing Cross. The remainder of the company followed on foot. As Zero Hour approached, there was a delay which allowed more time for the platoon commanders and Company Sergeant Major, WOII Frederick Spooner, to view the ground over which the attack was to take place. Previously, Butler had also studied the terrain:

> Although bodies are normally recovered during the night, there were still a few khaki-clad ones around to be seen through my binoculars that morning, which did not do much for my appetite.[7]

Nor, no doubt, did the news that 'A' Company was to assault without artillery cover. Tilney would later provide an explanation for this extraordinary decision:

> RA and medium machine guns were to stand by to support this attack by observation; no preparatory fire plan was possible due to the somewhat confused situation prevailing on the ridge at this time.[8]

Even as the British finalised their battle preparations, another enemy offensive was under way as *Kampfgruppe* Dörr and the *Küstenjäger* made a renewed effort to take Pandeli Castle. It failed due to a concerted effort by the guns on and around Mounts Vigla, Meraviglia and della Palma. At 0830, 'A' Company crossed its attack start line, just as Tarleton was reporting back to Tilney with his 'R' Group and Prendergast. By this time, Ju 87 *Stukas* were over Leros and dive-bombing Meraviglia and the Charing Cross area. From 0900 these attacks intensified, causing casualties at the latter location among personnel of Battalion Headquarters of the Royal West Kents. In addition, Meraviglia was constantly swept with machine-gun and cannon fire. For a while, German mortars on Point 100 also fell around the area of Brigade Headquarters. From the northern slopes of Meraviglia, the Faughs responded with machine-guns and mortars – although from their present location the latter were unable to reach Point 100. British 18/25-pounders added to the din, concentrating in particular on *P.L. 211*. The entire area was a deafening, smoke and dust-filled killing ground – a terrifying ordeal for troops on either side. Trenches became potential death-traps, with direct hits causing heavy losses among *7./Gren.Rgt.16*. It was, of course, worse for 'A' Company in the open. As soon as the leading platoons were past Searchlight Hill they were bombed by *Stukas* and subjected to sniper and mortar fire and Lieutenant H. D. T. Groom and six men were wounded. The remainder pressed on, straight into automatic fire from Point 100 and *P.L. 211.* With the King's Own and the Faughs providing supporting fire, small groups of men moved from cover to cover as they fought their way to within 50 yards of the German positions before withdrawing to reorganise in dead ground south-east of Searchlight Hill. There were four killed, among them Lieutenant Victor Hewett and WOII Frederick Spooner. Two officers and approximately twenty ORs were wounded. In the confusion, Major Butler found himself alone on Rachi for much of the morning. When he withdrew to rejoin his company, he was shot and wounded slightly in the wrist. Undeterred, Butler immediately formulated a plan for a second attempt to take the enemy positions.

Due to communication problems, a runner had in the meantime been sent from the Royal West Kents' Battalion Headquarters with a reminder for 'C' Company not to attack until ordered. The runner returned to report that Major Read had acted on his initiative and, contrary to orders, was already occupying Santa Marina. When he was informed, the brigadier sent word that the company was to halt its advance immediately. He then decided to proceed with the rest of his plan, regardless as to whether or not Point 100 could be taken. While Tilney was giving his orders, a message was received informing him of the failed attack by 'A' Company with a request by Butler for close mortar support and smoke from the 25-pounders for a renewed effort at 1430. This was agreed.

With a stream of constant interruptions, the 'O' Group dragged on for two hours. As a newcomer to the chaos and confusion that was Leros, Tarleton was able to observe events from a unique perspective. He had been shipped from a comparatively tranquil setting and pitched into a desperate battle, the organisation of which hardly filled him with confidence. As the 'O' Group continued in the cramped and overcrowded confines of the headquarters tunnel, Tarleton forced himself to ignore the continuous roar of gunfire and explosions. Meanwhile, Tilney had altered the objective of 'C' Company: ordering them to take not just Point 36 but to push on to the road junction of San Nicola and Villa Belleni. Supporting fire was to be provided by mortars and MMGs of the Faughs and all available coastal batteries and 25-pounders. The new CO of the Faughs, Major Shephard, was tasked with organising a composite company to be sent to Santa Marina to follow 'C' Company and mop up pockets of resistance. Shephard was doubtful whether he could find sufficient men in the time available. Tarleton, too, expressed misgivings, arguing that the forces to hand were hardly sufficient for the task ahead. Tilney concurred, but nonetheless was determined to proceed with the attack. H-Hour was fixed for 1500.

At 1315, Tarleton left by jeep with his 'R' Group to find 'C' Company. It was a perilous journey, with *Stukas* circling before swooping to unleash their bombs over Meraviglia. Tarleton's driver momentarily lost control and the vehicle careered off the road and became stuck. In desperation, the group took another jeep parked near by and drove off followed by a stream of oaths and several shots from its enraged owner! The runner from Fortress Headquarters had still not arrived when Tarleton reached 'C' Company's location south of Platanos. With fifteen minutes to spare the CO was able to prevent Major Read from moving against Point 36 – and into supporting fire scheduled for the same time! When Read called off his proposed attack it was already 1445, with no sign of the Faughs. Reluctantly, Tarleton postponed H-Hour until 1530, too late for the attacking troops to benefit from the prearranged fire plan. Two separate messages were sent by runner to notify Meraviglia of the change, but in the event only one got through later that afternoon.

The second attack along Rachi went in at 1425. Following the same route as before, it was made by two composite platoons led by Major Butler and the Company 2 i/c, Captain William Grimshaw, who was the only other effective officer. All available LMGs were grouped alongside Searchlight Hill under the wounded Lieutenant Groom and an officer of the King's Own. Smoke was laid over the enemy positions and mortar support provided by a detachment of the Faughs. The enemy responded with automatic and mortar fire and the King's Own officer with Lieutenant Groom's party was killed almost immediately. The attack had already commenced when two sections of 14 Platoon arrived in the Searchlight Hill area, having gone astray while moving up for the assault on Point 36. In the mistaken belief that they had been sent as reinforcements, Lieutenant Groom directed the soldiers forward against Point 100.

By this time, all that could be mustered of the Faughs to support the attack by 'C' Company of the Royal West Kents were approximately sixty men remaining from 'B' and 'C' Companies and 17 Platoon of 'D' Company. Ten minutes before H-Hour, two officers and nineteen men arrived (probably Captain J. W. Salter and Lieutenant J. Duffy with 'B' Company) and informed Tarleton that a similar number were on the way. The commanding officer of the Royal West Kents was appalled by what he saw: the Faughs were exhausted, with the strain of three and a half days of fighting evident in all their faces. They were given their orders during an ongoing aerial bombardment. At 1525, Brigadier Tilney appeared and demanded to know what the delay was. The attack began five minutes later, with a patrol team from Company Headquarters and one section from the reserve platoon attached to 14 Platoon to compensate for the two sections now fighting on Rachi. 13 Platoon took up position on the right followed by the Faughs; 14 Platoon was on the left and 15 Platoon (less one section) was reserve with the battalion 'R' Group following. The company commander and one runner was stationed between the two forward platoons with the company 2 i/c and Company Headquarters behind. The advance began as planned, but for 14 Platoon again moving too far west and ending up on Searchlight Hill. This time, the men were led from the area, and out of the battle, by the platoon commander, Lieutenant R. Norris. Lower down, Major Read was out of the fight after being severely wounded. Lieutenant Jode commanding 13 Platoon had also been wounded and his place taken by Sergeant Wallington, who took charge of clearing Krithoni. The area was covered from high ground by German machine-gunners and riflemen, and snipers concentrated on individual soldiers who dashed from cover to cover as they swept through the village. A soldier never knew when he was safe: in the open there was an awful sensation that at any moment one might be caught in the cross-hairs of a sniper-scope, while each and every house and villa was a potential enemy position. Whenever they advanced, the troops were targeted by *Stukas* whose pilots were directed by spotters firing red signal lights. As they pressed forward, and the Germans withdrew, the British came across large swastika flags laid out as indication markers by an enemy fearful of being wrongly identified by their own aircraft.

Meanwhile, Lieutenant Ted Johnson, commanding 'C' Company of the Faughs, had reached Platanos with no more than sixteen men. He was met by his friend, Lieutenant Austin Ardill, who provided a cursory briefing. Johnson was told to watch for a combination of Verey lights which would be his cue to follow up the line of advance, taking care of any enemy resistance along the way. Due to arriving late, however, he was left in ignorance of their actual objectives:

> As we waited on what could be loosely called a Start Line there was an air attack taking place on the steep slopes of Meraviglia immediately to our left. The noise of it made even shouted orders unheard by a man five paces away. The Verey signal was eventually seen and off we went ...
>
> My right hand section was stopped almost immediately by enemy who had allowed the West Kents to pass over them. But my centre section with Sergeant Wallace made uninterrupted progress up the line of advance and CQMS O'Neill with the left hand section also made good progress for about 200 yards when he came under fire from a house ahead. We could not afford the luxury of a company HQ and so I was located with this left flank section. Because of the noise I was unable to check Wallace's advance and lost all contact with him ...
>
> Because of the close nature of the undergrowth and rocks my visibility was not more than 15 yards. Unable either to see or hear my middle section I left Colour Sergeant O'Neill to extricate himself from his pinned down position and went in search of Sergeant Wallace who I had last seen going well up front. I failed to find him and, as might be expected, failed to find my left flank section when I returned to their last known position.[9]

By 1600 hours, the main advance was just 300 yards from Point 36. 15 Platoon of the Royal West Kents had swung left and was roughly in line with 13 Platoon on the coast and Company Headquarters, which had moved forward and was being followed by the battalion 'R' Group. The latter, comprising five men under Colonel Tarleton, was also caught up in the fighting and reinforced by a party of the Faughs. At about 1615, Lieutenant John Browne, OC 15 Platoon, was directed to seize Point 36. Using the cover afforded by a sunken road, the platoon advanced as far as the left flank of 13 Platoon and after being joined by those who were still fit to fight, rushed forward and took the height. It was quickly over: a number of Germans were killed and over twenty-five taken prisoner. Colonel Tarleton was treated to the satisfying spectacle of the enemy surrendering, clearly silhouetted against the evening sky. His pleasure was short-lived, for no sooner was the feature overrun than it was pounded by what seemed to be every German mortar and automatic weapon in the vicinity. Both the British and their German captives were fired on indiscriminately in a ruthless, and effective, attempt to clear the height. An unseen enemy position just north of the feature joined in, forcing the surviving British back down the east slope – and directly into an Italian minefield.

On Rachi the Royal West Kents had persevered in their attacks on Point 100 until no more than a dozen or so men reached their objective. In the final assault, Captain Bill Grimshaw was wounded in the wrist and Major Butler was shot and paralysed in his right leg. Realising that he could not hope to hold the position with a handful of riflemen, Butler dispatched a runner to chase 'A' Company's Bren gunners, who by then should have been following up the advance.

> The runner returned to report that the CO of the regiment [King's Own] through which I had attacked had refused to allow my men and their Brens to leave his Battalion area. I was absolutely shattered. I had been obliged to leave my Brens to provide my covering fire because the men of the regiment supposed to support me had been fighting more or less continuously for three days without sleep and seemed reluctant to put their heads up; and now their CO was keeping my men and their Brens to protect his own positions.[10]

Left with little choice, Butler called for stretcher bearers for the wounded and ordered those who were able, to withdraw. At dusk, 7./Gren.Rgt.65 reoccupied Point 36, enabling the enemy to regain his hold along a line south to Points 100 and 109.

Events on Rachi and along Alinda's shore overshadowed a follow-up attack at 1400 by the Germans on Appetici. After fighting for more than two hours, and supported by Stukas and mortar fire, the Küstenjäger, 6./Lw.-Jäger-Rgt.22 and 9./Gren.Rgt.440 overran 9 Platoon of the Faughs and took Pandeli Castle. Lieutenant Colonel C. W. M. Ritchie, G1 at Brigade Headquarters, was inspecting defences at Meraviglia at the time:

I appeared to be the only living soul at the south-east end of the hill top and in fact was the only person firing at the enemy who were entering the Castle unopposed at 1615 hours. If the very dirty Bren I was using had not kept jamming I could have caused a lot of casualties.[11]

With the enemy now in control of the castle feature, the scene was set for a link-up with *Kampfgruppe* von Saldern, whose forces were preparing to push east via Platanos to Pandeli for an assault on Meraviglia from the north and north-east.

It was an altogether different picture for the Royal West Kents. With the remnants of 13 and 15 Platoons scattered between the coast and Rachi, and with no sign of the whereabouts of 14 Platoon, Tarleton was unable to press on. He therefore ordered a withdrawal to the area of Battalion Headquarters which was situated on a spur which ran north from the defended slopes of Meraviglia to the sea.

As for the expected push by the Buffs, Colonel Tarleton would later claim that Brigadier Tilney had altered this aspect of the battle plan without his knowledge so that 'the operations by the Buffs were now to be limited to demonstrating only, in the direction of San Nicola and Alinda Bay Hospital'.[12] He goes on to state that at 1600, 'D' Company of the Buffs and 'B' Company of the Royal West Kents resumed their attack on San Nicola, but progress was slow and the troops were recalled after just two hours and relieved by the LRDG. Second Lieutenant Pav Pavlides of the LRDG records in his operation report that the Buffs had been warned to expect a series of Verey lights indicating that Rachi was in British hands, whereupon 'D' Company was to move east to the outskirts of San Quaranta/San Nicola. 'C' Company would then advance and clear the Villa Belleni area. No signals were forthcoming and the Buffs still occupied the same positions in the evening. Later still, 'C' Company sent a patrol towards Villa Belleni, only for the troops to return to Point 81 after meeting with strong resistance.

By evening the strength of the Buffs' three forward companies was reported to be just 160 men. That night, as the Royal West Kents' padre, Captain G. M. Young, assisted with the wounded, he unexpectedly encountered a column of enemy troops. The surprised officer was in the process of identifying himself when he was interrupted by the arrival of a stretcher party carrying Major Read. On being challenged, one of the stretcher bearers, Private Bett, immediately opened fire, causing the column, which he later estimated at company strength, to break up in disarray. Bett seized the opportunity to escape and subsequently reported the incident to the former 2 i/c 'C' Company, now OC, Captain E. E. Newbald. In the meantime, the Germans reassembled and continued on their way, taking with them the regimental medical officer, Captain J. C. Seddon, presumably to help with their own casualties. The padre was allowed to resume his work, and subsequently reported having seen over 1,000 lightly equipped troops pass by.

Battalion Headquarters received regular situation reports via Captain Newbald, but was prevented by ongoing communication problems from keeping the fortress commander informed. At 2000, an exasperated Colonel Tarleton placed the adjutant, Captain Donald Cropper, in charge of the whole defensive position and with his intelligence officer, Lieutenant R. A. James, left by jeep to see Tilney. Just after their departure, a runner arrived from Fortress Headquarters with new wireless frequencies and test call times, none of which made the slightest difference to communications. There was no let-up in enemy troop movements and at about 2030, Lieutenants Ardill and Duffy arrived at Captain Cropper's location with a number of men from the Faughs' forward position. They brought alarming news, claiming to have been bluffed by English-speaking Germans who had captured or scattered two-thirds of their number. The Faughs took up a new defensive position near by. It was an unusually clear night and before long, enemy soldiers were seen approaching along the coast road. On being engaged with rifle and Thompson fire by a party of the Royal West Kents, they took cover behind houses just off the road. The Faughs joined in with rifle and automatic fire, forcing the unfortunate Germans out into the open and straight into renewed fire from the headquarters area. At least eight of the enemy were killed. The remainder withdrew northward.

In the neutral waters off Turkey, shortly before 1800 hours, several MTBs each transhipped from HMS *Belvoir* twenty-five troops of the Royal West Kents. The remainder, including 'D' Company, were taken on board other vessels. The faster torpedo boats reached Lakki after nearly three and a half hours. On arrival, the senior naval officer was instructed to disembark all troops and then to proceed immediately to Alinda to engage surface vessels entering the bay. Just before the MTBs got under way, the order was countermanded. Puzzled, the force commander decided to ignore instructions and at 2206 set course for Alinda.

At Lakki, the new arrivals shouldered their packs and marched north towards the Anchor. A constant drone of low-flying aircraft heightened a noticeable air of tense expectation, before it was realised that most were Dakotas dropping supplies to the beleaguered garrison.[13] Ahead, the night sky was lit by flashes and all around the hills reverberated with the noise of battle. Peering at unfamiliar surroundings from beneath the rims of steel helmets, the men trudged on. At night, senses become especially acute and then a soldier's imagination can amplify his worst fears. For those who were unable to visualise what lay ahead, it was enough to know that they were listening to people fighting for their lives. None could have known, however, that this included their own Battalion Headquarters.

Within half an hour, the position was outflanked by the enemy who closed to within grenade-throwing range. Captain Cropper ordered a withdrawal to an RV further uphill. Soon afterwards, he, Captain C. M. Bernard and others were wounded by shrapnel. Cropper sustained a serious eye injury and set out to try to reach the RAP, only to be taken prisoner (he later escaped). A series of short withdrawals brought Bernard, the remnants of Battalion Headquarters and a few stragglers to a machine-gun post manned by the Faughs. By this time, the total strength of Bernard's party was little more than a dozen men, but they were spared a follow-up attack by the enemy whose intention seems to have been to clear the way for a link-up with their comrades on Point 189.

After being ferried overnight from Athens, *III./1.Rgt. Brandenburg*, assembled at Kalymnos. On Monday, these latest reinforcements embarked on four *Pi-La-Boote* and one *MFP* for passage to Leros with orders to liaise with *Kampfgruppe* von Saldern and safeguard the landing of heavy weapons in Pandeli Bay. Three *Flak* (anti-aircraft) guns, six *Pak* (anti-tank) guns and two light guns were loaded aboard two *Pi-La-Boote* which were to follow the troop transports and stand by off Leros, beyond reach of the coastal batteries.

In order to prevent further enemy reinforcements from arriving by sea, HM ships *Penn*, *Aldenham* and *Blencathra* had remained at readiness in Turkish waters throughout the day. At dusk *Blencathra* left Turk Buku to take *Rockwood* under tow to Cyprus. Later still, *Penn* was advised of enemy craft south-east of Kalymnos steering northward straight for Leros (evidently the *Brandenburg* reinforcements). By the time the information had been relayed through Alexandria, however, it was already an hour old and the captain of HMS *Penn*, Lieutenant Commander J. H. Swain, decided it was too late to act and to carry out instead previous instructions to sweep the east coast of Leros at dawn. It was a fateful decision which would result in a reprimand for Swain from the Commander-in-Chief, Levant (see Appendix G).

Under heavy fire from coastal batteries, the first wave of enemy landing craft with 280 men of *III./1.Rgt. Brandenburg* reached Leros at 2140, just as the port authorities at Lakki were supervising the disembarkation of the Royal West Kents. The second wave with heavy weapons remained offshore when it was realised that Pandeli Bay was not yet in German hands. The *Brandenburger* came ashore on the east side of Appetici and but a short march from Pandeli town. This was reached by the point troops at the same time as those of *Kampfgruppe* von Saldern, subsequent to their link-up with *Kampfgruppe* Dörr and the *Küstenjäger* at Castello di Bronzi. With enemy forces massed around the north and north-east slopes of Meraviglia, the scene was set for the final chapter in the battle for Leros.

After leaving Lakki, the British MTBs had proceeded to Alinda, but reported seeing nothing amiss. The three boats withdrew towards Kalymnos, eventually reaching Turkish waters without incident. The enemy off Pandeli watched their departure with interest, but made no effort to follow.

At 2030, Tarleton had reported to the brigadier with details of the afternoon attack. Also at Fortress Headquarters were Lieutenants Groom and Norris, who briefed their commanding officer on events on Rachi. Norris had an extraordinary tale and maintained that after joining 'C' Company's attack, he had continued unopposed all the way around Rachi and back towards Meraviglia. Others were of the opinion that the officer, having become disorientated by the bombing and mortaring, had actually led his platoon over the ridge south of Searchlight Hill and towards Gurna Bay before finally reaching Meraviglia. Norris was instructed to return to the Anchor and report to the Battalion 2 i/c, Major G. V. Shaw, newly arrived from Samos. Groom also left, with verbal orders for the King's Own to support yet another attack against Point 100 at 0900 hours the next day.

As the noose tightened around Meraviglia, Tilney issued orders for the 16th: Colonel Tarleton was to direct 'D' Company of the Royal West Kents in an attempt to secure Point 100 while the Buffs/Royal West Kents launched a simultaneous attack to clear San Nicola and the hospital area. As soon as Point 100 was taken, Tarleton was to take charge of all troops on Rachi and drive the enemy eastward into the sea. Tilney was interrupted by the arrival of two signallers with a situation report which had been dispatched by Captain Cropper shortly before he was wounded. It included news of a suspected enemy landing at Alinda Bay. Tilney, who could not possibly have realised the implications of the latest events, decided that the attack on Point 100 would continue regardless.

That night, Lieutenant Ted Johnson was briefed by Captain Mike Rochford, the battalion intelligence officer. His depleted company – now less than platoon strength – was to join 'A' Company in the morning to provide fire support for the attack against San Nicola. The main defence of Meraviglia was dependent on two platoons of 'A' Company situated on the spur projecting from the north-east towards Platanos, and fifty or so officers and men from Brigade under Lieutenant Colonel Ritchie covering the eastern approaches. It was considered that there was little likelihood of the enemy launching an attack from the west, which was virtually devoid of cover, and that any attempt to take the feature would come from the east. Accordingly, before midnight, Lieutenant Colonel Jake Easonsmith, commanding the Long Range Desert Group, was ordered by Tilney to send two patrols down either side of the east face towards Platanos in order to deny the area to the enemy. Both parties ran into German troops en route to Pandeli. There were casualties, including Easonsmith, who was killed, following which Colonel Prendergast resumed command of the unit.

After dark, 177 German prisoners of war embarked at Partheni Bay on an Italian F-lighter under the command of Lieutenant Stowell for passage to Tigani (Pythagorio) in Samos, and, ultimately, Egypt. Their departure was arranged by Lieutenant Commander Ramseyer:

> Whilst loading the lighter the Italians brought in some more Germans from a neighbouring island, where they had been sitting for some days since their barge had been sunk. As the island was no more than a large rock, they were wet, very hungry and devoid of any 'Master Race' touch. When the lighter was loaded, hatches were made fast and *MZ 722* left at approximately 1930B.[14]

Among the prisoners were *Feldwebel* Gustav Wehrs and *Unteroffizier* Andreas Hutter, who faced the next four years in captivity.

At Lakki, the evacuation of wounded also continued. One of the last to be shipped from the port was Major Robert Butler who was half carried on to a waiting ship by two casualties from his unit. He had been on Leros for just twenty-seven hours, a period that 'seemed like two lifetimes'.[15]

As usual, during the day, the Leros defenders had seen little or no evidence of their own aircraft whose crews were prevented by the *Luftwaffe* from venturing too close to the island.[16] Nevertheless, there were a number of sorties by RAF Beaufighters and USAAF B-25s. During the afternoon, Mitchells of 310th Bombardment Group carried out a cannon attack on two enemy warships, leaving one with a rising column of black smoke. Those on the ground had more respect for the Royal Navy whose efforts could often be seen and at least produced tangible results. During transit, many soldiers had also experienced something of what their colleagues in the senior service had to endure. But as with the air forces, many deeds passed unnoticed. In the evening of 15 November, the German *U-565* registered a torpedo hit on an enemy submarine south-east of Kos: her victim was undoubtedly the British submarine *Simoon*, which was reported missing with all hands.

Less was known about the clandestine war of Raiding Forces, whose disruptive efforts met with a minor success during the night of 15–16 November when a detachment of SBS raided Symi. An ammunition dump was destroyed, the power station and several caiques were damaged and nearly two dozen occupation troops were killed before the attackers withdrew without loss to themselves.

CHAPTER 12

Day 5 Tuesday, 16 November 1943

WHEN LIEUTENANT COLONEL B. D. Tarleton rejoined his battalion at the Anchor at about 0100 on the 16th, he deployed his men to cover likely approach routes from the north, and to support any move by 'D' Company. Lieutenant Richard Norris was ordered to take his platoon to a road 500 yards north-east of their present location. Accounting for the possibility that 'D' Company's task was liable to change, Tarleton took the added precaution of placing the new arrivals in some deep Italian trenches east of the Anchor road junction, which afforded some cover from air attack while enabling them to counter any threat from the direction of Appetici. The Mortar Platoon was also sited to cover the approaches from Platanos and Appetici and to support 'D' Company as required. The Anti-Aircraft (AA) Platoon under Captain M. B. Rickcord was tasked with moving as a fighting patrol along the road to Alinda Bay, to contact any members of the battalion en route, and to watch for and report any signs of enemy movement south.[1] Rickcord returned at 0445, having lost three men who were wounded when they entered an Italian minefield. No British troops other than Lieutenant Norris's platoon had been encountered, and no Germans were observed in Platanos.

At 0550, *Penn* and *Aldenham* arrived off the north-east point of Leros, far too late to have any effect on the latest German landing. Off Pandeli Bay the destroyers came under fire from an Italian-manned shore gun and *Penn* was hit on the starboard side, six feet above the waterline. Daylight brought an increased threat of enemy attack and at dawn both ships departed for Turk Buku.

By now, all German units on Leros had been placed under the command of *Major* von Saldern. Before dawn, the *Kampfgruppe* launched a major assault along the northern face of Meraviglia. At about 0515, Tarleton was informed that Norris had been killed and his platoon driven back towards the Anchor. Moreover, the enemy had reached the commanding south-eastern spur of Meraviglia. Lieutenant Colonel Ritchie, atop the height, recalled:

> A number of shots came from the direction of Leros town [Platanos], but there were still no signs of any movement on to Meraviglia. This firing did not last long ...[2]

Soon, more shots were heard:

> Going down to investigate I saw six Germans about 200 yards away moving up the hill towards us. Just then a grenade or 2-inch mortar bomb landed among them causing loud shrieks and checking their advance ... I went back to Fortress HQ to personally report the situation to Tilney and try to get more men to thicken up the alarmingly weak defences.
>
> From the area of the LRDG HQ I pointed out the apparent direction of the enemy attack up the southern spur. I was told to hang on at all costs and that an attack by 200 Italians or other troops would be put in astride the road from the Anchor to Leros. For various reasons, however, this attack unfortunately never materialised.[3]

Tarleton's immediate reaction was to redeploy Rickcord's platoon to meet the enemy. He also telephoned Fortress Headquarters with a situation report only to be told by the brigade intelligence officer that there was no cause for concern as an operation was already under way to clear the ridge. (At some point during the morning, Tilney had sent for 160 men gathered at Lakki to help defend Meraviglia.) Tarleton asked to speak to the brigadier and suggested to him that in view of developments 'D' Company's task be changed, but Tilney refused to alter his plan. Tarleton recalled:

> From now onwards fire from the dominating spur of Meraviglia increased and movement in the assembly area was becoming difficult as

automatics were brought to bear on the road to Portolago [Lakki]. There were no signs on Meraviglia of any clearing-up operations. The whole security of the assembly area depended on the dominating ridge being denied to the enemy. To move 'D' Company away from the position at this stage, however, would have allowed the enemy, either by infiltrating down the ridge or by an attack from Appetici, to occupy the Anchor road junction and cut off Meraviglia from Portolago.[4]

Meanwhile, Rickcord and his men pressed on in the face of constant enemy fire. Eventually, a route was found west of the Anchor and this enabled the leading elements to get within 250 yards of the German positions on the summit.

During the night, there had been an attempt to gather at the Anchor scattered personnel of 'C' Company. A composite platoon was formed under Captain E. E. Newbald and this was directed to take up a defensive position behind that of 'D' Company. At about the same time, a message was received by Captain C. M. Bernard instructing 'D' Company not to move and requesting the company commander to call Fortress Headquarters. The information was dispatched to Major A. J. M. Flint, but never reached him. Neither was Tarleton kept informed. Unaware of the change of plan, Tarleton and Flint left by jeep at about 0700 to reconnoitre the ground for 'D' Company's attack. With daylight, the *Luftwaffe* had returned and the vehicle was soon under air attack. Cannon shells and machine-gun bullets thudded into the ground, making further progress impossible. The jeep was abandoned. At the same time there was increased firing on the eastern heights of Meraviglia and aircraft were seen wheeling and diving over the south-eastern slopes. Fearing a major assault on the Anchor, Tarleton decided to return with his party on foot.

In fact, it was Meraviglia that was the focus of attention. Atop the feature, Ritchie had rounded up two Royal Signals officers, Captain Ramsay and Lieutenant E. B. Horton, and with half a dozen men taken up positions in and around the battery command post. Under constant machine-gun and sniper fire from the castle feature less than a kilometre away, the party watched and waited. Half an hour passed before the first Germans appeared over the top of the ridge. Ritchie fired and the group – about twelve strong

– went to ground. Two Germans were then seen within 150 metres of Ritchie's position:

> Taking the regulation aim for a walking target I fired at the leader who crumpled up with a loud 'plop'. His companion stopped for a fatal moment to look at his fallen comrade so I quickly shot him. Throwing his arms in the air he went over backwards just like the famous picture from the Spanish Civil War ...[5]

Earlier, Colonel Guy Prendergast had ventured from LRDG Headquarters to find out for himself what was happening outside:

> I found the top of the feature a very uncomfortable spot. It was under fire from the Castello feature and was also being mortared from the direction of Santa Marina. There were at least six *Stukas* permanently overhead looking for a suitable target to attack, and periodically Ju 88s would come over in formation and drop anti-personnel bombs on the feature. I lay for some time in a bombed and abandoned Italian ack-ack position and saw Germans ascending the feature from the direction of Vromolito. [This was possibly the same force encountered by Ritchie.] We exchanged a few shots and I then went down to the main HQ and told the Brigadier that in my opinion it was essential immediately to stage a counter attack on these troops to push them off the Meraviglia feature. He told me to return to my own HQ and he would see what could be done about collecting the necessary troops for this counter attack.
>
> At about 0800 hours Brigadier Tilney with one of his Staff Officers came to the LRDG HQ cave and said that he was unable to stage this counter attack, and was proposing immediately to evacuate his HQ from the Meraviglia cave, and that I must move mine similarly. He decided to try to resume control of the battle from Portolago [Lakki]. By this time the Meraviglia feature was certainly becoming a most unpleasant place on which to live. The bombing on it from *Stukas* and Ju 88s, which were able to come as low as they liked, as all the Italian ack-ack guns had by then run out of ammunition, was incessant, and heavy mortar fire was also spattering the feature. I told the LRDG HQ personnel to destroy all wireless sets and make their way to a certain house in Portolago which we all knew ...[6]

The LRDG, who held a position on the east side of the feature, were commanded by Lieutenant P. A. Mold:

> I was about to take a small party on recce round the corner when Colonel Prendergast arrived with the news that the enemy had occupied the Italian battery position on top of the hill and that HQ intended to evacuate and that if we did not move quickly we would be cut off. I gave orders for every man to take water bottle and a tin of food, his arms and as much ammunition as possible. Colonel Prendergast then said that the RV was to be the 'Turnbull House', Portolago [Lakki]. I thought at the time this was a suicidal decision, Portolago being under continuous heavy bombing. However, we destroyed all equipment, etc, in our area and made off down the hill under fire.[7]

To prevent their being captured and compromised, secret ciphers were also destroyed. At 0825 the Germans intercepted a signal sent in clear from Fortress Headquarters advising General Headquarters (GHQ) in Cairo that the enemy had landed reinforcements; *Stukas* had neutralised Meraviglia's defences and the troops were demoralised and facing a hopeless situation. When the message was translated and relayed to *Kampfgruppe* Müller, it was duplicated in leaflet form with an added word of encouragement from the German commander: 'Now let's finish them off!' Copies were then dropped over German positions by Arado floatplanes. Müller knew he was close to victory. Why such a signal was ever transmitted, and in plain language, is a mystery. For the Germans, it was an unexpected and welcome bonus and exactly what was required to boost the morale of their own forces, not least the *Fallschirmjäger* who were dispirited following a series of defensive actions.

Before Fortress Headquarters was evacuated, a telephone message was taken from Tilney by Major H. E. Scott, OC 'HQ' Company of the Royal West Kents, ordering 'D' Company to attack north along the Porta Vecchia–Platanos road with the intention of pushing the enemy back into the sea. A written message was sent to 'D' Company's location but there is no record of it reaching its destination. In any event, Tilney himself arrived soon after and reaffirmed the order, to the consternation of the Company 2 i/c, Captain P. R. H. Turner; for any movement along the road brought an immediate response from the Germans on the commanding heights.

At about 0830, Tarleton arrived back at the Anchor to a scene of disarray. The entire area was under fire from Meraviglia and troops had been dive-bombed, albeit without sustaining casualties. During ongoing air attacks against the battery on Mount Vigla, many bombs fell short, to land among what was left of 'C' Company, whose positions were also subjected to small-arms and mortar fire. To the north-west, the AA Platoon was still attempting to reach the top of Meraviglia, with supporting fire provided by the battalion's mortars. Through the dust and smoke, German snipers could be seen moving among the boulders and scrub on Meraviglia's slopes. They were engaged by troops posted as local defence for Battalion Headquarters, which had relocated to a house some 300 yards to the north-west of the Anchor's telephone exchange. With movement becoming increasingly difficult, 'C' Company, together with 18 Platoon 'D' Company, was also shifted slightly further west.

Tarleton was not informed about Tilney's earlier visit and was unaware either that Fortress Headquarters had been evacuated or that 'D' Company had been retasked. The brigadier had remained in the vicinity rather than proceeding to Lakki as originally planned, and returned during mid-morning whereupon he sought out Tarleton and updated him on developments. The battalion commander was dismayed to learn about the brigadier's intentions for 'D' Company, although he was kept in ignorance of any orders already given to Captain Turner:

> The company was to fight its way through Leros village [Platanos] and join up with the Buffs, who were to attack south-east towards Alinda Bay, having been joined by 'HQ' Company and 'C' Company 2/RWK, who were to proceed up the west of the island for that purpose.
>
> It was explained to the Brigadier that the 'HQ' Company available strength at that moment was the Mortar Platoon and a few men of 6 Platoon, ie about 45 in all, 2 Platoon [sic] being committed on Meraviglia, and that 'C' Company mustered about 23 very tired men ...
>
> 'D' Company could not attempt an attack up the Leros village road with any chance of success whatsoever whilst the slopes of Meraviglia and Appetici were held by the enemy. At this moment telephone communications was established with Colonel Prendergast, who was still either at Fortress HQ or the HQ of the LRDG nearby.[8]

The interruption, which saved 'D' Company from almost certain annihilation, resulted from an encounter between Major Ben Barrington of the Royal Irish Fusiliers and evacuees from LRDG Headquarters. Lieutenant Mold recalled:

At the double crested feature immediately below Meraviglia, I found myself with Sergeant Hughes and I paused to have a look round, only to be challenged for evacuating the hill by Major Barrington RIrF with a rifle. Fortunately, Colonel Prendergast then joined us and explained the situation and ordered me to proceed to Portolago [Lakki] to try and gather our chaps together with Captain [C. H. B.] Croucher who was already on his way.[9]

According to Prendergast:

I passed a wounded RIrF officer [Barrington] who asked me why we were pushing off. I told him that these were the Brigadier's orders, and sat down with him to discuss the situation. It seemed to us that if Brigade HQ did in fact evacuate its cave at Meraviglia, leaving all its wireless sets behind, it would be virtually impossible for the Brigadier to continue to control the battle.

I therefore decided to go back to the main HQ cave and see what could be done about moving the wireless sets to Portolago [Lakki]. I took with me Sergeant Hughes, the LRDG Signal Sergeant. When we got back to the cave, dodging bombs all the way, I found Captain Rochford RIrF, one signalman and a few very shaken Italians in the cave. The signalman said that he still had contact with the Buffs and with the RWK, and also with a set in Portolago. I therefore spoke on the R/T to these three stations, and was fortunately able to find the Brigadier on one of them. He told me to remain in the main HQ cave and to run the battle to the best of my ability until he should return and again set up his HQ there.[10]

While Tilney and Prendergast were discussing events on Meraviglia, Tarleton noticed some men doubling south-west from 'D' Company's location. He alerted Major G. V. Shaw, who was near by. The 2 i/c left, saying 'I'll fix it.' Possibly, the movement was 'D' Company forming up for the attack under Captain Turner (of which Tarleton and Shaw were still unaware).

When he arrived at 'D' Company's rear area, Major Shaw was hit by small-arms fire in the thigh and forearm, and died soon afterwards; a tragic and unnecessary waste of life.

On Meraviglia, Ritchie was in contact with the enemy throughout the morning. Soon after his initial skirmish, he was fired upon by two Germans:

> They were not very determined however, for after I had fired a few shots from my revolver and thrown some small Italian grenades at them (which all fell short) they disappeared out of sight down the hill. No sooner had they gone than Captain Booth and two men [appeared] ... saying that they had run out of ammunition. This seemed strange as I had not heard a single shot come from them although [they were] only 30 yards from me. Just after this the Marine '*Capitano*' of the damaged Italian battery emerged from his underground '*refugio*'... and shouted back, 'There are only two Germans. Come quickly.'
>
> Lieutenant Alan Phipps (RN) who had just joined me, carrying an enormous Webley automatic, asked if he could go and help. I told him he could, but to be careful. Telling Captain Ramsay to join him, they ran to [take up] position and together with the Italian they engaged the two Germans with pistols and grenades. I could not see what actually happened but very shortly afterwards the '*Capitano*' limped back with a hand almost blown off at the wrist and a leg badly wounded by a grenade. Ramsay returned a minute later to say that the two Germans had withdrawn down the hill but that Lieutenant Phipps had been killed by a burst of SMG in the chest.[11]

Capitano Werther Cacciatori, manning one of the gun positions, recalled that mortar fire from the castle and low-level strafing had reduced his force from two dozen or so to eight British and six or seven Italians. After firing the last remaining shells towards the enemy at almost point blank range, he and his men continued to defend the post with automatic weapons.

> Out of ammunition, we threw our last hand grenades. Number 4 gun was captured, but we re-took it in hand-to-hand combat. My faithful and heroic Cavezzale was always at my side. Driven back again, we took refuge in the emplacement of Number 1 Battery. With my Beretta pistol, I fired at six paratroopers advancing with sub-machine-guns.

I admired their officer who, after my every shot, popped up and renewed his firing, smiling remorselessly. Suddenly, I was blinded! I touched my temple; the wound was not deep. With my other hand I wiped away the blood so I could see again. It would not have happened if I had my helmet, but a metal splinter had knocked it off my head a few minutes earlier. I got up again and continued shooting; that captain still looking at me and still smiling! An explosion left me dazed. Next to me, Cavezzale grabbed his rifle with fixed bayonet and suddenly disappeared from view![12]

The sight of the wounded Cacciatori was altogether too much for Pietro Cavezzale. It is alleged that an Italian burial party later found his corpse beneath that of a German who had the Italian's bayonet embedded in his chest. As for Cacciatori:

My shoulder was broken and painful; a grenade exploded against it and my right arm was almost severed, dangling by only a few strands and bleeding profusely. I kept a grip on it with my left hand in order not to bleed to death. I was very thirsty, but choosing the moment I leapt clear and asked a sergeant at the command post to bandage the stump. The other side was still firing and one of our men was asking, 'Can we surrender?' Annoyed, I replied quietly, 'I will kill you first!'[13]

As the fighting continued, Ritchie was confronted by a German soldier in a nearby gun position:

He drew a bead on me with his schmeisser while I took very careful aim with my revolver. We must have both fired simultaneously as I felt nothing unusual in my shot, but when I aimed a second time I found my foresight a twisted piece of metal. His bullet had apparently hit the tip of my barrel and had been deflected past my face. Picking up my rifle, I waited for him to appear again and as his head rose above the parapet I shot him through the forehead ...[14]

Over the next hour there was a series of similar engagements:

Another German suddenly appeared from the dead ground in front and opened up at me with his SMG [sub-machine-gun]. Lying in the open a mere 40 yards away he was asking for trouble, but no sooner had I shot him than a comrade joined him so I disposed of him in the same way ...

One German with a SMG suddenly appeared in the far gun position ... fired a burst into the ammunition tunnel, then ran to the rear gun position and did the same. I got him as he came towards us, still shooting from the hip ...

Two Germans came from dead ground in front, jumped into the old built-up position [nearby] ... and with head and shoulders fully exposed began to recce my position through field glasses. Selecting the one I thought was an officer, I fired at him and he dropped out of sight. The other immediately ran away before I could get a shot at him.[15]

Due to the initiative and courage of such officers, Tilney was able to return to Fortress Headquarters. Before doing so, he ordered Tarleton to muster his available forces and to advance northwards via the western slopes of Rachi Ridge and establish contact with the Buffs. Tarleton was to place his men under command of Lieutenant Colonel Iggulden, whereupon the combined force was to attack south via Rachi and concentrate on Meraviglia. Tarleton made his way to Battalion Headquarters where he was informed about the proposed attack by 'D' Company. He at once countermanded the order, informing Captain Turner of the latest plan and instructing 16 and 17 Platoons to act as rearguard. Mortars were disabled and extra bandoliers of small-arms ammunitions issued. Efforts to contact the AA Platoon were less successful. It is possible that two of the sections tried, and failed, to rejoin the battalion, whereas the remaining two sections under Captain Rickcord remained in action on Meraviglia until the very end. The extra activity no doubt alerted the enemy that something was afoot. Air attacks increased, adding to the discomfort of those already under fire from the commanding heights. It was especially hazardous for runners, who constantly risked their lives to deliver messages and maintain contact between units and sub-units.

Earlier that morning, Lieutenant Ted Johnson had redeployed his men on the lower slopes of Rachi/Meraviglia, to cover the proposed attack on San Nicola. When this failed to materialise, Johnson found himself trapped in an increasingly precarious position where the slightest movement brought an instant response from enemy positions lower down:

We engaged what targets we could find, but I doubt we had much effect. At about 1000 hours the rocky position I was in, with about four others, of which Lieutenant Tom Massey Lynch of 'A' Company was one, became bracketed either side by sustained spandau fire. We had exhausted almost all ammunition and were hailed by our opponents to give up. Our immediate reaction to this suggestion was to let fly a short burst of fire from our one serviceable Bren and its dwindling ammunition and to move ourselves to another hole amongst the rocks, but we soon realised that a move was out of the question as any attempt even by a single man was met by a burst of very accurate and frightening machine gun fire from our opponents who had us pinpointed. Over the next half hour Tom and I discussed our predicament and from what we knew of the adverse situation of the overall battle, and our local situation, we could not achieve anything by launching ourselves and our three or four very tired soldiers into some heroic suicide action.[16]

In order to stay awake Johnson had been taking Benzedrine for the past three days. As the effect wore off, he was overcome with exhaustion and unable to think clearly. As far as both officers were concerned, there was only one solution:

We set about making our weapons and controlled stores unserviceable with a terrible feeling of failure. Disposal of ammunition was no problem as the few rounds we still had were quickly shot off and nobody had any grenades left. The rifles and the one Bren gun were stripped down to their component parts; in the case of the Bren, these parts were scattered into the rocks as far as we could throw them. The rifles were less easy to dispose of as only the magazine and the bolt could be detached. The sights were smashed with rocks. Any other small items of equipment such as bayonets were also disposed of. I had a prismatic compass, binoculars and pistol, all of which had to go. This wilful destruction of His Majesty's stores and equipment took us about as long as it takes to read about it. Meantime our opponents were getting restless in our failure to comply with their shouted instructions.

Now the hardest part of the entire battle came. We had to raise a piece of white vest which somebody produced from his pack and when we were sure that no fire was coming in our direction we eased our-selves out of our rocky position and commenced the sad and shame-ful trek down the hillside to the point where we could see our captors. The only part of this sad journey I clearly remember was that I picked up a soldier's abandoned greatcoat en route down the hill – my instinct of self welfare can't have been totally lost.[17]

In the neighbourhood of San Nicola, the Buffs and 'B' Company of the Royal West Kents had returned to the previous day's positions and taken over from the LRDG patrols after an uneventful night. The day dawned with none of the usual signs of enemy movement, prompting Captain Flood, OC 'B' Company, to send Lieutenants Caller and Gordon Huckle on a reconnaissance into San Nicola. When it was discovered that the Germans had abandoned the area, the company pushed forward on to Point 100 and Rachi Ridge, with 'D' Company of the Buffs advancing on their left. Only a few individual Germans were found in dug-outs. By 1030, 'B' Company of the Royal West Kents had established contact with the King's Own on Searchlight Hill. Captain Flood, Lieutenant Colonel Egerton of the King's Own, and Major E. W. Tassell, commanding 'D' Company of the Buffs, gathered for an impromptu conference after which Tassell left to report to his CO. At about 1130 Egerton told Captain Flood that as a result of what had been observed in the area of Fortress Headquarters, he was withdrawing all troops from the Rachi feature to join up with the Buffs at the north end of the island. 'B' Company was instructed to cover the withdrawal. Subse-quently, Egerton, Tassell and Flood were reunited on the north-western outskirts of San Nicola, where they encountered a non-too-pleased Lieutenant Colonel Iggulden.

In the meantime, the Royal West Kents – numbering little more than 160 all ranks – had started to leave the Anchor area with Captain B. A. Pond and 'B' Echelon leading the order of march. It is always difficult to disengage and withdraw when in contact with the enemy in daylight. To minimise losses, the Royal West Kents headed south-west and into cover before moving northwards towards San Giovanni. As soon as it was vacated, the battalion area was heavily bombed. Although the troops were harassed by small-arms fire there was no follow-up by German ground forces. It was probably assumed that the British were making for Lakki as the area was bombed soon afterwards. Large numbers of aircraft remained overhead throughout the rest of the morning and into the afternoon, but fortunately for the infantry the crews seemed more interested in the gun positions in the area of Mounts Patella and San Giovanni.

As the crow flies, the distance to be covered by the battalion before reaching San Giovanni was little more than two and a half kilometres. In reality, the country to be crossed was rough and undulating and intersected by ravines. Bordering the ravines and on the lower hill slopes, olive groves and terraced fields afforded a certain amount of cover, but higher up the vegetation was generally sparse, consisting mainly of the ubiquitous Greek spiny spurge. Progress was hindered by long-range sniper fire. Along the way, small parties from all units were encountered; some heading for pre-arranged RVs, others making for the beaches, but all moving away from Meraviglia and the enemy. It was evident that command had completely broken down and there was little hope of organising an effective counter-attack. Nevertheless, Tarleton pressed on and at around 1300, Battalion Headquarters reached the heights north-east of San Giovanni overlooking Gurna Bay. An hour later, Captain Mike Rochford turned up with written confirmation of Tilney's morning orders, for forwarding to Lieutenant Colonel Iggulden. It was assumed that Point 100 and San Nicola were still strongly defended by the enemy. No one seemed sure about Meraviglia any more. Under the circumstances it was decided to skirt around the south side of Rachi to try to reach the Buffs by moving south and west of Germano, using the cover afforded by broken ground at the base of the feature. Sub-unit RVs were allocated close to Condrida (Point 177) and, it was hoped, not far from the Buffs' positions.

After leaving Tarleton at about 1000 hours, Tilney had returned to Meraviglia and attempted to regain some semblance of control over the chaotic situation. His task was not helped by the premature destruction of secret ciphers which left signallers with no option but to continue using plain language during communications with the outside world. At 1105 a signal was sent to the Middle East suggesting Lakki as a suitable spot in which to insert airborne troops. It was a perilous drop zone; a built-up area with low-lying hills on three sides and the sea on the other. The War Office had already approved the deployment to Leros of 11th Battalion The

Parachute Regiment; fortunately the order was never implemented. Another desperate plea followed:

> If you reinforce LEROS we can restore situation. You MUST repeat MUST provide air cover. It is exhaustion we are fighting not numbers.[18]

The unrelenting cacophony of constant firing and explosions told its own story. After overrunning a vital defensive position in which Captain R. Ambrose of the Faughs was taken prisoner, there was nothing to stop the Germans from reaching the headquarters tunnel. Ritchie therefore ordered his party to fall back to where they could cover both the hilltop and the eastern approaches of the tunnel. He was joined by Major Richard Dixon of the Cheshire Regiment together with a Captain Duncan and about a dozen troops. They were instructed to join an attack to retake both Captain Ambrose's former position and that vacated by Ritchie, who recalled:

> I led my men off at the double, but before we had travelled 50 yards a rifle grenade landed in a hole about a foot from me. I had a strange feeling of hot needles shooting through my body and then must have blacked out for the next thing I remember was waking up in the LRDG signal tunnel, feeling very weak and extremely stiff with four or five field dressings on my left arm and leg. My tin hat had several holes through the left brim and I was later told that the butt of my rifle had been shattered by the blast and had no doubt saved my life by taking most of the shrapnel coming my way.[19]

Only Ritchie's position was taken. Minutes later, Major Dixon was shot dead by a sniper. The enemy assaults petered out soon after. Snipers were a problem for both sides. During the night, the *Fallschirmjäger* had reached Platanos where *Obergefreiter* Helmut Dassler and several comrades moved into a building once used as a pharmacy. Their arrival did not go unnoticed, and anyone who dared to show himself was instantly shot at by an unseen assailant. Dassler, who was unable to use his machine-gun after being wounded in one arm, had acquired a British sniper rifle. Here was an ideal opportunity to put the weapon to use. In order to lure the marksman into revealing his location, a steel helmet was placed on the end of a rifle and shown at an opening. Dassler's close friend, Walter Keller, described what happened next:

He [Dassler] said: 'The moment he fires I'll be able to see his muzzle flash.' So, he waited for the muzzle flash and then returned fire, whereupon everything went quiet. He announced: 'I'm sure I got him.' We were standing around and were quite happy with our achievement when all of a sudden, Dassler, who was within two metres of me, slumped towards me and said: 'I've been hit.' They had hit him with a dumdum bullet ... It had gone through his lung and left a huge hole in his back, and he said: 'Walter, they've got me.'[20]

Keller and his comrades attended to Dassler as best they could, reassuring him that his injuries were not at all serious.

We took him to the field hospital where he gave me his *Deutsches Kreuz* [German Cross]; I was to send it to his parents. He was transferred to Athens, but died there at the end of November. He was the bravest soldier I have ever known.[21]

At about 1245, Tilney left Meraviglia by jeep to find and brief Lieutenant Colonel Egerton and to reconnoitre Rachi Ridge. Searchlight Hill and Point 109 were found to be deserted. Neither was there any sign of movement by the Royal West Kents along the western slopes. Eventually, the brigadier found an SNCO, Sergeant Price, and a private, both of the King's Own, and learned that in view of the deteriorating situation, their CO had ordered a general withdrawal north. As it was apparent that Tarleton could not be expected to RV with the Buffs in time to organise a joint defence about Meraviglia, Tilney amended his plan and sent the two men by jeep with instructions for the Royal West Kents to concentrate in the area of Porta Vecchia. The message never got through, and Tilney and Tarleton were to stay out of touch for the remainder of the battle. Tilney's next move was to try to locate the Buffs and redeploy them on Meraviglia. Meanwhile, the CO of the battalion had been discussing events with Lieutenant Commander Frank Ramseyer, who recalled:

The Colonel [Iggulden] sent for me and explained that although we were doing well in the north, he had cause to believe that the central sector was not at all happy. Although no idea of surrender was intended he thought it would be as well if craft were prepared in Partheni Bay in case a sudden collapse occurred and evacuation became necessary.

During the early part of the invasion I had made provisional arrangements in case such an emergency was sprung on me, so Lieutenant [E.] Percy and I jeeped to Partheni to concert them. A tug was instructed to have steam up by 1700B and lighters ready to tow; a caique, and two motor boats were prepared and small craft checked over and placed with oars in them at what, we hoped, would prove strategic points round the harbour.[22]

The situation in the central part of the island was critical, as Ramseyer was about to discover:

On returning to [the Buffs] Headquarters at about 1300 I found Major Jellicoe preparing to leave to get through the enemy lines to Brigade Headquarters in order to find out the exact position so that the Buffs could co-ordinate their effort to greater advantage. To save Major Jellicoe and his party a long journey on foot we proceeded as far as Navy House [at the junction of the San Nicola–San Quaranta road] in the Jeep where I left them to make their own way by usual SBS methods of crawling under reeds, through hedges and around trees, and returned to Headquarters.

The Colonel then wished to go forward to see for himself how his sector was progressing so I accompanied him. En route we were amazed to see groups of British soldiers in open route order proceeding away from the battle area towards Partheni. The Colonel stopped and interrogated them, and they said they had orders to retire to the north. Many were without arms, very dejected and exceedingly tired.

These parties and subsequent parties encountered were ordered to go no further, disperse over the immediate area and await further orders. About a mile from Navy House the Colonel of the King's Own was located and he and Colonel of the Buffs discussed the position. During this conversation a Jeep drew up with a screeching of breaks and a very dishevelled Brigadier tumbled out. It was Brigadier Tilney and he appeared to be very angry. Apparently the units we had encountered had retired without orders from him and as a result the position in the centre was badly weakened. Colonel in command of the Buffs was ordered to take over all stragglers and co-ordinate them with his own, and the other Colonel was placed under his orders.[23]

With so many troops concentrated in one place, San Nicola had become a prime target for the *Luftwaffe*. Tilney therefore instructed Iggulden to send one company to reinforce by dusk the scattered troops still on Meraviglia, with the remainder to follow under cover of darkness. Tilney was unaware that the majority of the Royal West Kents were then only a short distance away, still heading towards San Nicola. 'B' Echelon had gone ahead to try to contact the Buffs, leaving 'C' Company to lead the way through the vegetation and trees below Rachi's southern slopes; 'HQ' Company, Battalion Headquarters and 'D' Company followed at ten-minute intervals. En route, caves and tunnels were checked lest they concealed the enemy. More often than not, they were found to harbour Italians and stragglers from other units. It was a time-consuming process accompanied by much shouting and movement and before long it attracted fire from Point 100. Either the Germans had never relinquished possession of the feature, or else had filtered back during the day. From Rachi, signal lights were fired to indicate the position of the Royal West Kents. Moments later, aircraft carried out a low-level sweep, but left after only a superficial search. The troops continued towards the Germano–Condrida area where they took up defensive positions. The precise location of the Buffs was still unknown and Tarleton did not want to risk moving at night in unfamiliar terrain. He therefore dispatched a search patrol under Lieutenant J. A. Myers who returned at around 2200 with a message from the Buffs 2 i/c, Major D. B. Pyke. The battalion, together with all other troops in the area (including Captain Pond and 'B' Echelon of the Royal West Kents), had been ordered south to Meraviglia. To Tarleton's astonishment, there was no mention of his expected arrival: during his orders at San Nicola, Brigadier Tilney had apparently failed to mention that he had countermanded the move. Tarleton decided to stay where he was until daybreak, unaware, as was Iggulden, that the outcome of the battle had already been decided.

The situation was no less confusing for those further south. Earlier in the day, Lieutenant Clifford Clark and his party had rounded up many who were fleeing from Meraviglia. Shortly afterwards, Clark was contacted by an officer with orders from Tilney for all troops to RV at the Anchor preparatory to launching a counter-attack to recapture Meraviglia. Clark therefore withdrew his force from San Giovanni. Each man took only his personal weapon and ammunition; leaving behind all six Vickers machine-guns (the bolts of which were buried) and any excess kit. Few doubted that they would be back. After a slow and hazardous journey under continual air attack, Clark reached the outskirts of Lakki. A patrol was sent to reconnoitre the Anchor and the remaining troops were deployed under cover while Clark went forward to enquire about events at port headquarters:

The HQ, which was an Italian one, and in which we had one room, was deep underground. I had to push my way through hundreds of Italian soldiers, all scared out of their wits and cringing against the walls and on the floors, before I got to it. I found one British Staff Officer with some Italian officers of high rank poring over maps and interrogating a German prisoner who had just been brought in. I reported that I had the equivalent of one complete company of British troops outside. What was the position and where could I get instructions? The Staff Officer was about as helpful and useful as a cold in the head. He said he was completely out of touch; thought the Anchor was already held by the enemy, and suggested I went back to Giovanni. He finished up by saying 'You do what you think best old chap.' When I suggested the 'possibility' of using the Italian soldiery, they looked as if they thought I was off my head. I went, treading hard on quite a few of the bodies sleeping on the floor as I forced my way out.

Things were pretty warm overhead as I made my way back to where I had left the chaps. The recce patrol was back, having been shot up by automatics – the Anchor was held!

On the way down I had picked up Colour Sergeant Hayward, Corporal Hunt and Private Thompson, all of the 2nd Battalion. Their news was bad: the battalion had 'bought it' good and proper. [Lieutenants] Vic Hewett, John Browne and Lieutenant Johns had been killed, and a whole string badly wounded from the officers alone. They joined my party.

It was now getting dark, and I finally decided to move the Company back to Giovanni and to occupy our old positions. We moved off. I pulled in every odd man I saw and went into every air raid shelter en route. Any who weren't 'keen' on coming, luckily there were few, I put with my reliable men, who had orders what to do 'if'!

When we had gone about a third of the way we had a false alarm.

What we thought was a German force turned out to be an RA officer and a party of his men who had destroyed their Bofors and were heading for Porto Lago [Lakki]. I explained the position to him and suggested that he joined me. He and his men agreed eagerly, and we moved off stronger still. We must have been about 150, with a lot of automatics with us. My idea, which I told the officers and passed on to the men, was to hold Giovanni until the morning, and then launch an attack, under cover of our six Vickers, along the ridge in an attempt to recapture Meraviglia ...

We were about half way back when an LRDG runner dashed up to us and said: 'The Brigadier capitulated at 1600 [sic] hours.'[24]

After having been evacuated from Meraviglia, *Capitano* Cacciatori had to endure a painful journey by stretcher to Lakki:

En route, we were machine-gunned by a bomber descending over us, but my orderly shielded me with his body. When we reached the Anchor, a German officer ordered us to stop. By the way the Germans were walking about as if they owned the place, I realised that something awful had happened up top. The officer scrutinised me and I expected to be shot. He asked my orderly if I was the one in command of Mount Meraviglia.

'We are done for', I thought. Another sailor understood and nodded. The expression of the blond officer hardened; he obviously wanted to vindicate the deaths of so many of his soldiers, but a sense of honour prevailed and he walked away. At the infirmary, I was suddenly aware of a pain even more severe than my wound: could it be that the fighting had ceased on the mountain and throughout Leros?[25]

Tilney had returned to Meraviglia and the disappointing news that the expected 160 reinforcements from Lakki had failed to materialise. An officer was therefore sent to hasten the arrival of the Buffs' advance company. Like so many others, the message never reached its destination. At the same time, word was received from GHQ that the Aegean was to be evacuated the following night. Further details were to follow, but if there was a follow-up signal, it was sent too late to have any effect. (Earlier in the day, the Navy had, in fact, received instructions to collect all small craft at Turk

Buku under the orders of HMS *Fury* – who had arrived in the area with *Exmoor* and the Polish *Krakowiak* – in preparation for a possible evacuation of Leros.) Prendergast was dispatched to Lakki to fetch whoever he could for a counter-attack. He left just in time. Mortar, machine-gun and small-arms fire intensified as the enemy launched the final assault on Meraviglia. It became impossible to leave Fortress Headquarters by the east exit. Before long, troops from *III./1.Rgt. Brandenburg* were also covering the west side, as Naval Lieutenant E. A. I. Crowder discovered:

> The Brigadier ... told me that I would be sent on an important mission to try and get to Colonel Tarleton [sic: Lieutenant Colonel Iggulden] of the Buffs, who was supposed to be concentrating on Meraviglia from the north. I said that it was not much my line of country but I would do my best to get through and asked him for some advice as to route, and started for the western entrance of Battle Headquarters. I was stopped there by the soldiers defending same and told I could not possibly get out as a machine gun had been so placed as to cover the entrance. I told the Brigadier this and said the chances of his message getting through seemed pretty small, but I would have a shot. He said 'No, no, wait till I see just what is happening' ...[26]

Tilney described what happened next:

> Somewhat incredulous, I went to investigate. I went far enough out of the western exit to draw MG fire on to my raised helmet. I endeavoured to look over the entrance to the summit towards the east. As I did so, I saw a German standing over the top of me and Colonel Douglas Brown [Commander Royal Artillery] who had followed. The German missed with both automatic and grenade, but neither of us quite knew why. The eastern exit was also under heavy MG fire and being on the enemy side it was to be assumed that it too was closely guarded. I knew the enemy were on the top by the exit to the OP, for part of the MG fire was coming from there on my recce of the western exit. Moreover, the OP would be bound to have communicated with HQ if the enemy had not been there. The HQ appeared completely trapped. The Germans commanded the exits as men on a rabbit shoot stand over a warren.[27]

Crowder's account continues:

> He [Tilney] came back to me and said 'It's all up, chaps, I am glad I
> did not send you out Crowder, or you would be dead now.' He asked for
> anyone who could speak German and gave orders for a white flag to be
> shown at the OP. One OR was found to speak with the Germans, but
> unfortunately was shot and wounded in the chest before he made them
> understand.
>
> When a final understanding was reached, we were allowed to come
> out without incident, except that one German soldier took Colonel
> [M. C.] Waddilove's watch. The Brigadier, when he arrived outside,
> asked to speak to the Senior Officer; he then said 'I am the Commander
> of the Island, and to avoid further bloodshed, I surrender the Island.
> Tell your General I wish facilities to tell my Senior Officers the battle is
> over and to stop fighting and march the men in.'[28]

The time was 1630 hours. Meraviglia had been overrun by units of
II./Gren.Rgt.65, II./Gren.Rgt.16 and *III./1.Rgt. Brandenburg* – the latter
under *Oberleutnant* Max Wandrey following the wounding earlier in the
day of the *Bataillon Kommandeur, Hauptmann* Gustav Froböse. Major
Jellicoe arrived soon after to find Tilney in discussion with a German officer. The brigadier apologised for the situation in which the SBS commander
found himself and then informed him about Lieutenant Phipps:

> 'Incidentally, your friend, Alan Phipps is missing and I don't know
> whether there's any chance of finding out what's happened to him.' I
> turned to the German ... and explained the situation. I said I'd like to
> look for him and he said, 'Fine, if you give me your parole.' He was
> very correct. I suppose I must have spent the best part of an hour look-
> ing for Alan Phipps but I couldn't find him. I found four or five quite
> badly wounded people. I was glad I had morphine on me and I was
> able to inject them, including one or two Germans, and then went back
> and surrendered my parole. Then we were all marched down to the
> little port on the west of the island.[29]

The task now facing the Germans was how to convince the garrison
that the battle was over. A bizarre situation unfolded as British officers
and their captors travelled together in jeeps to locate the many scattered

TOP San Nicola: a weary *Obergefreiter* Walter Keller of *3./Fallschirmjäger-Rgt.*2 immediately after the British surrender. (*W. Keller*)

Fallschirmjäger of the signal platoon relax after the battle. (*H. Weiser via P. Schenk*)

ABOVE One of the contested gun positions at Battery Lago on Appetici. (*E. Johnson*)

The battle over, victors and vanquished leave Appetici. (*P. Schenk*)

TOP Alinda Bay from Meraviglia, photographed immediately after the battle. (*E. Johnson*)

The castle on Point 189 seen from a gun position at *P.L. 127* on Meraviglia. (*E. Johnson*)

RIGHT After accepting the British surrender, *Generalleutnant* Friedrich-Wilhelm Müller (left) tours Meraviglia. (*E. Johnson*)

Brigadier Robert Tilney in conversation with *Generalleutnant* Müller on the road to Santa Marina. (*E. Johnson*)

TOP After the battle, German paratroopers march to a rest area just inland from Alinda Bay. (*E. Johnson*)

17 November 1943: *Leutnant* Karl Franz Schweiger (left) and *Kompaniechef, Hauptmann* Rabe (centre), with members of *3./Fallschirmjäger-Rgt.2* at Alinda. (*W. Keller*)

ABOVE *Fallschirmjäger, Obergefreiter* Hans Weiser (left) and *Obergefreiter* Lutz Popp, unwind in Platanos. (*H. Weiser via P. Schenk*)

San Nicola: *Oberfeldwebel* Walter Lünsmann (second from left) reports with survivors of *6./Gren.Rgt.16* to the *Kompaniechef, Hauptmann* Heinrich Michael (left). (*W. Lünsmann*)

TOP A *Marinefährprahm* (F-lighter) approaches shore near the Villa Belleni field hospital. (*H. Weiser via P. Schenk*)

At Villa Belleni, wounded await their turn to be evacuated. (*G. Symonds*)

ABOVE Sea mines at a captured storage depot at Partheni. (*G. Symonds*)

Santa Marina: *Fallschirmjäger* with Italian captives. (*G. Symonds*)

TOP Clearly delighted that their war is over, British prisoners are marched towards Santa Marina. (*M. Dülken*)

Prisoners of war en route to Lakki. The camouflage paint pattern on steel helmets distinguishes some of these men as Malta veterans. (*W. Lünsmann*)

TOP British and Italian graves on Meraviglia. (*E. Johnson*)

Wooden crosses mark temporary German graves at San Quaranta chapel cemetery. (*H. Weiser via P. Schenk*)

LEFT Italian 102mm anti-aircraft gun at *P.L. 211* on Rachi Ridge. This was probably the gun used to cover the *Fallschirmjäger* assault against Meraviglia on 14 November. (*P. Schenk*)

BELOW December 1943: German troops clear up at the site of an Italian 152mm coast defence gun at Battery Ciano on Clidi. (*G. Symonds*)

TOP LEFT The privations of serving in Malta at the height of the island siege are evident in this portrait of Lieutenant Colonel Maurice French, commander in Leros of 2nd Bn The Royal Irish Fusiliers. (*J. Chatterton Dickson*)

TOP RIGHT End of the line for most of the Leros garrison: Lieutenant Ted Johnson of the Faughs as a prisoner of war at *Oflag VIIIF* near Märisch Trübau, in Sudetenland (present-day Czech Republic). (*E. Johnson*)

ABOVE LEFT Air-gunner *Unteroffizier* Andreas Hutter, of *II./T.G.4*, who was taken prisoner when his Ju 52 was shot down off the coast of Leros. He was evacuated by the British just before the end of the battle. (*A. Hutter*)

ABOVE RIGHT Recognition for the victors: among those decorated after the battle for Leros was *Hauptmann* Martin Kühne, commander of *I./Fallschir-mjäger-Rgt.2*, seen here after his award of the *Ritterkreuz* (Knight's Cross) on 29 February 1944. (*M. Kühne*)

Three of those who got away:

TOP LEFT Lieutenant Clifford Clark of 2nd Bn The Queen's Own Royal West Kent Regiment in Malta in 1942. (*C. Clark*)

TOP RIGHT Lieutenant Commander Frank Ramseyer of Force 133. (*M. Ramseyer*)

Major Lord Jellicoe (left), commanding officer of the Special Boat Squadron, photographed in Turkish waters in 1944. (*M. Ramseyer*)

ABOVE One of two *Schnellboote* heads for Samos with an advance party subsequent to the surrender of Italian forces on the island. (*U. Walther*)

22 November: arrival of the German delegation at Tigani (Pythagorio), Samos. (*U. Walther*)

TOP Photographed just after Operation 'Taifun', the commander of
12. R.-Flottille, Oberleutnant zur See Hansjürgen Weissenborn (right),
on the bridge of *R 210* with the commander of *21. U.-Jagdflottille*,
Korvettenkapitän Dr Günther Brandt. (*H. Weissenborn*)

At the conclusion of operations in the Dodecanese, *R 210* arrives at Piraeus
flying the white ensign from BYMS *72*, captured off Kalymnos on 12
November 1943. (*H. Weissenborn*)

TOP *Oberleutnant* Max Wandrey, who took over command on Leros of *III./1.Rgt. Brandenburg*, is awarded the Knight's Cross at a ceremony at Lamia, Greece. (*U. Walther*)

Oberleutnant Wandrey (centre) with the commanding officer of *1.Rgt. Brandenburg*, *Oberstleutnant* Uwe Wilhelm Walther (left), and *General der Flieger* Hellmuth Felmy of the *Luftwaffe*. (*U. Walther*) units still holding out. Disbelieving troops were informed of Tilney's decision and ordered to lay down their arms. The brigadier and Captain Edmund Baker were escorted by two German officers, including *Hauptmann* Heinrich Michael, OC *6./Gren.Rgt.16*, and driven to Lakki to co-ordinate the surrender of the garrison with *Contrammiraglio* Luigi Mascherpa. Signals were also sent in clear advising Italian and British command headquarters of events. *Generalleutnant* Müller was at sea en route to Leros when news of the surrender reached him. Initially, he was dubious, failing to understand how a commander could continue to influence his forces when he was a prisoner of war. Müller landed at Castello di Bronzi at 2130 and was assured by *Major* von Saldern personally that the garrison had indeed capitulated.

As the battle entered its final phase, the Royal Air Force had continued to operate out of sight to those on the ground. Beaufighters of 603 Squadron on an offensive sweep in the Leros area attacked two Arado seaplanes, claiming one as destroyed and the other damaged. At 1320, seven Beaufighters of 47 Squadron and one of 603 Squadron struck at enemy shipping three miles west of Kalymnos. Seven Arado 196s, four Ju 88s and four Bf 109s were supposed to have been protecting the convoy, which consisted of a Siebel ferry (*SF 105*) and two landing craft en route from Amorgos to Kalymnos. Before the Germans could react, the Beaufighters swept in at low level, using their cannon fire with deadly effect. The Siebel ferry was hit and blew up, leaving only burning wreckage and two columns of black smoke. In the ensuing air battle, a Ju 88 was also destroyed. At least three Beaufighters failed to return.[30]

During the day, up to ninety-six badly wounded from Leros were transferred from MMS *103* to the destroyers *Penn* and *Aldenham* at Turk Buku for onward passage to Cyprus. That evening, both ships sailed with instructions to bombard enemy positions in the centre of Leros before leaving the area to rendezvous with *Blencathra* and *Rockwood*. When under way, Lieutenant Commander J. H. Swain on board the *Penn* was handed a signal from Fortress Headquarters:

Island surrendered. Stop bombardment, assurance has been given German convoy expected this evening not be attacked.

The message was sent in clear and without a code word. Swain reported:

> I called Leros and asked for one but there was no reply. *Exmoor* was heard relaying the message to Alexandria and I asked for instructions. I was ordered to cancel the bombardment and to bombard Kos roads instead ...[31]

That night, patrols were maintained by MTBs in a fruitless effort to intercept further invasion craft. It was far too late. After being subjected to an ineffectual glider bomb attack, the boats withdrew to Pharlah Bay. After the battle, the senior officer 10th MTB Flotilla, Lieutenant Commander C. P. Evensen noted:

> It must be admitted that the enemy are masters of the art of secreting their ships at night; the nature of the Aegean Islands assisting them tremendously. Sweeps were carried out at only a few yards offshore in the endeavour to locate them, but never during the whole of the invasion of Leros was a torpedo target sighted.[32]

CHAPTER 13

Escape

AS A RESULT OF THE CONFUSION surrounding events at Meraviglia on Tuesday morning (16th), Second Lieutenant Pav Pavlides had wasted no time in initiating a withdrawal from Leros of LRDG personnel. After joining in the premature evacuation from Meraviglia, he encountered the unit's medical officer, Captain Dick Lawson, and Major L. Bindon Blood (Royal Irish Fusiliers) and advised both to head for an RV on the west side of Lakki (probably Scrofe).[1] In company with a Rhodesian, (probably Les) Berry, Pavlides made his way to Scumbarda where, at 1240, he contacted Second Lieutenant R. F. White and persuaded him to prepare to pull out the New Zealanders of 'A' Squadron LRDG. White sent one of his men, Private Lennox, to ensure that two boats were still at a hidden location below Scumbarda, warning him that the OP was to be evacuated at 1715, and Berry and five others left to find Lawson with instructions to RV off the coast between 1930 and 2000. Efforts were also made to contact Lieutenant Folland (LRDG) at his OP on Marcello, following which all wireless sets and other equipment were destroyed; but without explosives, the battery guns had to be left intact. At 1700, OP No. 4 at Scumbarda closed down and Lieutenants White, Pavlides and the four remaining LRDG set off towards Serocampo Bay, where Pavlides had a boat prepared for departure. The group arrived an hour and a half later to find a 12-foot rowing boat into which they clambered and headed for the bay entrance. There appeared to be complete disorder ashore, with much shooting by Italians at Serocampo and Bren gun fire in the direction of Lakki. For ten long minutes a searchlight at Diapori Point played on the boat as its six occupants attempted to make the RV with Lawson. When no other boats were seen, the party continued north, past Pega and towards Turkey.

After parting company with Colonel Guy Prendergast in the morning, Lieutenant P. A. Mold reached San Giovanni and met Captain C. H. B. (Dick) Croucher on his way with a party from Lakki. Following the example of the Royal West Kents, some of whom were encountered near by, the officers agreed to attempt to link up with friendly forces further north. Due to the ongoing bombing and strafing, the party continued in two less conspicuous groups, with Mold's consisting of a Lieutenant Bell and an OR. At about 1400, Mold met some SBS signallers who had arrived the night before and whose wireless sets had been delivered to Meraviglia. With the senior man, Sergeant Cartlidge, Mold set off in search of the equipment, only to be prevented by enemy fire from reaching their destination. They returned to Lieutenant Bell's position where they also found a very tired Captain Mike Rochford who had arrived from Meraviglia. In time-honoured fashion, it was announced to be 'brew time' and while enjoying tea the men maintained watch on Meraviglia. After a while, the occupants of Brigade Headquarters were observed through binoculars emerging with their hands up and individuals were seen fleeing with Germans in pursuit. The first stragglers arrived to confirm that Fortress Headquarters had been overrun, although Mold was as yet unaware that Tilney had surrendered his entire command. He therefore withdrew two Vickers machine-guns from San Giovanni, gathered all the stragglers in the area – about fifty men – and prepared to make a stand on a hill between San Giovanni and Patella, in the area where it was assumed that Croucher would be. Mold pressed ahead and found Captain Lawson awaiting the return of Signalman King (presumably the runner encountered earlier by Lieutenant Clifford Clark) who had gone with Captains Croucher and Ron Tinker in search of Colonel Prendergast:

> He [Signalman King] returned some minutes later with the truly astonishing news that the surrender had been agreed upon at approximately 1630 hours – roughly at the time we saw the 40 bodies coming out of the [headquarters] 'tunnel'.
>
> We got all the chaps together round a well and told them to have a good drink – fill their water-bottles – get something to eat and have a

rest. We gathered the officers together, approximately six, and mutually decided to try and get the chaps away by splitting up in small parties, each under an officer.

To add to the confusion, Jerry decided to drop AP [anti-personnel] bombs in our area but fortunately not near enough to do any real harm. We decided to make for the sea-side of the Patella feature and move off at 10 minute intervals.[2]

Unaware of developments, Prendergast was still on his way to Lakki to collect reinforcements to help with the defence of Meraviglia. He was overtaken by a jeep with Tilney, Captain Edmund Baker and their German captors and informed of events, whereupon the vehicle continued on its way watched by a bemused Prendergast. Eventually, he encountered Croucher and Tinker and learned that the remainder of the LRDG Headquarters personnel were on their way to the escape RV at Scrofe.

After discussing with Captains Croucher and Tinker what was our best move, we decided to make for an escape point [Porto Cassio] situated on the east coast of Monte Tortore just opposite the island of Pega. We chose this one as we all knew of a cave there which was in a very deserted part of the island. We decided to make our way there at once and were joined before leaving by Captain Craig who had been the Brigade IO. It seemed impracticable for us to join the LRDG HQ party at Patella as our own chances of finding them were small and we thought the enemy would soon search that populated area.[3]

Five days of non-stop action took effect as men were overcome with fatigue. For the British and Italians, the news that the battle really was over was received with mixed feelings: there was anger, disappointment and puzzlement over the outcome; few relished the prospect of months or years in a prison camp. At the same time there was an indescribable sense of relief and an overwhelming desire simply to lie down and sleep. Lieutenant Mold, physically and mentally exhausted, was, like many, nearing collapse when at about 2000 he set off across country towards Patella:

All went well until I bumped into Michael Rochford's party. He was almost done and as he had come across some barbed wire had convinced himself that the obstacle was a minefield. I remarked I couldn't remember a minefield in the area and decided to go through with Michael, his party and my party following. I made a point of passing back that the LRDG party (mine) were to follow on. We proceeded cautiously at first and after about three quarters of an hour walking, bumped into Doc Lawson's party almost on the Patella track. I told Michael to follow on Doc Lawson's party and I waited for my chaps to go by – They did not materialise and I went back for about half an hour [and] met two or three Royal Sigs chaps who said that they had come all the way round the track and had not seen my party of LRDG. From then on I did not see my party again. I went on myself and eventually made the coast at a point inside the harbour boom. There, I found Michael flat-out. It appeared that he had decided to rest and told his party to split up into twos and threes and make their own way. I skirted the area and found the greater majority resting with the intention of packing in the next day. I could persuade none of them that I was on a good thing in escaping chiefly because we now only had water-bottle and chocolate ration. I returned to Michael who had apparently tried to get on to the beach and nearly broken his neck but I persuaded him we could find a way which I eventually did through an Italian gun position. My idea then, although it now seems a little absurd, was to get along the coast, over the boom and round the point on to the sea-side of the island. We made [our way] along the coast cautiously, in fact too cautiously, for it took us several hours to reach a position 200 yards from the boom. By this time we were wading waist deep manoeuvring round rocks, etc, and I last remember seeing red tracers covering the boom and could only assume I had a blackout.[4]

Colonel Prendergast's party had also headed for the coast:

Our resources were very limited. Between us we could muster one small bag of sugar and one or two tins of bully. We were all very lightly clothed, and both Captain Tinker and Captain Craig were in considerable pain through having been buried in slit trenches by very near misses of bombs. Captain Croucher had a bad leg from falling into a bomb hole. I sent these three officers and a Private [H.Thompson] of the King's Own Regiment who had joined us to the cave on Monte Tortore with instructions to wait for me there. I decided to go myself to Monte Scumbarda to find out what had happened to Lieutenant White and his patrol who had been doing very useful work there. Before leaving I tried to contact any other LRDG personnel from the large crowd of rather demoralised troops in Portolago [Lakki], but failed to find any. I advised as many officers of other units as I could find to try to reorganise their men and to make for one or other of the escape points. Everybody, however, appeared too tired to want to do anything but sleep.

I made my way along the road to Scumbarda. After a very steep climb, I arrived there about midnight. Lieutenant White's patrol had used a cave as a store and place for the wireless set. I found at this cave Private Lennox, who told me that he had been sent down the cliffs to Cape Scumbarda to try and find a boat Lieutenant White knew was there. The boat had been destroyed by a bomb, and when Private Lennox got back he found that Lieutenant White and the patrol had pushed off and he did not know where they had gone. He therefore readily joined me, and we loaded up two rucksacks which were in the cave with blankets and as much rations as we could carry.

While we were at work in the cave, some Italians came in and stole my field glasses which I had put down. I told them to give them back and they retaliated by producing revolvers and a Tommy gun and told us that we were their prisoners. They tried to disarm us both, and when we refused, they started shooting into the cave. I demanded to see their CO and Lennox and I, with heavy rucksacks on our backs, were pushed rather ignominiously to the flat top of Scumbarda on which the coastal gun position was located. The Italian officers were in a subterranean control room and appeared to be pretty tight. Their men were all gesticulating and talking and drinking, and I found it very difficult to get any sense out of anybody. The Italian Commander told me that the British had let them down and that he was proposing to hand us over to the Germans. We decided to make a break for it and ran off down the road to the best of our ability. The Italians then opened fire but missed us because it was fairly dark. I turned round to see if Lennox was following and saw what I thought was him lying on the ground; I went back and found that he had tripped over, and we were immediately collared by the Italians and brought back to the gun position. We made another break for it and this time got away without being hit.[5]

Although the SBS and the LRDG appear to have been the only units to have formulated contingency plans, information was sometimes shared with individuals from other regiments. Major Pat McSwiney of 3rd LAA Battery recalled:

I made my way to Portolago [Lakki], fighting a rather futile rearguard action with a Bren gun as I retreated, before hearing news of the final surrender. I was utterly exhausted, both mentally and physically, and found that my legs would barely respond to orders from my brain. By chance I met up with Eric Rawlinson [Captain, Royal Artillery] and together we made for the northern end of Portolago Bay where we found a deserted house and a dump of NAAFI goods. Among them was a bottle of whisky; I drank almost the whole of it in half an hour but it had no intoxicating effect. It did clear my head and co-ordinate my limbs: it proved to be a real life saver!

I knew the geography of the island well because of my earlier responsibilities, and both Eric and I had maps showing the original rendezvous points on the coast, that had been arranged with the SBS, should the island fall into enemy hands. One of these was relatively close to where we were at this moment, and yet it was unlikely to be swamped by would-be escapers, as Mount Zuncona was quite a steep climb and the wadi where we should be lying up could only be reached by tackling it. It was obvious that the vast majority of the troops would be taken prisoner, but it was the duty of officers and senior NCOs to escape if possible, and we reckoned that unless we were in our hiding place by dawn the chances of not being rounded up were slim. While discussing these plans, three more [Royal Artillery] officers arrived: Lieutenant John Davies, Majors Reed and Hall (the latter pair had been on the island for a relatively short time and I had not met them before), together with a couple of artillery sergeants, making a party of eight [sic]. We each collected a two-gallon water can, tins of bully beef and a few packets of biscuits, which we assumed would be sufficient for the two or three days, while we waited for an SBS boat to put in at midnight at the given rendezvous. Major Reed, considerably my senior in age, was elected leader of the party and I was voted Navigator and Second-in-Command.[6]

Other troops had to fend for themselves. Lieutenant Clifford Clark was determined not to become a prisoner of war and to spare his family the shock and anguish of receiving a telegram advising them that he was missing in action:

I gathered the men together, told them what had happened and advised them to try and escape. I told them to break up into small parties, to get food and water, and to take to the hills until they decided on a plan. Unfortunately, there was no laid on plan of evacuation or escape, so I could do no more for them. I picked my party carefully and wished the rest the best of luck. Quite a lot wanted to come with me, but I finally decided on the following: Lieutenant Stokes, UDF; Colour Sergeant Hayward, RWK; Colour Sergeant Milton, RWK; Sergeant [George] Hatcher, RWK; Corporal Hunt, RWK; Private Moore, RWK (my batman); Private Thompson, RWK (requested by Colour Sergeant Hayward) ...

Our little party found a house with some stores, where we ate some bully and biscuits and, after putting either a tin of bully or M&V or a packet of biscuits in each of our pockets, we moved off down towards Porto Lago [Lakki]. We also took a greatcoat or a blanket each; I took a blanket ...

Our rough plan was to get down to the harbour and try and find a boat. We knew it was now or never, as it would be the first place the Germans would cover. If this did not succeed we intended taking to the hills and making further plans.

We moved carefully. We could hear planes overhead, but for the moment the harbour seemed to be clear of Germans. We searched around, but every boat seemed to be a wreck or badly holed from the bombing and useless. We met other groups doing the same thing, but there was nothing. Just when we thought we had drawn a blank, we found an Indian RE Sergeant and an Indian Sapper uncovering what appeared to be flat pieces of canvas and wood from underneath some debris. There were two other groups doing the same thing. What a find – three RE canvas folding assault boats! We decided there and then that we would take one boat, and the two Indian REs, and make for Turkey.

While we were fitting up our boat, with the able assistance of the REs, I sent Colour Sergeant Milton to get a two gallon can of water from a pump in Porto Lago. It should take about ten minutes, but I said I'd give him half an hour.

One of the other boats had just been launched, but it had not been fitted up properly and it sank almost immediately. It had been crowded and I think some chaps were drowned. The rest looked a sorry sight as they pulled themselves back on to the quay. And then there were two!!

The second boat seemed to fare better, had a successful launching, and moved off into the darkness of the harbour. By this time we had got our boat fixed up properly, only to find there were no oars. Were we to be beaten at this stage? The RE Sergeant dashed away and in a few minutes was back with four oars and some flat pieces of wood which others could use. We didn't ask where he got them![7]

While Clark awaited the return of Milton, Major Barnett, a Raiding Forces officer who claimed to know his way round the islands, was allowed to join the group. In effect, he replaced Milton, who failed to arrive back after the appointed time. Clark could not afford to wait any longer and at 2100 the boat pushed off with its ten occupants – and just two water-bottles between them. Clark, who was suffering from the effects of malaria, was thankful for the reassuring presence of Stokes, who quietly urged the paddlers to keep going. They had not gone far before machine-gun fire from the harbour entrance indicated that the enemy had spotted the other boat. For these unidentified men, all hope of escape vanished within seconds as their boat was torn apart and sunk. The survivors, some of whom were wounded, struggled in the dark, cold water with no option but to head back for shore – and into captivity. In the last remaining boat, everyone knew that at any moment they might be next. They had to trust to luck and a flimsy, flat-bottomed craft just 18 inches deep and measuring 15 feet by 4 feet:

We were rather quiet for a bit but no one suggested turning back. Our first problem still remained negotiating the boom across the harbour, avoiding the machine gun and getting clear of the harbour.

When we got to the boom, we found there was only one break, in the middle, the rest being heavily spiked, which would have sunk us straight away. We crawled around this and back to the opposite side of the harbour where we knew there was at least one gun. Perhaps there were more, and on our side! We had to chance it.

We hugged the bank and made slow progress, hardly daring to breathe in case the slightest noise brought our journey to an abrupt end with a hail of lead. It took us literally hours before we even got to the end of the harbour, but we did get there, and decided to make straight out to sea for at least a mile before we headed north.[8]

Amid the confusion, someone apparently neglected to keep the RAF informed of events, for during the night 216 Squadron flew twelve supply sorties to Leros. As a result of this wasted effort, one Dakota (FD 790) was obliged to ditch off Turkey; fortunately, the crew of six survived.

Dawn on Wednesday, 17 November. All over Leros, men on both sides stirred in their defensive positions. In stark contrast to previous days, there was virtually no gunfire. Instead, German troops were happily singing, 'Deutschland über Alles'. It made little sense for those who were unaware that Brigadier Tilney had surrendered his command. The sense of unreality was heightened by the arrival of German seaplanes which alighted unimpeded in Lakki Bay. The victors could hardly believe their good fortune as they laughed and joked and were able to walk in the open for the first time. For those who awoke as prisoners of war, it was altogether different. Many, on learning that the fighting was over, had simply rolled themselves in blankets and slept. Having had a few hours to recover from their exhaustion, they now faced the shocking reality of months or years in captivity. After four years of war, some may have considered death or injury a possibility; for others a victorious homecoming had become a virtual certainty; few could contemplate surrender.

The Royal West Kents on the northern shore of Gurna Bay learned about the capitulation just after daybreak.

The whole Battalion was tired, hungry and bewildered by the news. A meal was got together from various food dumps, articles of value destroyed and escape parties improvised.[9]

For most, however, there was to be no escape.

Individuals and small parties ... lay up for various lengths of time, but had to give themselves up for want of food or water, or were picked up by German patrols.[10]

At Lakki Bay, Lieutenant P. A. Mold was still suffering from the rigours of the previous few days:

I awoke to find myself sprawled across the rocks (some 100 yards or so beneath the MG position covering the boom), very wet and cold – dawn was just breaking. I climbed in amongst the rocks and found a spot where I could hide. I took off my wet clothes and having dried myself on my handkerchief (I can distinctly remember covering my feet with it apparently thinking it would keep them warm) I stayed thus until the sun was up, when I had a bite of my chocolate ration and some water. I had an excellent view of several E-boats, seaplanes and other craft entering the harbour and I rested thus until the evening.[11]

Others met with varying degrees of success. The party under Majors Reed and Pat McSwiney reached the tiny inlet of Porto Cassio on the southeast coast, set up camp in a gulley 400 yards inland and then settled down to await the arrival of the expected rescue vessel.

Colonel Guy Prendergast had made his way with Private Lennox to Point 228 (Mount Tortore). There they found Trooper McLean (who had become separated from Lieutenant White's patrol) and, shortly afterwards, Captains Croucher, Tinker, Craig and Private Thompson. Officers and men teamed off and took up residence in two small caves in order to recuperate and plan their next move.

Lieutenant Clifford Clark and his group of nine had paddled for all they were worth until they reached an islet off the north coast. At daybreak, they hauled their little boat ashore, hid it under a ledge and then collapsed exhausted.

During the night, Major George Jellicoe had persuaded his captors to allow him to return to his men, ostensibly to persuade them to lay down their arms. In fact, he had no such intentions and in the early hours of the 17th, relocated Lieutenant Commander Frank Ramseyer. Together, they rounded up some ninety personnel and left on a motor boat for Turkey. At 0630 on the 17th, they reached Lipsi, north of Leros. Theirs was one of several vessels which put to sea at the last moment, thereby avoiding falling into German hands.

An equally determined effort was made by four escaped prisoners who had taken advantage of the chaos and confusion to give their captors the slip: Corporal Taffy Kenchington, fellow Faugh, Fusilier Ryan, and two soldiers of the LRDG and SBS made their way to Gurna Bay where they found a small boat. Their voyage to freedom was relatively uneventful and after rowing through the night and for much of the next day, they reached Turkey where they were apprehended by local forces and handed over to the British vice consul.

Others were less fortunate: on Tuesday night around 100 men were seized on the beach opposite Scrofe after mistaking a German patrol vessel for a rescue craft. Just two soldiers, both of the Royal Corps of Signals, escaped.

At least one person seemed to be in no hurry either to surrender or flee. In the morning, Captain John Olivey ordered his men to make for an escape RV. Two attached subalterns, Freeman and Price, were instructed to make their own way to Alinda. Olivey remained on Clidi to gather his belongings and to change into clean clothes. When he was interrupted by the arrival of several Germans, he played dead until the patrol moved on. Having armed himself with a sniper rifle and a German pistol, Olivey then went in search of a suitable hiding place and settled down to sleep. That evening he returned to Battery Ciano with the intention of destroying the last remaining gun and the main magazine and, if possible, the local magazines at each gun position. Olivey was able to prepare explosive charges, but unable to find a pull switch with which to ignite the fuse. The only option was to light the fuse himself, except that he did not have any matches.

> I returned to the fort where I knew I had concealed a box. I was surprised to find the fort occupied by two Germans who took me for one of their officers. I was forced to shoot them both, but the noise attracted others, and I had to make a hasty withdrawal.[12]

Hungry, thirsty and indescribably weary, Olivey spent the rest of the night evading capture. Others were similarly engaged all over Leros. For some, their ordeal was to continue for days. Major McSwiney's party waited in vain for the arrival of a rescue vessel until the evening of 20 November when two Greek shepherds led them to a 12-foot rowing boat which had been abandoned following an earlier, unsuccessful, escape attempt. After applying a makeshift patch to a gaping 6-inch hole just above the water line, the eight men put to sea. McSwiney recalled:

> Our boat was leaking fast and shipping water over the windward gunnel; we were being blown almost due south and were being driven nearer and nearer to the huge cliffs of the island of Kalymnos. At a crucial moment I insisted that if we did not make a mighty effort to turn the boat into wind, and attempt to row against it, we should soon be dashed against the rocks and our chances of survival would then be very slim. Although a wave nearly capsized us as we made the turn, we were still just afloat and, bailing furiously, we pulled slowly away from the hideous noise of that vicious sea, which was pounding the cliffs with such force that we had to shout to be heard at all.

> Ten minutes later, the boat was steered into a sheltered inlet.

> The transformation was extraordinary, as the moon remained strong enough to enable us to collect sticks and build a fire, around which we all sat, partially drying out our saturated clothing, and soon our teeth stopped chattering. A minute Greek chapel had been built in the cove and, with one of us on guard, we slept fitfully on the stone floor until a weak sun filtered through the windows ...[13]

Over the next two days, the men rested and regained their strength by feasting on goat boiled in sea water. The boat was made seaworthy using material found along the seashore and on the evening of 22 November, the men again put to sea. They reached the Turkish coast after daybreak on the 23rd.

The nine men with Lieutenant Clark had resumed their journey late on Wednesday (17th) and several hours later reached Lipsi where they were befriended by local Greeks. In the early hours of Saturday (20th) contact was made with a caique of the Levant Schooner Flotilla. The men were taken on board whereupon, to Clark's surprise, the vessel proceeded to the northern coast of Leros. There, she embarked two soldiers of the Royal Irish Fusiliers, one of whom was injured, and a wounded Italian before steering east for Turkey which was reached at dawn.

During the night of 20–21 November, contact parties were landed at Leros from High Speed Launches 2531, 2539 and 2542, the latter coming ashore close to McSwiney's former hiding place near Porto Cassio. The boats were scheduled to return at the same time for three consecutive nights. At 0110 hours on the 22nd, HSL 2542 arrived at the RV to be greeted by someone using a light to flash the letter N. As this was not the prearranged signal, Private Miller of the SBS volunteered to investigate and took a dinghy to within 50 yards of the coast. When it was realised that there was no immediate threat, Sub Lieutenant Tuckey put out in the remaining dinghy. They had located Colonel Prendergast and his party who had maintained a nightly watch in the hope of being picked up from the escape RV below Tortore. Prendergast described the moment when help finally arrived:

> We went down to the beach as usual, and about midnight heard a craft approaching the coast. It hove to about half a mile from the RV and for a long time did nothing. We could just see the dim black shape on the water. It then came inshore a little and we decided to risk everything and flash our torch.
>
> This was a very exciting moment as we did not know whether we should be greeted with a hail of bullets or whether we should be taken off. Presently a small boat appeared and the occupant hailed us. We could not understand what he said or in what language he was talking, but shouted our names. After a lot of hesitation he came in closely and eventually came right up to us and took us off to the waiting craft, which turned out to be an Air Sea Rescue launch.[14]

On Wednesday evening, Lieutenant Mold had again found Lieutenant Rochford. Subsequently, they teamed up with the two signallers who had avoided capture at Scrofe. On 21 November, contact was made with a civilian and the next night the signallers were taken to an escape RV at Nikolaos Bay on the west coast. When the two officers followed on 23 November, they were met by Captain Ashley Greenwood. After escaping with Ramseyer and Jellicoe, he had returned with a Greek known as Spanias as one of the three teams put ashore by HSL. Each night the tiny chapel at Nikolaos Bay was packed, as desperate men gathered in hopeful antic- ipation of being rescued. Unfortunately, Greenwood and Spanias were unable to re-establish contact with the RAF launch which left them with no option but to arrange an alternative method of escape. By 30 November the situation had deteriorated further when several German soldiers took up residence in the chapel. As a result, the Faughs' medical officer, Captain J. Barbour, was captured when he unsuspectingly entered the building. Soon after, Greenwood got away in a rowing boat together with Rochford and, it is thought, the two signallers. During the night of 1 December, Mold managed to find a place aboard a fishing boat with four Greeks (including the skipper); 'Tony', an Italian sailor; Captain Donald Cropper, Lieutenant John Browne and Private Cliff Hodges (all of the Royal West Kents), Lieutenant Harold Price (the forward observation officer on Clidi), and a Faughs medical orderly, Lance Corporal McGuire.

Captain Olivey was taken prisoner in the most unlikely circumstances. Driven by hunger and thirst, he had made his way back to the Italian barracks on Clidi after daybreak on the 18th. After finding and devouring some mouldy bread and bacon fat, washed down with sour wine, he undressed, climbed into bed and slept for several hours. He awoke at 1500 just as two German officers entered with three of their men.

> The junior officer spoke perfect English and, coming in, asked what I was doing there. Before waiting for a reply, he spotted my battle dress coat with the three pips hanging over a chair. He was obviously very pleased with his capture.[15]

Olivey later 'demoted' himself and, disguised as an ordinary private, managed to escape twice only to be recaptured. On 21 November, he was transported with 2,700 prisoners by sea to Piraeus. From the docks, the men were marched towards Athens where Olivey again gave his captors the slip, this time by fleeing down a side street. Within minutes he was befriended by two Greek women and so began a long journey to freedom during which the LRDG officer was passed from house to house until being taken by sea to Turkey. Olivey eventually reached Cairo on 25 April 1944.

The fifteen men comprising Olivey's patrol were prevented by the presence of enemy soldiers from reaching their escape RV. After waiting in vain for two days for their OC to join them, they had divided into four parties. The largest of these (seven men) surrendered on 20 November; two more groups were evacuated between the 20th and the 22nd (probably by HSL

2539). The last man, Gunner Jack Rupping, was looked after by Greeks until his escape could be arranged on the night of 4–5 December.

Many owed their lives to the courage of ordinary Greeks. After his heroic rescue efforts in the early hours of 13 November, Midshipman Rankin of HMS *Belvoir* had watched helplessly as his ship made off without him. Resignedly, he struck out towards the nearest island and at about 0900 struggled ashore on the east coast of Kos wearing only his shirt and a lifebelt. Befriended by farmers, Rankin was taken to a nearby house where he was provided with food and clothing. But he was impatient to rejoin his ship and on 29 November, while reconnoitring before to attempting to swim to Turkey, Rankin and a Greek friend were captured by the Germans and incarcerated in Kos castle. Three days later, after an Italian had revealed the whereabouts of a tunnel, they managed to escape. Soon after, Rankin joined thirty-one others on board a tobacco caique bound for Turkey. After journeying by sea, road and rail, he reached Beirut where, on Christmas Eve 1943, he boarded a train for the last leg to Alexandria, in Egypt.

On the neighbouring island of Kalymnos, local Greeks also took care of the three escapees from BYMS 72. Within a few days, Leading Wireman Crichton and Stoker I. Yuill were evacuated by caique to Turkey. The fate of Able Seaman Mariner, who remained on Kalymnos, is unrecorded. One more crew member was released from captivity in unusual circumstances. Stoker S. A. Hudson had been severely traumatised and was put ashore when the minesweeper called at Alinda. Later, he was taken prisoner and joined other casualties on board the hospital ship *Gradisca*. The circumstances surrounding the freeing of those aboard the vessel is related by Lieutenant Geoffrey Hart of the Buffs:

When we left the hospital at Portolago it was at night. The *Gradisca* was in the bay and our stretchers were put on lighters (flat-topped pontoons or barges). I suppose there were about 40 stretchers. The German crew took off all the stretchers except for mine and that of another Buffs officer, Lieutenant Gore. It was the end of November and cold. We were just left there at the side of the ship, but I could hear German voices inside shouting 'Zwei Offiziere – Boofs'.

After about half an hour a German Naval officer and orderlies came and apologised for the delay but they were making a two-bedded stateroom on the promenade deck available to us and had sent the previous occupant, an Italian colonel, 'down into the hold'. The Germans were as good as their word. We had a stateroom with windows overlooking the promenade deck. Lieutenant Gore had a bed against the window side and I had a bed on the inside. The German captain was an elderly Naval officer – of the Imperial German Navy, he said, 'not a U-Boat officer'. He was punctilious, a typical Edwardian-type senior officer, and did his rounds every morning asking if we were alright. The food was awful but I believe it was the same as the Germans had. The British Field Surgical Unit stayed with us all the time and operated on all wounded, regardless of nationality, but told us that they could do little as the theatre equipment and medical supplies were totally inadequate. I was told that there were the two of us (Buffs officers) and about 34 ORs from the Battalion. The Padre of the King's Own [Captain Edward F. Johnson] had also stayed. I do not know how many other British there were but there were a number of German wounded, Italians and, I believe, some French and Greeks.

We sailed about dawn and after a day or so called at a harbour in Crete. Here, a long column of German soldiers carrying full kit were formed up and marched on to the ship. Although I was unable to get out of bed I caught a glimpse of them through the window. Lieutenant Gore, who was only slightly wounded in the ankle, was able to give a running commentary. Later, I learned that the ship was reported to have also been used as a trooper ...

After a couple of days we left and sailed northwards for Trieste. My own condition was not good. My wounds were very gangrenous and nothing could really be done on the ship.

On the evening of 8 December, Hart went to sleep as usual, but was woken shortly afterwards:

Lights illuminated the promenade deck; the German crew were all shouting and running about and there was the sound of ropes being thrown and, I thought, of life-boats being lowered. At first I thought we had struck rocks and were sinking. After a while the noise lessened and Lieutenant Gore opened a window and tried to find out what was happening. I then saw a blue British steel helmet at the window and, in close proximity to the wearer's nose, a shining 1914 style bayonet passing back and forth. We called out and asked who he was and were greeted with a flow of expletives in a broad Scots accent the like of which I have seldom heard. In effect, he was saying that he had found blank-blank Germans, likewise Italians, likewise French and now he had found blank-blank English: what was this blank-blank ship, the blank-blank League of Nations?

The *Gradisca* had been stopped by HM destroyers *Troubridge* and *Tumult* and the incredulous Scotsman was a Royal Navy rating. As soon as Hart and Gore realised what was happening, the seaman was sent to fetch an officer:

> Almost immediately, a very young Lieutenant came in to our cabin and asked us if the ship was carrying arms. He did hope that this was the case as boarding a hospital ship was really not on. We, of course, assured him that she must be as the column of German soldiers had boarded at Crete and at that stage of the war troops were bound to have arms secreted in kit-bags if they were not openly carrying them. He thanked us and said he would report back.
>
> The waiting was ghastly. Our own forces were obviously all around us and I longed to get to them but could not really move from my bed let alone get over the side of the ship. Eventually the ship moved off very slowly. There seemed to be a lot of light and Lieutenant Gore thought he could see a naval vessel quite close.
>
> Eventually, somebody – I think the King's Own Padre – came to our room and said that the German captain had invited the British officers to the wardroom for drinks. He considered that we were still his prisoners but he had a British Naval officer on his bridge who had really taken over his ship. I, of course, could not go, but they sent me down a bottle of beer! Lieutenant Gore did go for a time. Apparently, the German and the British officers sung alternate English–German marching songs accompanied on the piano by the Padre, whilst the ship slowly crossed the Adriatic to Brindisi.
>
> The next day we were taken off. The Germans were left on board. The Italians were asked if they were for Mussolini or Badoglio. If Mussolini, they were left on; if Badoglio, taken off.[16]

Among the latter was *Capitano* Cacciatori. Naval Lieutenant Austin Crowder, who had been evacuated with jaundice, was also freed. For the vast majority of the garrison, however, their journey would have an altogether different ending. After capture, officers and men were segregated and held in transit in Greece until they could be transported in railway goods wagons to prison camps in the Reich. According to German statistics, 3,200 British and 5,350 Italians were taken prisoner.[17]

CHAPTER 14

Aftermath

North of Leros is the island of Samos; for the Germans, the last major obstacle in their conquest of the Aegean. Resident troops of the *Ieros Lohos* (Greek Sacred Squadron) only just escaped the fate of the Royal West Kents when an order to send the force to Leros was countermanded late on 16 November.[1] The following morning, the port of Vathi was bombed and strafed by at least fifty German aircraft. An hour later, at 1230, Tigani (Pythagorio) was subjected to a heavy raid that lasted two and a half hours. Two days later, the British prepared for a general withdrawal of servicemen and civilians alike. Subsequently, it was reported that 138 British (including four officers and some seventy ORs of the Royal West Kents), 358 soldiers of the Greek Sacred Squadron, 400 Greek guerillas and 2,978 Italians had been evacuated from Samos; another eighty-four British were taken off Ikaria.

On Sunday, 21 November, the Germans made an initial attempt to occupy Samos. The landing party included the commanding officer of *Jäger-regiment 1 Brandenburg, Oberstleutnant* Uwe Wilhelm Walther:

> As the motor torpedo boat under my command approached the island of Samos in the early evening hours, the signaller on board used a large signal lamp to flash in morse: *Parlamentario a bordo* [Negotiator on board]. *General* Müller ... had ordered me to take the two motor torpedo boats and proceed to Samos as negotiator to request the surrender of the English and Italians there. The coast was before us with its romantic little harbour of Tigani. No one was visible, a situation which we soldiers did not feel at all happy about, as we could

be fired upon at any moment. Having received no reply to the repeated messages sent by the signaller, I therefore left one of the boats to provide cover while I tried to approach the island in the other. Just as well, because all of a sudden, we came under fire, albeit without suffering any damage. As it was getting dark and it was proving impossible to land under the circumstances, I was ordered by wireless to return to Leros. We raced back at top speed at sunset and trailing a long, bright wave that lit the sea; quite an impressive picture which would be difficult to beat even in peace time.

The following morning (22nd) the Germans made a renewed effort to reach the island. Walther's account continues:

The order had not yet been carried out, therefore new instructions were issued and at dawn we again set out across the calm waters. Maybe, this time we would have more luck, maybe our opponents had still not quite woken up. So, we went through the same procedure all over again. While I left one boat to cruise along the coast, the other took me at top speed into the harbour, this time without being fired at. Yet again there was no one to be seen, except for a solitary Englishman who acted like a one-man reception party. He was a typical commando-type, very dashing, but unfortunately no use to me as apparently he 'didn't know anything'; he didn't even know about an island *Kommandant*. At last, an Italian officer arrived, looking like a peacock in full plume and accompanied by an armed escort. Initially, he refused to negotiate with me until I was able to convince him that his war was over and that he should prepare to surrender weapons and any units as the German *Wehrmacht* would soon arrive and occupy the island. Eventually, he had no choice but to accept all terms and conditions.[2]

The identity of the mysterious British soldier has not been established, and while he was exempt from capture during negotiations, his subsequent fate is unknown. Walther described him thus:

He was dressed in olive green and wore a jumper and beret and had a colt [handgun] in his belt. As an old *Brandenburger* I realised that he was a British Commando who had presumably been left behind to monitor events. He was courteous and polite and helped the crew to moor the boat.[3]

However, Walther was less than impressed by the local commandant, whom he nicknamed 'Papagallo'. When the Italian officer enquired if it was really necessary to surrender those with womenfolk on the island, Walther, a tough and experienced veteran, was unmoved:

Matey, if one surrenders, it generally means everybody.[4]

Negotiations were swiftly concluded and troops who had taken part in the fighting for Leros were ordered north for what would become an unexpectedly pleasant sojourn, as described in the diary of *Oberjäger* Haat Haacke of *III./1. Rgt. Brandenburg*:

Monday 22.11.43: Wake up call at 6.00. Ready to march at 7.00. I read my mail from yesterday. Towards midday we cook English tinned vegetables. At around 12.00 we receive news that Samos has surrendered. We are being transferred onto boats straight away. Departure 13.00. We are a convoy of 26 boats ... We land on the south coast of Samos without incident at 20.00. We move through a mined area to Vathi, where we arrive at 1.00.

Tuesday, 23.11.43: We have been placed with nice people, who immediately offered us tangerines. At around 9.00 I take over from [*Unteroffizier*] Zintle at the *Batteriestellungen*. There, people bring us *Wurst* and wine. Towards midday we march to the south coast. En route a car gives us a lift. We move into nice quarters in Tiganion [Pythagorio]. The town has been virtually destroyed by bombs. From today, I lead the operation.

Wednesday, 24.11.43: Got up at 6.00. I take my *Gruppe* on a reconnaissance patrol. In a monastery we loot some provisions. In the afternoon I go for a swim.

Thursday, 25.11.43: Slept until 7.00. For breakfast fried sausage and coffee with milk.

Wednesday, 1.12.43: The last few days have been taken up with 'house-keeping' duties, we stacked ammunition, rolled petrol drums, did laundry etc. We also cooked lunch ourselves. We lived as if in paradise ...[5]

For the Italian former occupation forces, life was far from pleasant. By 29 November, the Germans had taken 4,355 prisoners, including ninety-three officers. One officer and twenty-six men were executed as 'armed insurgents'. Only 527 'Blackshirts' were allowed to retain their arms.

By this time, Santorini had surrendered and the last 'out' patrols of the Long Range Desert Group had been evacuated from Mykonos and Serifos, leaving the Cyclades to the Germans. In the south-east, only a token British force remained on Kastellorizo which was retained as a base for MTBs. The German assault troops on Leros were also withdrawn and replaced by garrison units.

After the fall of Leros, Allied submarines continued to intercept enemy vessels, and achieved a significant success on 19 November by sinking the steamer *Boccaccio* at Monemvasia (south-east Greece). Although offensive operations including hit-and-run attacks by Raiding Forces would also continue, some islands remained under German occupation until the end of the war.

In the wake of events in the Aegean islands, New Zealand was quick to make known her anger. Remembering, perhaps, the sacrifices made by the Dominions in the Great War at Gallipoli, the New Zealand Prime Minister, Peter Fraser, wrote to the High Commissioner in London on 27 November 1943:

> A number of Long Range Desert Group patrol troops were ordered to take part in the attack and occupation of some of the Dodecanese Islands without either the knowledge or consent of the New Zealand Government or apparently of General Freyberg, who would have immediately consulted us. This was a breach of our agreement with the British Government and Army authorities. The circumstances surrounding the loss of Leros have already largely destroyed my own faith in the present Mid East command, if it was responsible, and when it becomes known that a number of New Zealanders were stupidly sacrificed without even consent for their inclusion in the task force being asked from our Government, the disappointment and bitterness here will be intensified many times over ...
>
> The decision to leave the force of Leros to become the easy prey of German air and land forces combined was wrong, and indeed most reprehensible. The useless sacrifice of fine men in such a fashion is proof

that the tragic lesson of Greece and Crete has not been fully assimilated and understood by some of those in the high command, or else they are prepared to take a risk, as stated by [Britain's Deputy Prime Minister] Mr Attlee, as to gamble on a poor chance with men's lives. I strongly protest against any of our men being sacrificed in such a fashion.[6]

Britain disputed some of the issues raised by Mr Fraser, but it was a moot point whether or not General Bernard Freyberg had agreed to New Zealanders in his command being deployed with the LRDG in the Aegean and whether he had, in turn, informed the New Zealand government, when the latter had made representations to Britain as early as 3 November for the withdrawal from Leros of the LRDG New Zealand Squadron. After the disasters in Levitha and Leros, the British government was hardly in a position to argue. Of eighty New Zealanders who began the Aegean venture, six officers and forty-four other ranks were all who could be mustered on 1 December prior to being released back into the service of their own country.

Only too aware of the backlash to be expected from his critics, a few days after the fall of Leros Winston Churchill recommended that the Foreign Secretary adopt an evasive policy when the issue was raised in Parliament:

Not advisable to answer in detail such questions as to why lessons of Crete were not learned. If we only proceed on certainties we must face prospect of a prolonged war. No attempt should be made to minimise poignancy of loss of Dodecanese. Stress tremendous effort made by Germans. Don't forget we probably drowned best part of 2,000.[7]

If Mr Churchill's reference was to German deaths, the figure quoted was well in excess of actual losses; if the total included Italian and Allied prisoners, it was a gross underestimation. According to German naval sources, of nearly 4,000 mainly Italian prisoners of war on board the transports *Donizetti* and *Sinfra*, close on 3,400 went down with both ships. Many more were lost while in transit outside Aegean waters.

Generalleutnant Müller recorded German casualties during the battles for Kos and Leros as 260 killed, 746 wounded and 162 missing: this does not tally with other reports. Certainly, 177 German prisoners of war were evacuated by the British before the fall of Leros, while the records of the *Volksbund Deutsche Kriegsgräberfürsorge* (German War Graves Commission) show that in 1960, 135 dead were exhumed from cemeteries and field graves in Kos for reburial at the main German war cemetery at Dionyssos-Rapendoza on the Greek mainland. Nine bodies from field graves in Leros were also transferred subsequent to the relocation in 1972 of all 316 of those interred at the wartime cemetery near Alinda Bay. Müller himself survived the war only to face trial for war crimes committed during his command on Crete. He was executed by the Greeks on 20 May 1947 and also lies at Dionyssos-Rapendoza.

In the British and Commonwealth war cemetery at Leros there are 183 dead, mostly from the fighting in November 1943. Another 135 officers and men of the Buffs died when HMS *Eclipse* was mined while en route from Samos to Leros. Those killed on Kos and elsewhere are buried in Rhodes. In November 1943, it was estimated that there were between 400 and 500 dead or missing naval personnel. Add to these figures casualties among Allied aircrew and one is presented with well over 700 fatalities. Many more were wounded.

According to German records, nearly 4,600 British service personnel were taken prisoner on Kos and Leros together with approximately 8,500 Italians. As well as the Italians who perished en route to prison and labour camps, were those who died in battle or were executed in accordance with the *Führer*'s directive. Among the latter were *Ammiraglio* Inigo Campioni, governor of the Italian Aegean Islands, and *Contrammiraglio* Luigi Mascherpa. They were sentenced to death by a German military court and executed on 24 March 1944 in Parma.

And, of course, there were the civilians: some died or were maimed in the fighting between opposing forces, others were casualties of bombing raids and some fell victim to unexploded ordnance which still litters the islands.

Both sides also suffered in terms of material losses: tons of shipping including civilian vessels pressed into military service were sunk or damaged beyond repair, and numerous aircraft were lost in the air or destroyed on the ground. Vast quantities of Allied arms and equipment also fell into German hands.

With Leros went any hope of a British victory in the Aegean. Someone had to be held accountable and rightly or wrongly, for many that man was the unfortunate Brigadier Robert Tilney. He was liberated from captivity by the Americans in 1945 and shortly afterward retired from the Army. In later life he was left severely brain damaged as a result of a tragic riding accident. He never recovered and died sixteen years later on 1 May 1981.

After his departure, temporary Major General Ben Brittorous returned to England and the ignominy of a home command before retiring as brigadier in 1946. Following a long illness, he died on 25 March 1974.

In the end, the battle for Leros and the Aegean was one of improvisation and daring, but not just for the British. In a final twist of irony, Winston Churchill's heroic bluster was unintentionally echoed in Adolf Hitler's congratulatory message to his commanders on completion of Operation 'Taifun'.

> The capture of Leros, embarked on with limited means but with great courage, carried through tenaciously in spite of various set-backs and bravely brought to a victorious conclusion, is a military accomplishment which will find an honourable place in the history of this war.
>
> The military and political importance of this victory is great and cannot yet be assessed.
>
> I express my full appreciation to commanders and troops, and particularly to *Generalleutnant* Müller.[8]

In London on 20 November 1943, the War Office concluded:

> Our available resources compared with those required for the operations in Italy, were very small. Activities in the Aegean were, after all, a minor affair. The balance sheet is against us, but, in view of the undoubted distraction of enemy strength from other theatres and of the very great results which might have been achieved had the Italians fought stoutly with us, our losses were not in vain.[9]

The limitation of available resources was understood at the outset. Furthermore, British efforts in the Aegean led to relatively few German forces having to be diverted from other fronts. As for Italian involvement, no one seriously expected any more or less from a nation whose previous war record spoke for itself.

The painful truth is that Churchill had gambled and lost dearly. The cost, of course, was borne by others: men who gave their lives and their freedom, or who were crippled by terrible wounds. Some carry the physical and emotional scars to this day. In November 1943, Reg Neep was a twenty-year-old signals corporal in Headquarters Company, the King's Own. He fought at Appetici and finished the battle as platoon sergeant before being taken prisoner and spending the rest of the war in Germany. He revisited Leros for the first time in September 2001 and spent many hours walking over familiar ground. Yet, he was unable to face returning to Appetici.

Today, on Kos, there is little to remind one about the war. The island is hugely popular with young holidaymakers. In summer, the once idyllic seafront of Kos town is packed with those who have no idea about what took place there more than half a century ago. What tangible evidence there is attracts barely a glance: reminders such as the rusting remains of a wrecked F-lighter in the shallows at Marmari are all but ignored by passers-by.

Leros is different. With little to offer as a tourist destination, it has remained relatively unspoiled. Because of its proximity to Turkey, there is a noticeable military presence. Certain areas are off-limits, including the summits of Clidi, Appetici and Meraviglia. All have been requisitioned for their strategic importance, with original Italian constructions having been repaired and renovated for use by the Greek armed forces.

There are remnants of wartime battery positions throughout the island, but much of the damage to so many bunkers is due to post-war demolition orders. The tunnel that housed Tilney's headquarters escaped destruction and is preserved within the restricted military zone on Meraviglia. Hillsides where much of the fighting took place are unchanged and littered with war debris: barbed wire, shrapnel, cartridge cases and live ammunition. In the residential areas some buildings lie in ruin to this day, their walls pock-marked by bullets and scarred by shrapnel. Fine examples of Italian military architecture, some with murals created by bored German occupation troops, also remain. On an interior wall in the former Italian wireless station near 'the Anchor' there is an impressive painting of an eagle and swastika and an inscription: *Es gibt für uns nur einen Kampf – und dann den Sieg* ... 'We have just one struggle – and then victory ...' On the facing wall is the rest of the message, but it is no longer legible, the words having faded with time, like the distant memory of an all-but-forgotten battle.

German unit designations

In the *Wehrmacht*, Roman numerals were used to indicate *battaillone* while, generally, Arabic numerals were used for other unit formations. There are several ways in which unit designations can be abbreviated. For example, *II. Battaillon/Grenadierregiment 65* can be shortened to *II./Gren.Rgt.65*, *II./G.R.65*, or simply *II./65*. Although it has become popular to modernise abbreviations by omitting most of the stops, for consistency and with the possible exception of variations used in direct quotes, a style commonly used in wartime reports has been adopted for use throughout this book, in this instance *II./Gren.Rgt.65*.

The original German for unit components has been retained. Most are self-explanatory, but readers may be unfamiliar with the term *Zug*: three *Gruppen* (sections) formed a *Zug* (platoon) and three *Schützenzüge* (rifle platoons) and a *schwerer Zug* (heavy weapons platoon) made up a *Kompanie* (company). There were four *Kompanien* in a *Bataillon* (battalion) and three *Bataillone*, with support weapons, comprised a *Regiment* (regiment). Typically, a *Zug* was commanded by a *Feldwebel* or, sometimes, a *Leutnant*; a *Gruppe* by an *Unteroffizier*, and a *Kompanie* by an *Offizier*. As with British units, the number of personnel could vary, but as an example, the complement of *5. Kompanie* of *Grenadierregiment 65* just prior to the battle for Kos was two officers and 157 other ranks.

Time Zones

Between September–November 1943, Allied forces in the Aegean operated under various time zones including Greenwich Mean Time (GMT) and Time Zones A, B and C. A (–1) was local time and one hour ahead of GMT; B (–2) and C (–3) were two and three hours ahead of GMT. The Germans kept to the equivalent of Time Zone B until 0200 hours on 4 October, when their forces on and around Kos switched to Time Zone A. The British, on the other hand, displayed a curious tendency during September and October to deviate between the four time zones, although on Kos units appear to have adhered mainly to Time Zone C. By November, the British were at last all operating under Time Zone B. For consistency, a universal system has been adopted for use throughout this book. Accordingly, Time Zone C (–3) is used wherever possible up to 31 October 1943 and Time Zone B (–2) thereafter.

Italian batteries on Leros

Coastal Defence batteries

NAME	ARMAMENT	LOCATION
Ducci	4×152/50, 1×120/45	Point 155/Cazzuni
Ciano	4×152/40	Point 320/Clidi
San Giorgio	3×152/40, 1×102/35	Point 334/Scumbarda
Farinata	4×120/45	Point 256/Marcello
Lago	4×120/45	Point 180/Appetici

Anti-Aircraft batteries

NAME	ARMAMENT	LOCATION
P.L. 262	6×76/40	Point 327
P.L. 248	6×76/40	Mount della Palma
P.L. 113	4×76/40	Point 226/Zuncona

Dual purpose batteries

NAME	ARMAMENT	LOCATION
P.L. 306	6×102/35, 2×76/40	Mount Vigla
P.L. 388	4×102/35	Porto Cassio
P.L. 211	4×102/35	Rachi
P.L. 227	4×102/35	Lakki Point
P.L. 127	6×90/53	Point 204/Meraviglia
P.L. 281	6×76/40	Point 74/Diapori Point
P.L. 899	4×76/50	Point 48/Vaies Point
P.L. 906	4×76/40	Point 284/Muplogurna

NAME	ARMAMENT	LOCATION
P.L. 989	4×76/40	Point 61/Cape Timari
P.L. 888	4×76/40	Point 61/Blefuti Bay
P.L. 749	4×76/40	Arcangelo (islet)
P.L. 250	3×76/40	Cazzuni Point
P.L. 432	3×76/40	Point 81/La Madonna
P.L. 690	2×76/50	Castello di Bronzi
P.L. 508	2×76/50	Point 138
P.L. 763	2×76/40	Alinda Bay
P.L. 763	2×76/40	Gurna Bay

(*P.L.*: *Pezzo Leggero*: light piece/gun)

Recommendation for award to *Sottotenente di artiglieria* Ferrucio Pizzigoni

Confidential.

2nd Lieut. PETSIGONNE –
The Alpine Regt – serving with the Italian Marines – Pt. 320 – LEROS.

At the approach of enemy shipping from the North East on [sic] Nov. 1943 2nd Lieut Petsigonne showed considerable skill – having taken over command of the Marine battery on Pt 320. His guns being responsible for the sinking of at least two of the enemy landing craft before they could reach the island.

During the approach of the enemy to Pt 320 he personally – with the assistance of one marine maintained and fired his one remaining gun – successfully repulsing attempts to land barges in the North of Leros.

When his ammunition in the local (No. 2 Gun) magazine was exhausted he personally – under enemy machine gun fire – carried shells from the main magazine until assisted by British troops.

On the near approach of the enemy he organised the carrying forward of the Seotti Fascisti [sic] gun so that this could bring fire on the approaching enemy. This gun immediately became the target for mortar and rifle fire but he continued to fire until the gun was wrecked by the enemy.

2nd Lieut Petsigonne then taking with him an Italian machine gun and ammunition advanced to the cave to the West. His gun was heard in action up to 14.00 hours when his position was overrun and captured by the enemy.

No remains of 2nd Lieut Petsigonne being found in the cave when the position was retaken – it is concluded that he was captured.

Throughout the battle 2nd Lieut Petsigonne had shown great courage and complete disregard of danger.

I have the honour to recommend 2nd Lieut Petsigonne for conspicuous skill and bravery in the face of the enemy on Point 320 Leros on the 10th [sic] November 1943.

[signed] J. R. Olivey, Capt., L.R.D.G.

Letter of condolence to family of *Uffz.* Andreas Hutter from his commanding officer

Copy
Auer *Oblt.*   Command Post, 1.12.1943
Staffelkapitän 6. Staffel

My Dear Hutter Family !

On 13.11.1943, your son, *Unteroffizier* Andreas Hutter, did not return from a combat mission to the Aegean island of Leros and has since been missing. During its approach to the island in order to drop paratroopers, the aeroplane carrying your son was attacked by enemy fire along with all the other machines. The machine with your son was hit in the rudder and flew over the island and after 2 km had to make an emergency landing on the sea. Both the crew and the paratroopers, who had not been dropped, had to leave the aircraft to either swim to safety or try to reach land with the rubber dinghy. This happened at around 5.30 in the morning; the machine flew separately, as did all the others, after your son had also taken part in the first joint mission to Leros on 12.11. Three men from his crew swam for 1½ hours before reaching dry land and returned to their *Staffel* after the Island surrendered. My immediately launched investigations only revealed that your son Andreas was swimming in the water near the dinghy, which could not be inflated due, presumably, to bullet damage. *Uffz.* Langos, who belonged to the same crew, called out to your son to try to swim back to shore. However, the survivors were separated by high seas, with the aeroplane sinking soon after. When three men reached the shore after 1½ hours, they remained there for another three hours to wait for their other comrades. Your son Andreas, as well as *Uffz.*

Meyendicks from the same crew have not been seen on the island and have been missing ever since.

I am writing these painful words with a heavy heart, my dear Hutter family, but send you all our wishes, that your son might have been rescued and might have been taken prisoner. I will personally inform you forthwith, if I hear any further news.

With *Uffz.* Hutter, the *Staffel* is losing an honest, very decent soldier and comrade, who has proved himself as a courageous and brave soldier on 64 combat sorties. I have recommended your son for the silver *Frontflugspange* [combat mission clasp] and the *EK II. Klasse* [Iron Cross 2nd Class] and I will forward these decorations to you as soon as they arrive. Your son's possessions will be dispatched to you today. Your local Armed Forces welfare office will be delighted to assist you with any advice and counselling you might require.

If your son has fallen to the enemy and has met his fate as a soldier, I would hope – my dear Hutter family – that you would draw comfort in this difficult time in knowing that he has given his life for the greater good and continuance of the people, the *Führer* and the Fatherland.

My sincere condolences and best wishes

Yours

Auer

Letter home from Lt Col M. French

2 R. Ir. F.
M.E.F.

12 Oct. 43

My own Di,

It looks just possible, my sweetheart, that we may be in for a sticky time for the next day or two and I am seizing an opportunity to get a letter away to you.

If anything should happen to me, remember that our separation is only temporary. Thank God you have the two pussies [children] and Di, my darling, don't hesitate to marry again if you meet the right chap because I couldn't bear to think of you alone. Mother will help you (if my pessimistic outlook turns out to be true which it probably will not!) more than anyone.

It is cruelly hard that we should have been four and a half years apart, but the remaining separation will only be like a continuation of this and I will be close to you, dearest Di – always.

What fun it will be to read and tear this letter up 'one day'. Be happy, my darling. It may be hard at first but it will pass and then you will know that death cannot separate us.

What a gloomy letter! You say you will be all right financially. I wish you would be better off but you are so good at managing that you should be able to make do – you and the pussies. I am glad they have not seen me for so long and are so young. You having them makes me so much happier about you.

We are all in good heart and if it becomes necessary will go on in good heart to face whatever may be before us. You have been the sweetest possible wife that any man could have. Oh how fortunate I have been in my womenfolk! No more now, my darling. I will cable if the situation changes. I am not able to do so now.

I love you, my precious Di, and our love will never end. Whatever happens, one way or the other, this is NOT good-bye but merely till we meet again.

God bless and care for you and ours always. Kiss the pussies.

> With the dearest love
> I can offer to anyone
> Maurice.

Letter of reprimand to Lt Cdr J. H. Swain from Vice Admiral A. U. Willis

MOST SECRET AND PERSONAL.   Office of Commander-in-Chief,
Levant.
27th December, 1943.

Levant 00230/6.

THE COMMANDING OFFICER,
    H.M.S. PENN
    (Through Captain (D), 14th Destroyer Flotilla).

With reference to your No. 1671/21 of 19th November 1943, I consider that with one exception, the operations described were well carried out by the Force under your command and that valuable assistance was rendered to the garrison of LEROS.

2. The exception was that you did not immediately leave PHARLAN BAY on receipt of the first enemy report of landing craft East of LEROS on the night of 15th/16th November in accordance with the instructions contained in my signal 15 1527.

3. It is true that these two enemy reports were both an hour old when they reached you, but even so there was a good chance that you could intercept before the enemy craft reached LEROS, or at any rate that you could have interfered with the landing operations which would have been nearly as good.

4. The decision to keep your force at anchor that night was based on the

experience of the night before when it appeared that enemy landing craft were able by reports from their continuous night air reconnaissance, to evade your patrol. As however, no reports were received of any enemy reinforcements reaching the island that night, the presence of your force in the area appears to have persuaded the enemy landing craft to return whence they came, which in itself must have been of great assistance to the garrison.

5. In these circumstances, you should have acted on your instructions and proceeded to try and intercept. Had you succeeded the effect in the battle raging in LEROS which you knew from my signal 15 1955 was very critical, might have been considerable.

6. I consider therefore that your appreciation of this situation was faulty and that you committed an error of judgement at a very critical time.

(sgd) A. U. WILLIS

VICE ADMIRAL.

Correspondence relating to the death of Lt A. Phipps, RN

Subject:-

Casualties Officers.

Lt Alan Phipps RN.

To:-   H. V. Markham Esq

Admiralty CW Branch

(Officers Casualties)

Queen Anne's Mansions

London SW1

I the undersigned would like to make the following statement regarding the death of the a/m Royal Naval Officer, whilst performing duties ashore on the Aegean Isle of Leros on Nov 16th 1943.

After conversation with the Officer's widow, Mrs Alan Phipps, of 10c Hyde Park Mansions, London, it appears that Lt Phipps is still posted as missing.

I can confirm that this Officer died in action on the last day of battle on Leros, at some time between 1000 hrs and 1700 hrs Nov 16th 1943.

I was assisting this Officer and two others to retake and defend a gun position on the slopes of the Island HQ Mount at about 1000 hrs. Shortly after the site had been taken, Lt Phipps was hit above the waist, apparently in neck and chest, by rifle fire from the enemy. He fell to the ground inside and close to the parapet.

Owing to accurate enemy mortar, grenade and sniper fire, the site had to be evacuated.

After capitulation the site was revisited later the same day at about 1700 hrs, conducted by an enemy guard for express purpose of ascertaining the condition of this Naval Officer and another unknown Army Officer. Both Officers had been dead for a considerable time.

I should like to comment on the outstanding bravery of this Officer, who initiated and led the attack on the position advancing across open ground exposed to fire. It was due to his leadership only that the position was retaken. His actions in this area prevented the enemy from further advance until much later in the day. At one stage in the fighting when the supply of grenades had been exhausted, he stood at the parapet hurling rocks upon the advancing enemy below.

Two other Officers known to have witnessed Lt Alan Phipps brave actions are Lt/Col Ritchie of a Scottish Regt of Infantry and Capt Ramsey R. Sigs at the time Sigs Officer to 234 Inf Bde.

E. B. Horton

12th Aug 1945   Lt R. Sigs
'UPLANDS' 20 PRIEST HILL. CAV. READING.

H. & A. 218/44

21st August 1945.

The Secretary of the Admiralty desires to acknowledge Lieutenant Horton's letter of 12th August 1945 and to thank him for the information contained therein concerning Lieutenant Alan Phipps, R.N.

The services of this gallant officer were most carefully considered for recognition, and he was awarded a Posthumous Mention in Despatches, by His Majesty's gracious command. A copy of the relevant Gazette is attached.

As Lieutenant Horton is probably aware, this is the highest honour, except the Victoria Cross, which may be given to Officers and Men who are killed in action for services in the action in which they lost their lives.

Lieutenant E. B. Horton,
Uplands,
20, Priest Hill,
Cav.
Reading.

Notes

CHAPTER 1 Italy and the Aegean

1 Place names in the Aegean can be spelt a number of ways and sometimes differ altogether according to source. For the purpose of this work, a modern Anglicised version has been adopted, except when quoting original wartime reports when the modern name is also given in brackets.

2 See Prime Minister Winston Churchill's message to President Franklin D. Roosevelt of 7 October 1943, pp. 81–2.

3 *Operations in the Dodecanese Islands, September–November 1943*, p. 2. PRO: AIR 41/53.

CHAPTER 2 Calm before the Storm: February–September 1943

1 *Dodecanese. December, 1942 to the Loss of Leros 1943. Report by M.O.1. (Records).* PRO: WO 32/11430.

2 Between May 1943 and January 1944, no fewer than seven such plans were produced. Initially, these were designed to overcome German and Italian resistance in the Aegean as well as mainland Greece, while later proposals were for the capture of Rhodes or Crete against German opposition. On four occasions a force was assembled and partially prepared to undertake the capture of Rhodes.

3 *M.O.1. Report,* op. cit.

4 Landing craft for 'Accolade' had been provided from among those designated for a proposed combined operation against the Arakan, codenamed 'Bullfrog'. As the latter had priority over 'Accolade', the vessels were subsequently withdrawn and reallocated in order for 'Bullfrog' to be implemented. The operation was later cancelled.

5 In his Dispatch 0143/4793 (PRO: WO 32/11430), General Wilson wrote: '... a carefully planned and rehearsed operation had just been jettisoned and no urgent action was contemplated in the near future, since I was not kept informed of what was afoot and first learned that Italy was discussing terms only twenty-four hours before the public announcement that the Armistice had been concluded.' His statement was later amended to read: '... a carefully planned and rehearsed operation had just been jettisoned and no urgent action was contemplated in the immediate future, since I was not kept informed of what was afoot and first learned that Italy was discussing terms only a few days before the public announcement that the armistice had been concluded.' (*Supplement to The London Gazette*, 13 November, 1946, p. 5585).

6 The Royal Irish Fusiliers and the Royal West Kents were in Malta throughout the siege, which began on 11 June 1940 and continued until 20 November 1942. The Durham Light Infantry arrived in Malta from Egypt in early 1942. In June, all three battalions were shipped to the Middle East for retraining in preparation for the intended assault on Rhodes.

7 *Operations in the Dodecanese Islands, September–November 1943*, p. 7. PRO: AIR 41/53.

8 On 11 September 1943, 11 Battalion The Parachute Regiment, two detachments of the Special Boat Squadron (SBS), two squadrons of the Long Range Desert Group (LRDG), the Greek Sacred Squadron (formed in the previous year with officers of the Royal Hellenic Army), the Kalpaks (an especially fearsome and ruthless small unit of indigenous troops under the command of a British officer) and one troop of 133 Light Anti-Aircraft Battery (Royal Artillery) came under the operational command of Force 292. The remainder of the SBS, LRDG Headquarters and Headquarters Raiding Forces remained under General Headquarters in Cairo. Soon after, Raiding Forces became an umbrella organisation for the SBS; LRDG; the Holding Unit, Special Forces (which included officers and men of 30 Commando); the Greek Sacred Squadron, the Kalpaks, 42nd Motor Launch Flotilla and the Levant Schooner Flotilla with command and control exercised by Headquarters Raiding Forces, Aegean, under Colonel (later Brigadier) D. J. T. Turnbull.

9 The Rt. Hon. The Earl Jellicoe KBE, DSO, MC, FRS, interviewed on 13 March 2001.

10 Ibid.

11 Ibid. According to Peter Smith and Edwin Walker, *War in the Aegean*, p. 78, the Italian minefield plans Campioni gave to Jellicoe 'were so inaccurate as to be valueless ...'

12 Colonel L. F. R. Kenyon, *Appendix 'A', Narrative of the Cos Operation, 1943*. PRO: WO 106/3145.

13 Colonel L. F. R. Kenyon, *Narrative of the Cos Operation, 1943*.

14 According to British sources, on 31 August 1943, the *Luftwaffe* South Eastern Command fielded 271 serviceable aircraft comprising: 79 Messerschmitt Bf 109s (reconnaissance and fighters); 24 Messerschmitt Bf 110s (reconnaissance and fighters); five Dornier Do 17s (bombers); 19 Junkers Ju 88s (reconnaissance and fighters); 68 Junkers Ju 87s (dive bombers); 41 Junkers Ju 52s (transports); 34 Arado Ar 196s and one Blohm und Voss Bv 138 (coastal aircraft). *Appendix 1, Operations in the Dodecanese Islands, September–November 1943*.

15 At the time of the Italian armistice, Admiral Sir John Cunningham, Commander-in-Chief, Levant, had at his disposal six 'Fleet'and two 'Hunt' Class destroyers (8th and 22nd Destroyer Flotillas), fifteen submarines (1st Submarine Flotilla and part of 10th Submarine Flotilla), and various small craft including motor boats and Royal Air Force High Speed Launches.

16 According to *Operations in the Aegean Area by Aircraft of the Middle East Command (8th September–16th November, 1943)* (PRO: AIR 23/6143), the first five Spitfires of 7 (SAAF) Squadron reached Kos at dusk on 14 September. This is unsubstantiated by the squadron Operations Record Book (PRO: AIR 27/105), which merely states that on 12 September, Lieutenant A. E. F. Cheesman took off with sealed orders from El Gamil [Port Said] for advance [Kos] followed a day later by three more pilots and, on the 15th, by the commanding officer [Major Cornelius van Vliet]; with additional personnel, including four pilots, travelling by Dakota. An entry in the ORB of 46 Squadron (AIR 27/460) also shows that its Beaufighters escorted Spitfires to Kos on 15 September.

17 Lieutenant Commander Ramseyer, RNVR, *Report of Proceedings for Occupation of Kos, Samos, Leros and Simi*.

18 Air Commodore W. H. Dunn was placed in charge of these operations. He was responsible to the Air Defence commander, Air Vice Marshal R. E. Saul, in Cairo; Group Captain Riccard of No. 201 (Naval Co-operation) Group was attached to the Advance Headquarters Staff for liaison duties. Lieutenant General Sir Desmond Anderson commanded all army and air forces in the Aegean and at Kastellorizo; local command of all army and air forces in Kastellorizo was vested in Major G. V. Shaw (Royal West Kents) and command of the naval forces in the Aegean and at Kastellorizo was exercised by the Commander-in-Chief, Levant, Admiral Sir John Cunningham.

CHAPTER 3 **Reinforcements: September 1943**

1   *War Diary, German Naval Staff, Operations Division, Part A, Volume 49* (a translation of *Seekriegsleitung, Teil A, Kriegstagebuch*). IWM: EDS 233.

2   Navigator, Flight Sergeant Thomas Lumsden of 252 Squadron was killed. His Beaufighter IF (V8335) and Beaufighter VIC (JL766) of 227 Squadron crash-landed on returning to Cyprus. *Unteroffiziere* Fritz Schaar (pilot) and Herbert Schneider of *Seeaufkl.Gr.126* were lost when their Arado 196 (*Werknummer* 185) was shot down off Ios by a 252 Squadron Beaufighter crewed by Squadron Leader K. L. Faulkner (pilot) and Flight Sergeant G. V. Goodes. An Arado was also attacked by two aircraft of 227 Squadron flown by Canadian, Pilot Officer Percy Glynn with Sergeant Timothy Barrett, and Canadian, Flying Officer D. Anderson with Flying Officer J. Timmons. This may have been 1017 of *Seeaufkl.Gr.126* which crashed in the Gulf of Patras; both crewmen were injured.

3   There were on Astipalaea up to 131 survivors from this convoy. At least four German officers were taken to Leros by Major David Lloyd Owen on 18 September; fifty-five prisoners were evacuated by MLs 354 and 355 during the night of 20–21 September and seventy-two more left for Leros with 'Y1' Patrol on 21 September. Others may also have remained at large on Astipalaea.

4   Peter Smith and Edwin Walker, *War in the Aegean*, pp. 105–6.

5   *War Diary, German Naval Staff, Operations Division, Part A, Volume 49*.

6   *Feldwebel* Heinz Keller of *11./J.G.27* was credited with shooting down the first Spitfire five kilometres north of Kos at 1608 followed by a second eight kilometres north-west of Kos at 1613; the latter victim was evidently also attacked by *Fahnenjunker Unteroffizier* Manfred Hientzsch of *10./J.G.27* who claimed a Spitfire destroyed eight kilometres north-west of the island at 1612.

7   The Operations Record Book of 7 (SAAF) Squadron states that Lieutenant I. M. Seel 'was definitely not fired at during the engagement, but may have been engaged in the earlier stages of the operation'. According to German records, two pilots of *12./J.G.27* were credited with shooting down a Spitfire west-south-west of Kos: *Leutnant* Hans Hetzler (at 0917) and *Oberleutnant* Dietrich Boesler.

8   At 1218, *Unteroffizier* Hannes Löffler was credited with destroying a Spitfire north-west of Antimachia, followed two minutes later by *Oberfeldwebel* Fritz Gromotka who claimed a Spitfire north of the aerodrome; at 1617 Gromotka claimed another Spitfire in the same area as his previous victim; three minutes later, *Oberfeldwebel* Johannes Scheit also claimed a Spitfire north of the aerodrome. All three pilots belonged to *9./J.G.27*.

9   On this occasion three pilots were each credited with the destruction of a Spitfire, although *Major* Ernst Düllberg of *Stab III./J.G.27* who made his

claim east of Cardamena at 1708 and *Oberfeldwebel* Johnannes Scheit of *9./J.G.27* who carried out his attack over Kos at 1710 may have attacked the same aircraft. Five minutes later, *Oberfeldwebel* Fritz Gromotka of the same unit accounted for his victim between Kos and the island of Yalli.

10 On 1 October 1943 *Luftwaffe* operational aircraft in the Greece/Aegean area are reported to have comprised: 44 reconnaissance machines, 54 fighters, 68 long range bombers, 69 dive bombers, 50 coastal and 77 transport aircraft. *Operations in the Dodecanese Islands, September–November 1943*, p. 21. PRO: AIR 41/53

CHAPTER 4 Operation *'Eisbär'*: 3 October 1943

1 Although the combat report of 6. *Kompanie/Grenadierregiment 16* identifies the attached *Pionier Zug* as belonging to *3. Kompanie/Pionierbataillon 22*, this is almost certainly an error and should read 2. *Kompanie/Pionierbataillon 22*.

2 *Operations in the Dodecanese Islands, September–November 1943*, p. 24. PRO: AIR 41/53.

3 Colonel L. F. R. Kenyon, *Narrative of the Cos Operation*, 1943. PRO: WO 106/3145.

4 The Germans on Kos kept to Time Zone B (-2) until 0200 hours on 4 October when they switched to Time Zone A (-1). For consistency, all timings have been converted to Time Zone C, believed to have been that kept by the British garrison troops throughout the two-day battle (see Appendix B).

5 Gustav Wehrs, unpublished manuscript.

6 The five pilots who all reached safety were: Flying Officers H. F. Norman, T. H. Bates and F. G. De Pass, Flight Sergeant D. N. Maxwell and Sergeant S. B. Harris.

7 Captain George Sivewright was killed. The fate of his unidentified driver is not known.

8 A 227 Squadron Beaufighter VIC (JL760) was shot down with the loss of the pilot, Flying Officer Percy Glynn and observer, Sergeant Timothy Barrett (another crew from this unit was injured when their machine crashed on take-off). The commanding officer of 46 Squadron, Wing Commander George Reid, was reported missing when Beaufighter XIC (JM238) was hit by *Flak* and later attacked by Arado 196s whereupon it spun in near the Turkish coast. His observer, Flying Officer W. R. Peasley, was picked up and taken to Turkey.

9 Wehrs, op. cit.

10 Only later did the British on Kos discover that a landing had been effected seven kilometres further west than had been indicated by initial reports; even so, this was thought to have been supplementary to the (non-existent) landing at Cape Foca.

11 One aircraft failed to take off due to mechanical problems; another turned back after missing its rendezvous with the others. The twenty-four men assigned to these machines parachuted in twenty-four hours later.

12 Some Germans were ruthless in their behaviour towards their erstwhile allies: Major Hugh Vaux witnessed the execution of two Italians who were unable to carry their loads.

13 The only available report which mentions the battle for the ammunition dump is that of 6./Gren.Rgt.16. The identity of the defending forces has not been established, but it is likely that the action involved Italian troops. This is supported by a reference in the after-action report by Major Hugh Vaux which states that sometime after 0900 hours: 'The two Italian companies on the left of 'A' Company were ... engaged by the enemy coming down from the hills and were fighting well and, in fact, held those positions until dusk although there was some enemy infiltration on their left flank.' (PRO: WO 106/3146).

14 Squadron Leader William Cuddie (pilot) and Flying Officer Leonard Coote were killed when their Beaufighter XIC (JL907) reportedly flew into the explosion resulting from their attack; Warrant Officer E. Ledwidge (pilot) and Flight Sergeant J. T. Rowley, and Flight Sergeants C. Holmes (pilot) and W. Bell survived when JL903 and JM264 ditched due to battle damage. In the course of the day, other Beaufighters returned to base damaged and with wounded crew. The *Luftwaffe* acknowledged the loss of three *Stukas* during operations on 3 October: *Unteroffizier* Jordan Stifter (pilot) and *Gefreiter* Arthur Achenbach (wireless operator) died in Ju 87D-4 (1113/SU+FH) of *I./St.G.3*, while the crew of Ju 87D-3 (110288) of *II./St.G.3* survived as did a *I./St.G.3* crew when their Ju 87D-4 (1072/S7+LH) made an emergency landing on Syrna. Although the loss of all three aircraft was attributed to anti-aircraft fire, two were apparently victims of Beaufighters of 227 Squadron: Squadron Leader J. R. H. Lewis (pilot) and Flying Officer G. J. Matthews were credited with one *Stuka* shot down into the sea (possibly *Werknummer* 110288), and Flying Officer A. G. Deck (pilot) and Sergeant J. Templeton claimed another (probably 1072) which was reported to have crashed on Tilos.

15 War Diary of 1st Battalion The Durham Light Infantry: *Appendix 'A': Statement by CSM W. Carr 1 D.L.I. of D Coy (at Antimachia)*. PRO: WO 169/10202.

16 *Loss of H.M. L.C.T. 3 at Kos – 3rd October 1943*. PRO: ADM 199/1040.

17 Statement by Flying Officer B. W. Purcell. PRO: AIR 23/6743.

18 Letter to the author from Walter Lünsmann, 22 January 2001. The willingness of the British to surrender evidently surprised the former soldier, who added: 'I hope and wish that these men survived the war. To this day I am still

grateful to them. As I confronted them all on my own, they had a good opportunity to shoot me.'

19 Kenyon, op. cit.

20 Ibid.

21 *Generalleutnant* Friedrich-Wilhelm Müller, *Gefechtsbericht über die Einnahme der Insel Coo – Unternehmen 'Eisbär' [Combat Report on the taking of the island of Kos – Operation 'Polar Bear']*.

22 Report by Flight Sergeant R. S. Taylor. PRO: AIR 23/6742.

23 Ibid.

24 Deciphered Enigma signals. PRO: ADM 223/588.

CHAPTER 5 The War on Land: October 1943

1 Wing Commander R. C. Love, *Notes on Operations in the Aegean, September/October 1943*. PRO: AIR 23/6743.

2 The remainder of the party is believed to have been Sergeant Burridge, Lance Bombardier Thompson and Gunner Webb (all Royal Artillery), and Leading Aircraftmen Moreton, Prince, Terry, Nichols, Gargon, Edwards, Luke, Scott and Riley.

3 Report by Flight Sergeant R. S. Taylor. PRO: AIR 23/6742.

4 Ibid.

5 Peter Smith and Edwin Walker, Appendix 6, *War in the Aegean*.

6 Edited extracts from *Aegean Oct. 1943. An Impression*. PRO: WO 201/818.

7 Ibid.

8 Captain A. G. Redfern, *Operation Report No. 99*. IWM: LRDG 2/1.

9 *Appendix 'B' to Operation Report No. 103* [Long Range Desert Group]. IWM: LRDG 2/1.

10 Captain John Olivey, *Long Range Desert Group Story in the Dodecanese Islands, Fee, Fie, Foe, Fum*. IWM: 11/3.

11 *Brandenburg Division* report dated 23 October 1943. IWM: AL 2557/1.

12 Long Range Desert Group, Operations in Aegean. 11/9/43 to 30/11/43. IWM: LRDG 2/1.

13 Olivey, op. cit.

14 The prisoners, all of whom were presumably from *11. Luftwaffenfelddivision*, were *Jäger* Gerhard Lau, *Obergefreiter* Hans Riechoff and *Gefreiter* Franz Luboska.

15 Gunner J. Patch, *Report of attack on Levitha 23–24 Oct. 1943*. IWM: LRDG 5/2.

16 Ibid.

17 Trooper W. R. Hill, *The Levita Raid – October 23rd 1943*. IWM: LRDG 5/2.

18 Immediately after the battle, the Germans reported that four LRDG men had

been killed; German casualties were one killed, two wounded (one of whom may have died of his wounds) and two missing, 'presumably removed by English'. Subsequently, a number of those taken prisoner on Astipalaea and Levitha gave their captors the slip, among them Trooper Ronald Hill and Gunner Jim Patch. After breaking out of a moving train while en route through Yugoslavia, they joined Dragoljub Mihailović's Četnici and remained with them until September 1944, when they were recruited by the British Military Mission. They were evacuated from Yugoslavia three months before the war's end, in February 1945.

CHAPTER 6 The War at Sea: October 1943

1 *Operations in the Dodecanese Islands, September–November 1943*, p. 29. PRO: AIR 41/53.

2 PRO: FO 954/32.

3 On 14 October 1943, Vice Admiral Sir A. U. Willis, KCB, DSO superseded Admiral Sir J. H. D. Cunningham, KCB, MVO as Commander-in-Chief, Levant.

4 PRO: FO 954/32.

5 According to the *War Diary, German Naval Staff, Operations Division, Part A, Volume 50* (IWM: EDS 223), German air reconnaissance also reported seeing more than one submarine attacking the *Olympos* convoy.

6 *Oberleutnant zur See Schunack*, combat report dated 26 October 1943. It is uncertain whether the Royal Navy was under orders to finish off survivors of this particular convoy, but it is possible in view of the fact that the troops were assumed by the British to have been destined for an invasion of Leros.

7 The five *Marinefährprähme* lost with the *Olympos* convoy were F 308, F 327, F 336, F 494 and either F 523 or F 532. Although only one F-lighter is believed to have reached Astipalaea, a British cipher dated 8 October (Cositrep No. 18) indicates otherwise: 'After naval action, one enemy LC [landing craft] one small escort vessel both badly damaged arrived Stampalia [Astipalaea] and captured by GRN [garrison] with 80 prisoners.' (PRO: WO 106/3149). Another, LRDG, report records that 93 Germans were taken prisoner but makes no mention as to the number of craft captured.

8 Casualty figures from HMS *Penelope* Ship's Log (PRO: ADM 53/118344). According to Captain P. W. B. Brooking, commanding HMS *Sirius*, there were seven fatalities and sixteen wounded on *Penelope*. Bomb splinters from near misses seem to have also taken their toll, with two officers and eleven ratings killed and twenty-nine wounded on *Sirius* alone.

9 The *Luftwaffe* acknowledged the loss of two aircraft, both to anti-aircraft fire: *Unteroffizier* Siegfried Herrmann (pilot), *Gefreiter* Kurt Auer (observer),

Gefreiter Werner Persch (wireless operator) and *Gefreiter* Walter Flegel (air gunner) were posted missing when a Ju 88A-4 (888872/3E+KM) of *II./K.G.6* crashed in the sea north of Karpathos, while *Leutnant* Wolfgang Wendel (pilot) and *Feldwebel* Georg Scheller (wireless operator) were picked up injured after their Ju 87D-4 (2376/S7+OL) of *I./St.G.3* crashed south-west of Rhodes.

10 Flight Sergeants John Hey and Eric Worrall of 603 Squadron were reported missing after ditching their Beaufighter VIC (JL761) following an attack by *Oberleutnant* Alfred Burk of *11./J.G.27*.

11 By 9 October the Germans had picked up 1,027 survivors of the *Olympos* convoy, leaving 150 unaccounted for. Of these, eighty or more captured with *F 496* were subsequently freed from captivity on Levitha and Astipalaea. By 10 October, 302 of the 366 men on the *Bulgaria* had also been saved; others were picked up by British submarines, and four survivors were freed from captivity on Amorgos in November.

12 Major William L. Leverette, combat report.

13 L. F. S. Forster, '*The Admiralty regrets to announce the loss …*' (two-page account about the loss of HMS *Panther* dated 2 February 1977). IWM: 87/15/1.

14 Leverette, op. cit.

15 The *Luftwaffe* acknowledged the loss to fighter attack of no less than seven Ju 87D-3s of *II./St.G.3* south-west of Rhodes, with the crew of one machine (*Werknummer* 1007) having been picked up by German air-sea rescue. It was reported that the wireless operator in 110336/S7+MP, *Feldwebel* Rudolf Malina was injured while the pilot, *Leutnant* Heinz Spielmann, was killed. The remainder who died or were reported missing were *Leutnant* Rolf Metzger (pilot) and his wireless operator *Unteroffizier* Hans Sopnemann in 100375/S7+GM; *Hauptmann* Peter von Heydebrand (pilot) and *Oberfeldwebel* Herbert Bluschke in 110535/S7+AU; *Unteroffizier* Heinrich Manger (pilot) and *Obergefreiter* Erfried Primissl in 100380/S7+DN; *Unteroffizier* Josef Rose (pilot) and *Gefreiter* Franz Neumann in 110322/S7+FP; *Leutnant* Horst Skambreck (pilot) and *Unteroffizier* Georg Peters in 100374/S7+KP. *Oberfeldwebel* Hans Birkner (pilot) also perished when his Ju 87D-3 (100378) was damaged and had to make an emergency landing at Rhodes. *Einsatzkampfgruppe Ju 88/General der Flieger Ausbildung* lost one Ju 88A-4 (*Werknummer* 4579) south-west of Kos due to engine trouble (the crew was rescued) and another (8830/K5+JL) disappeared somewhere in the Adriatic together with the pilot and *Staffelkapitän*, *Hauptmann* Helmut Schüler and *Oberfeldwebel* Ullrich Thomas (observer), *Gefreiter* Josef Gruber (wireless operator) and *Oberfeldwebel* Fritz Czech (air gunner). AA gunners apparently accounted for Ju 87D-4 110461/S7+AK of *I./St.G.3*, together with

Unteroffizier Siegfried Martens (pilot) and *Oberfeldwebel* Ernst Kröger, who were reported missing east-west of Karpathos. *Leutnant* Otto Hecht (pilot) and his wireless operator, *Unteroffizier* Hans Krajacic, of *II./Schl.G.3* were also reported to have been wounded as a result of fighter attack south of Rhodes.

16 When the *Sinfra* was torpedoed, the order went out: 'Send rescue vessels ... Rescue the Germans first.' By the end of the day, 566 survivors, including 163 Germans, had been saved. In the process, Allied aircraft destroyed one Dornier Do 24T-3 rescue plane (probably *Werknummer* 3214 of 7. *Seenotstaffel*; the air gunner, *Unteroffizier* Mathias Schneider and the flight engineer, *Obergefreiter* Heinrich Seilkopf were injured).

17 In spite of rough seas and notwithstanding the loss during take-off of a rescue Do 24, by 18 October, 320 survivors from the *Kari* had been saved.

18 By 2 November 1943, 306 of *Ingeborg*'s 408 crew had been rescued. Another thirteen survivors were later freed from captivity on Amorgos.

19 Edited extract from Commander J. N. Toumbas, *Report of Proceedings in HHMS Adrias, 21/23rd October 1943*. PRO: ADM 199/1040.

20 Commander R. H. Wright, *Loss of His Majesty's Ship Hurworth*. PRO: ADM 199/1040.

21 Toumbas, op. cit.

22 Ibid.

23 *Report of Proceedings of Lieutenant H. C. A. Middleton, RN, subsequent to the mining of HMS Hurworth*. PRO: ADM 199/1040.

24 Wright, op. cit. According to the War History of the Royal Navy (PRO: ADM 199/1044), by 25 October, eighty-five crew, including Commander Wright, had been rescued.

25 4th Battalion The Royal East Kent Regiment (The Buffs) had served in Malta from November 1940 until its departure to Egypt in September 1943. Instead of being redeployed as expected for the Italian campaign, the battalion was ordered in October to proceed to Leros.

26 *HMS Eclipse and HMS Petard's Report of Proceedings, 22nd–26th October 1943*. PRO: ADM 199/1040. According to the War History of the Royal Navy, by 25 October, 136 of those on board HMS *Eclipse* had been rescued. The War Diary of 4 Buffs (PRO: WO 169/10185) records that 135 all ranks from the 187 who embarked were still missing on this date.

27 *The wartime experiences of Mr Lukehurst of The Royal East Kent Regiment 1940–1946, Malta Leros Stalag IVB*. IWM: 96/41/1.

28 Peter Wood, *One Man's War* (unpublished manuscript). IWM: 94/43/1.

29 Lukehurst, op. cit.

30 Ibid.

CHAPTER 7 **Leros: Prelude to Battle**

1   Frank Smith, recorded memoirs sent to the author on 4 March 2001.

2   Commander C. A. de W. Kitcat, *Report of Proceedings* dated 5 October, 1943. PRO: ADM 199/1040. At least seventy perished on *Vasilissa Olga*.

3   G. W. Searle, *At Sea Level*, pp.128–9.

4   Athanasios Paraponiaris via Ioannis Paraponiaris. The German bomber seen to be hit by anti-aircraft fire may have been a Ju 88A-4 (885875/3E+GM) of *II./K.G.*6 which was lost over Lakki with its crew: *Unteroffizier* Radunz (pilot), *Unteroffizier* Breuer (observer), *Gefreiter* Tillwicks (wireless operator) and *Unteroffizier* Stutz (air gunner).

5   Ibid.

6   Major G. J. Ryan, unpublished manuscript. Further testimony of the volatile nature of Brittorous is provided by Bob Earle in a letter to the author dated September 2000:

   'It was my misfortune to be posted from The Buffs to 234 Brigade HQ as the Motor Transport Sergeant. This was unfortunate in as much as the Brigade Commander, Brigadier Brittorous, was much hated for his violent manner and terrifying and unpredictable behaviour.

   The first morning of my duties at Brigade HQ, I bent down to polish my shoes at my billet doorstep, a stone hut with a corrugated iron door, when there was a violent bang just above my head and a stone the size of a house brick dropped on my foot. Behind me a voice was screaming, 'You didn't salute me.' 'The Hun will get you', etc, etc. That was my introduction to the Brigadier.'

7   Ibid.

8   Ibid. Two British and five Italian submarines delivered to Leros up to 325½ tons of cargo. In addition, on 22 October, six Bofors guns arrived on HMS/M *Severn* with the barrels and working parts stowed inside the hull and the gun mountings lashed to her outer casing. She was followed by HMS/M *Rorqual* carrying six more guns and a jeep.

9   Captain John Olivey, *Long Range Desert Group Story in the Dodecanese Islands, Fee, Fie, Foe, Fum.* IWM: 11/3.

10   Ryan, op. cit.

11   Major J. M. McSwiney DSO MC, *The Aegean Dodecanese Venture* (unpublished manuscript).

12   Ryan, op. cit.

13   Royal Navy War Diary. PRO:ADM 199/2281.

14   Edward B. W. Johnson, *Island Prize, Leros, 1943*, p. 36.

15   1st Battalion The King's Own Royal Regiment was actually a composite unit

comprising the remnants of 1st Battalion The South Wales Borderers, 1st Battalion The Duke of Cornwall's Light Infantry and 1 King's Own; all of which had suffered heavy casualties, mainly during the fighting in North Africa.

16 According to a report by the War Office dated 23 November 1943, British (including imperial and colonial) troops on Leros would eventually total 3,282 all ranks comprising: 2,468 infantry, 244 (anti-aircraft and field) artillery, 65 (Indian) engineers, 135 Long Range Desert Group and 64 Special Boat Squadron personnel and 306 officers and men from other units. This was in addition to a headquarters staff of one Royal Air Force and 12 Royal Navy officers (PRO: WO 365/49).

17 According to Italian sources (see Appendix C) there were on Leros twenty-five batteries with 103 guns ranging in calibre from 76mm to 152mm, not all of which were effective on 12 November 1943.

18 Brigadier R. A. G. Tilney, DSO, *The Battle of Leros, 12–16 November 1943*. PRO: WO 32/12271.

19 Ibid.

20 Johnson, op. cit., p. 41.

21 Tilney, op. cit.

22 The Henschel Hs 293 glider bomb was a remote-controlled anti-shipping missile with a 500-kilogram warhead. That which hit HMS *Rockwood* was launched from a Dornier Do 217 of *12./K.G.100*.

23 Decoded German ciphers. PRO: ADM 223/589.

CHAPTER 8 **Operation '*Taifun*': Day 1: Friday, 12 November 1943**

1 The sometimes conflicting information in available reports fails to provide a satisfactory explanation as to why the British failed to react to preliminary sightings of the German invasion fleet. In the Admiralty publication, *Aegean Operations – 7th September to 28th November, 1943. British occupation and German re-capture of KOS and LEROS*, it states on p. 24: 'These [sightings] were, in fact, the invading barges, though this was not appreciated by Captain (D), 8th Destroyer Flotilla, nor, until later, in the Commander-in-Chief's Operations Room.' Yet, according to the Admiralty's, *HMS Faulknor – Report of Proceedings 8th to 15th November, 1943* (PRO: ADM 199/1040): 'It had always been expected that the enemy would launch his assault in daylight from the cover of the minefields at the northern end of Kalymnos. Captain (D), Eighth Destroyer Flotilla appreciated that the forces now reported were moving up to these bays and that he would be unable to interfere with them on account of the minefield. Due to an erroneous appreciation in the Commander-

in-Chief's Operations Room it was not believed that these might in fact be the assaulting forces until it was too late to order Captain (D), Eighth Destroyer Flotilla to intercept.' Curiously, in his own *Report of Proceedings* (PRO: ADM 199/1040) for the same period, Captain (D), Eighth Destroyer Flotilla (Captain M. S. Thomas) makes no mention whatsoever of the enemy sightings.

2 *Report of Proceedings of HMML 456 from 3rd to 26th November 1943.* PRO: ADM 199/1040.

3 *Capture of BYMS 72, Interrogation of survivors.* PRO: ADM 199/1040.

4 Report by *Oberleutnant zur See* Hansjürgen Weissenborn from the war diary of *12 R-. Flottille.*

5 *Generalleutnant* Friedrich-Wilhelm Müller, *Gefechtsbericht über die Eroberung der Dodekanes-Insel Lero (Unternehmen 'Taifun') [Combat Report on the conquest of the Dodecanese island of Leros (Operation 'Taifun').]*

6 *Report of Proceedings of HMML 456 from 3rd to 26th November 1943.* By 15 November ML 456 had completed temporary repairs and joined MLs 299, 461 and HDML 1004 at Samos.

7 Ibid.

8 Combat report by *Leutnant zur See* von Zatorski, who added: 'According to a *Pionieroffizier* who landed in his *Pi-La-Boot* near Alinda Bay, his group found a heavily damaged English gunboat lying in a bay. It was destroyed by the *Pi-La-Boot* without any resistance. According to prisoners, the boat had been attacked at sea by a small German unit and was badly damaged. It could reach the bay only with maximum effort …' The flotilla commander, *Oberleutnant zur See* Hansjürgen Weissenborn commented: 'The attack was carried out with courage and planning. The heavily damaged boat could have been destroyed completely with a second attack. However, as the main objective was the landing of troops on Leros, the commandant's actions were correct. Request acknowledgement of the destruction of the English gun-boat for *R 195*.' Another, unsubstantiated, account maintains that ML 358 sank at Lakki where at least three of the crew reached shore: one man was seriously wounded and subsequently died in captivity; the others survived as prisoners of war.

9 Müller, op. cit.

10 The consensus of the British on Leros is that the Italians contributed little or nothing during the battle. The Germans were equally harsh in their assessment of the fighting abilities of their erstwhile allies. Significantly, when British veterans organised a reunion in Leros in 1988, they invited their former opponents to attend but refused to allow any Italian participation.

11 Captain John Olivey, MC and Bar, *Long Range Desert Group Story in the Dodecanese Islands, Fee, Fie, Foe, Fum.* IWM: LRDG 11/3.

12 Ibid.

13 Gustav Wehrs, unpublished manuscript. The pack mule referred to was one of several being transported on what was actually a *Pi-La-Boot*. All of the mules were killed during the approach.

14 Edward B. Johnson, MC, *Island Prize, Leros, 1943*, p. 47.

15 Account by Eric Ransley, 14 January 2001.

16 Wehrs, op. cit.

17 Account by Eric Ransley, November 2001.

18 Wehrs, op. cit.

19 Olivey, op. cit. 'Major M' is named as 'Major Millar, OC, the King's Own' in Olivey's official after-action report, dated 1 June 1944 (see also note 33).

20 Ibid.

21 Ibid.

22 Ibid.

23 Second Lieutenant R. F. White, *Report on operations on LEROS*. IWM: LRDG 3/1.

24 Walter Keller, memoirs.

25 Olivey, op. cit. By all accounts, the *Fallschirmjäger* deployment came as a complete surprise to the Leros defenders. Yet, British intelligence had known for at least a week of the presence in Athens of German paratroopers. It was surmised: 'Although Leros topographically difficult for mass landing parachute troops it is possible that limited number might be employed to neutralise key positions such as guns and beach defences ...' (PRO: ADM 223/589). One wonders why those on the ground in Leros were not also informed.

26 *Unteroffizier* Fritz Näpflein (wireless operator) was the sole survivor of a Ju 52 (6763) of *I./T.G.4*; those who died were *Leutnant* Helmut Günther (pilot), *Feldwebel* Hans Mahr (observer), and *Leutnant* Werner Bockelmann (air gunner). Also lost over Leros on this date were an Arado 196 of *Seeaufkl.Gr.126*, whose crew was rescued unharmed, and two Ju 88C-6s of *11./Z.G.26*: *Leutnant* Hans Sukowski (pilot), *Unteroffizier* Karl Ustrabrowski (observer) and *Obergefreiter* Günther Holstein (wireless operator) were reported missing in 750453/3U+PV; *Obergefreiter* Winfried Kröll (observer) was killed and *Unteroffizier* Gregor Merva (pilot) was reported missing with *Unteroffizier* Joachim Lieb (wireless operator) in 750908/3U+JV. *Leutnant* Jürgen Wellmann (pilot) and *Unteroffizier* Richard Köhlmann (wireless operator) of *I./Schl.G.3* were killed when their Ju 87D-3 (110594) was shot down by AA fire south of Antimachia, Kos, and Ju 87D-4 110598/S7+CH of the same unit was written off after an emergency landing on Paros.

27 Leonard Marsland Gander, *Long Road to Leros*, p. 187.

28 Major J. M. McSwiney, DSO, MC, memoirs (IWM: 97/36/1), pp. 139–40.

29 Major a. D. Martin Kühne, *Sprungeinsatz auf Leros [Parachute mission on Leros]*, *Der Deutsche Fallschirmjäger*, March–April 1984.

30 Sergeant Daniel P. O'Connell was a cousin of Sergeant Daniel J. O'Connell, who was mortally wounded on Appetici on 12 November. The cousins joined the Army together, sharing consecutive service numbers (6979443 and 6979444). Sergeant D. P. O'Connell was killed on the last day of the battle.

31 Brigadier Robert Tilney, DSO, *The Battle of Leros, 12–16 November 1943*. PRO: WO 32/12271.

32 Gander, op. cit., p. 188.

33 Olivey, op. cit. In describing this particular episode in his after-action report, Olivey identifies 'Major M' as 'Major Martin'. Both Major Millar (see note 19) and Major Martin appear to be one and the same officer, almost certainly Major W. P. T. Tilley.

34 Ibid.

35 Ibid. The 'fort' was a two-storey pillbox on top of Point 320 with the lower level housing an underground control room.

36 Ibid.

37 IWM: LRDG 2/3.

38 Tilney, op. cit.

39 9 Platoon of the Faughs under Second Lieutenant R. J. Hillman was sent to help defend Pandeli Castle, but this was almost certainly prior to the morning attack by 'C' Company.

40 Johnson, op. cit., p. 51.

41 Clifford A. L. Clark, *Leros – From Invasion to Surrender*, published in *The Echo*, September 1997.

42 Clifford Clark kept note of events throughout the battle. He assured the author that he is 'absolutely certain' about the times recorded.

43 Diary of Ted Johnson.

44 New Zealander, Flying Officer Athol Greentree (pilot) and Sergeant George Freeman of 47 Squadron were reported missing in Beaufighter X LX912.

CHAPTER 9 **Day 2: Saturday, 13 November 1943**

1   As many as six officers and 114 ratings may have been recovered by HM ships *Echo* and *Belvoir*. Subsequently, at least two more survivors were picked up by the German minesweeper *R 210*.

2   Walter Keller interviewed by Sonja Stammwitz, 27 December 2001.

3 Leonard Marsland Gander, *Long Road to Leros*, p. 192.

4 Letter to the author from Andreas Hutter, dated 3 February 2001.

5 Gander, op. cit., p. 192. According to the *Luftwaffe*, just one Arado float-plane appears to have been lost (on 12 November).

6 Edward B. W. Johnson, MC, *Island Prize, Leros, 1943*, p. 55.

7 Letter to the author from Walter Pancott, dated 28 August 2000.

8 *II./Lw.-Jägerregiment 22, Gefechtsbericht über den Einsatz auf Leros [II./Lw— Jägerregiment 22 combat report on the operation in Leros]* dated 22 November 1943.

9 Letters to the author from Geoffrey R. Hart, June–July 2001. It is not clear who held Quirico at this time. Possibly, the feature was defended by paratroopers who had earlier landed in the area.

10 Both sides were provided with 1:25,000 maps which were derived from those used by the Italians. German commanders were also provided with a 1:20,000 aerial photo-montage marked with targets and other key points. British maps were noticeably inferior to those of the enemy, and in any case were rarely issued at platoon level.

11 Brigadier R. A. G. Tilney, *Report of Operations on Leros, 12–16 November, 1943*.

12 R. A. Ardill, account written for Ted Johnson in 1989. Austin Ardill's recollections are controversial in that it is generally accepted that Lieutenant Colonel French planned and led the counter-attack on Appetici. In a conversation with the author on 25 June 2001, Ardill reaffirmed his story, stating that French told him: 'You will lead the attack, but I'll go with you.' After discussing the matter at length with Ardill, it seems likely that he was entrusted with taking charge of the leading company, while French retained overall command of the operation.

13 *Statement by Second Lieutenant Pavilides, LRDG on operations in Leros 10–16 November 43*. IWM: LRDG 2/1.

14 Another theory attributes the reports of a major German attack on Meraviglia to misinformation spread by enemy troops in British or Italian uniforms. Although it has never been proved that the Germans used such tactics on Leros it is interesting to note that on 30 October 1943, *Admiral Ägäis* received the following signal (from a source named only as Löhrl): 'Have arrived in Syra with all vessels ... Request permission to seize Italian uniforms for Brandenburg for purpose of disguise.' Of more significance, perhaps, is a signal emanating from Meraviglia at 1840 hours on 13 November: 'Many Germans in Italian uniform. You can tell them by their alpine boots.' Colonel B. Tarleton, in *The 2nd Battalion The Royal*

West Kent Regiment on the Island of Leros, November 1943 (IWM: LRDG
11/5) also records that towards the end of the battle, 'It is possible ... that there were
German snipers wearing Italian uniforms, and several suspected cases were
reported by NCOs of the unit.' German veterans, including Hans Schädlich, commander of *Kampfgruppe* Schädlich, were unable to substantiate the reports.

15 *War Diary of the German Naval Staff, Operations Division, Part A, Volume
    51.* IWM: EDS 144.

16 At 0955 hours on 13 November 1943, *Leutnant* Emil Clade of 7./J.G.27 shot
    down Beaufighter X LZ127 of 47 Squadron north of Levitha; American, Flying
    Officer Edgar Clary (pilot) and Flight Sergeant Walter Finbow were killed. At
    1042, during an earlier operation, Warrant Officers Frank Cox (pilot) and N.
    S. Ferguson, two Australians in 603 Squadron, were reported missing when
    Beaufighter X LX977 ditched with engine trouble. In the afternoon, Beau-
    fighter X LX928 also ditched after being hit by return fire while engaging
    bombers over or near Leros; Squadron Leader S. R. Muller-Rowland (pilot)
    and Pilot Officer J. D. Anderson, who had only just arrived with other rein-
    forcements for 47 Squadron from Number 5 Middle East Training School at
    Shallufa, were rescued by a Greek fishing boat and later returned to their unit.

CHAPTER 10 **Day 3: Sunday, 14 November 1943**

1   R. A. Ardill, account written for Ted Johnson in 1989. Ardill's description of the
    death of Lieutenant Colonel French differs from that provided just after the battle
    by Captain Michael Rochford, one of only two officers of the Royal Irish Fusiliers
    to escape from Leros. On 21 December 1943, he wrote in a letter to French's
    widow: 'On the second day of the battle, he [Lieutenant Colonel French] was
    leading a counter attack on an enemy occupied hill. The attack was carried out by
    three companies of the King's Own – the only other members of the Regiment
    present were Lieut Ardhill [sic] and Fus Hardy (Col French's runner) ... I spoke to
    his runner in the morning – he told me that Col French and the King's Own had
    reached the top of the mountain, but had been held up by heavy machine gun
    fire from the front. Your husband armed with his pistol at once rushed forward to
    attack the machine gun nest. He was killed immediately by machine gun fire.
    After this, the Germans drove us back and your husband's body was left on the bat-
    tlefield. I understand that he was afterwards buried in a little Greek churchyard.'

2   Letter to Mrs Diana French, widow of Lieutenant Colonel French, from
    Brigadier Robert Tilney.

3   Letter to Mrs Diana French from Captain H. Dougall. The regimental
    motto, *'Faugh a Ballagh'* ('Clear the Way!') is an anglicised form of Gaelic

whence derives the nickname of The Royal Irish Fusiliers: the Faughs.

4   Captain John Olivey, MC and Bar, *Long Range Desert Group Story in the Dodecanese Islands, Fee, Fie, Foe, Fum* (IWM: LRDG 11/3). In his after-action report, Olivey names those involved in clearing the cave as Corporal Coventry, Gunner Rupping and Rifleman van Heerden. As many as seventeen Germans may have been taken prisoner.

5   Ibid.

6   According to former Private A. Goodman, batman to Major V. G. Bourne, seventy-three Germans were taken prisoner.

7   Account by Major V. G. Bourne sent to the author in November 2001. A PIAT (Projectile Infantry Anti-Tank) was a shoulder-fired anti-tank weapon.

8   Clifford A. L. Clark, *Leros – From Invasion to Surrender*, published in *The Echo*, September 1997. These events are recorded by Clark as having taken place soon after midday on 13 November 1943, on orders relayed via Lieutenant Colonel French. Other reports fail to mention such an attack on this date. Significantly, in his *Report on operations on Leros* (IWM: LRDG 3/1), Second Lieutenant R. F. White recorded at 1025 hours on the 14th: 'From HQ. GERMANS retreating in disorder North from RADIC [sic] RIDGE. We could observe our infantry doing a counter attack behind a smoke screen down the spur running North from WINDMILL 083405 [San Giovanni] no mention of this action in any SITREP …' This clearly refers to the move by 'B' Company of the Royal West Kents, who linked up with 'D' Company of the Buffs later the same day.

9   Diary of Ted Johnson.

10 Letter to the author from Vic Kenchington, 16 January 2001.

11 Johnson, op. cit.

12 Clark, op. cit.

13 Letter to the author from Vic Kenchington, 16 January 2001.

14 Brigadier Robert Tilney, DSO, *The Battle of Leros, 12–16 November 1943*. PRO: WO 32/12271.

15 Letter to the author from V. G. Bourne, 15 January 2002. Commenting further, Bourne admitted: 'I confess I thought we had lost 'C' Company. The fire was very intense and much more frightening than anything else in the whole battle.'

16 Two 46 Squadron crews, Flight Lieutenant D. J. A. Crerar (pilot) and Pilot Officer L. Charles, and Flying Officer B. F. Wild (pilot) and Flight Sergeant R. Gibbons, shared in the destruction of Heinkel He 111H 8011/6N+EP of *II./K.G. 100* which was shot down north of Leros with the loss of the air-gunner, *Gefreiter* Helmut Grundke. In turn, two Beaufighter XICs of 46 Squadron were lost together with their crews: Warrant Officer Ronald Lindsey (pilot) and Flight

Sergeant Alfred Gardener in JL894, and Canadian, Flight Lieutenant John Horsfall (pilot) and Flight Sergeant James Colley in JM248. Two Messerschmitt Bf 109 pilots were each credited with shooting down a Beaufighter: the claim by *Major* Ernst Düllberg (*Stab III./J.G.27*) was timed at 1435 north-east of Leros, and that of *Oberfähnrich* Alexander Ottnad (*8./J.G.27*) at 1436 north-east of Agathonisi. *Unteroffizier* Herwarth Mandelkow (wireless operator) and *Unteroffizier* Kurt Hanuschek (flight engineer) of *II./T.G.2* were killed when their Junkers Ju 52 (7607) was shot down by AA fire. A Ju 52 (4046) of the same unit was badly damaged by AA fire and the wireless operator, *Gefreiter* Urban Pfeifer, killed. Three Hurricanes of 94 Squadron and four of 336 (Hellenic) Squadron also failed to return from strafing attacks over Crete. A Ju with human remains still in the cabin was recovered from Alinda Bay on 3 October 2003 and identified as *Werknummer* 7607.

17 The commander of 'A' Company was, in fact, Captain Derek Thirkell-White of the Suffolk Regiment; Captain Cecil Blyth was second-in-command. Neither survived the attack on Appetici. The party reported by Lieutenant White is thought to have included at least one other officer. It is not known whether these men were among the seventy or so accounted for after the attack.

CHAPTER 11 Day 4: Monday, 15 November 1943

1 The precise number of troops transported by HM ships *Echo* and *Belvoir* varies according to reports from 350 to 377 officers and men. According to Captain C. M. Bernard and Captain R. A. James (*The 2nd Battalion The Royal West Kent Regiment on the Island of Samos, September–November 1943*), 'A' Company embarked on a minesweeper [MMS 103] at 2100 hours on 13 November and after laying up in Turkish waters during daylight hours arrived at Leros at about 2300 on the 14th; Battalion Headquarters, the Signal Platoon, RAP and 'C' Company embarked on HMS *Echo* on Sunday night (14th) and reached Leros in the early morning hours; Major Shaw (second-in-command) with 'D' Company, the AA Platoon, the Mortar Platoon and the remainder of HQ Company embarked on another destroyer [*Belvoir*] and proceeded to Turkish waters where, on the 15th, 'D' Company was taken on board a minesweeper [MMS 103] and Major Shaw and the remaining troops transhipped to five torpedo boats [thought to have included MTBs 266, 315 and the repaired 307 plus a motor launch, HDML 1004] for the final leg to Leros; the small craft arriving at 2200 that night and the minesweeper about two hours later.

2 Lieutenant Commander C. P. Evensen, RNVR, *Senior Officer 10th MTB Flotilla. Report of Proceedings, 4–18/11/43*. PRO: ADM 199/1040.

3   Ibid.

4   Leonard Marsland Gander, *Long Road to Leros*, pp. 208–9.

5   Letter to the author from Hans-Walter Lünsmann, April 2001.

6   Raiding Forces Aegean was formed on 15 October 1943 in order to control LRDG and SBS operations in the Aegean. Colonel G. L. Prendergast was promoted as OC five days later, whereupon Lieutenant Colonel Jake Easonsmith assumed command of the LRDG.

7   Lieutenant Colonel Robert Butler, MBE, MC, *Nine Lives, Through Laughing Eyes*, p. 120.

8   Brigadier Robert Tilney, DSO, *The Battle of Leros, 12–16 November 1943*. PRO: WO 32/12271.

9   Edward B. W. Johnson, MC, *Island Prize, Leros, 1943*, p. 66–7.

10 Butler, op. cit., p. 125.

11 C. W. M. Ritchie, from his account written while in captivity.

12 Colonel B. Tarleton, *The 2nd Battalion The Royal West Kent Regiment on the Island of Leros, November 1943*. IWM: LRDG 11/5.

13 Some of the supply aircraft may also have been Halifaxes or Liberators of 178 Squadron which was by this time operating with the overworked Dakotas of 216 Squadron.

14 Lieutenant Commander Ramseyer, RNVR, *Report of Proceedings during and after invasion of Leros – 12th November to 4th December, 1943*. The prisoners brought in by the Italians were survivors from *Pi-La-Boot 'H'* lost on the first day of the battle near the islet of Strongilo.

15 Butler, op. cit., p. 128.

16 According to *Luftwaffe* records, a wireless operator in *Stab/Schl.G.3*, *Gefreiter* Günther Härtner, was wounded and his Ju 87D-3 (*Werknummer* 110592) written off in an emergency landing at Athens-Kalamaki after being damaged by a fighter. The unit responsible has not been identified.

CHAPTER 12 Day 5: Tuesday, 16 November 1943

1   In describing events during the last day of the battle, Colonel Tarleton is consistent in identifying 2 Platoon as that which fought under the command of Captain Rickcord. Generally, however, 2 Platoon was the designation of the Mortar Platoon (commanded in this instance by Lieutenant D. A. Cruickshank). It would appear that Rickcord, who was 2 i/c of Headquarters Company, actually led the Anti-Aircraft Platoon. This was created with surplus NCOs and men from the Carrier and Anti-Tank Platoons who were formed into four Bren gun sections. They had attained a high standard of efficiency

and physical fitness after being deployed on foot in Samos as a mobile covering force under Company Sergeant Major Dunton.

2   C. W. M. Ritchie, from his account written while in captivity.

3   Ibid.

4   Colonel B. Tarleton, *The 2nd Battalion The Royal West Kent Regiment on the Island of Leros, November 1943.* IWM: LRDG 11/5.

5   The 'famous picture' referred to purportedly shows the death of a Loyalist soldier in the Spanish Civil War: actually a staged image taken in 1936 by Robert Capa.

6   *Report by Colonel G. L. Prendergast DSO on his escape from Leros.* IWM: LRDG 5/3.

7   Lieutenant P. A. Mold, *The story of my adventures following the capitulation of Leros island, Aegean.* IWM: LRDG 5/4.

8   Tarleton, op. cit.

9   Mold, op. cit.

10 Prendergast, op. cit.

11 Ritchie, op. cit. For his actions on 16 November, Lieutenant Alan Phipps was recommended for a decoration by Lieutenant Commander L. F. Ramseyer. He was considered for an award of the Victoria Cross but due to a lack of eyewitnesses eventually received a Posthumous Mention in Despatches. Six months too late, the Admiralty was sent a letter outlining events by Lieutenant E. B. Horton. This was followed by another, more detailed, report in August 1945 (see Appendices H and I).

12 Gino Manicone, *I Martiri dell'Egeo, L'Amaro volto di una tragedia Italiana*, p. 104.

13 Ibid, p. 105. *Capitano* Cacciatori impressed everyone with his courage, as testified by Naval Lieutenant Austin Crowder: 'One officer in particular was declared by all who fought alongside him an exceptionally brave man. He was the Captain in Command of Meraviglia battery and fought alongside the British. When his ammunition had gone, he started hurling rocks. A number of British Senior Army Officers said his conduct was exceptional.' (PRO: AIR 20/5465). Even Brigadier Tilney, a man who was not lavish in his praise, acknowledged 'the greatest gallantry' displayed by Cacciatori during the defence of Meraviglia.

14 Ritchie, op. cit.

15 Ibid.

16 Edward B. W. Johnson, MC, *Island Prize, Leros, 1943*, pp. 69–70.

17 Ibid, pp. 70–1.

18 IWM: LRDG 2/3.

19 Ritchie, op. cit.

20 Walter Keller interviewed by Sonja Stammwitz, 27 December 2001. Dumdum (named after the town and military establishment near Calcutta) is used to define a soft-nosed bullet that expands on impact. An improvised dumdum can be made by filing down the copper tip of a standard round to expose the soft lead core. Such a projectile generally causes a small entry wound and a large exit wound, as described by Keller. A bullet that breaks up inside the body can cause similar injuries.

21 Walter Keller, unpublished manuscript.

22 Lieutenant Commander Ramseyer, RNVR, *Report of Proceedings during and after invasion of Leros – 12th November to 4th December, 1943.*

23 Ibid.

24 Clifford A. L. Clark, *Leros – From Invasion to Surrender*, published in *The Echo*, September 1997. Of the listed fatalities, only Lieutenant Victor Hewett was killed. Lieutenant John Browne was wounded but escaped from hospital and subsequently reached Cairo (see chapter 13).

25 Manicone, op. cit., p. 105.

26 Lieutenant E. A. I. Crowder, RNR, *Report on Proceedings at Leros during and after the Battle*. PRO: AIR 20/5465.

27 Brigadier R. A. G. Tilney, *Report of Operations on Leros, 12-16 November, 1943.*

28 Crowder, op. cit.

29 The Rt. Hon. The Earl Jellicoe KBE, DSO, MC, FRS interviewed on 13 March 2001.

30 On 16 November 1943, the *Luftwaffe* acknowledged the loss of a Ju 88A-4 (800632/9K+CN) of *II./K.G.51* together with its crew: *Leutnant* Martin Franke (pilot), *Oberfeldwebel* Willi Wagner (observer), *Unteroffizier* Willi Steffens (wireless operator) and *Unteroffizier* Fritz Leinweber (wireless operator). At least three Beaufighter Xs of 47 Squadron were shot down: LZ125 with Flying Officer William Thwaites and Flying Officer John Lovell, LX904 with Flying Officer John Fletcher and Sergeant Jack Dale, and LX883 with Flying Officer Anthony Bond. Bond's navigator, Sergeant Alfred Cottle, survived. The victors were *Major* Ernst Düllberg (*Stab III./J.G.27*), *Leutnant* Emil Clade (*7./J.G.27*) and *Oberfähnrich* Alexander Ottnad (*8./J.G.27*).

31 *HMS PENN. Report of Proceedings, 12–19/11/1943*. PRO: 199/1040.

32 Lieutenant Commander C. P. Evensen, RNVR, *Senior Officer 10th MTB Flotilla. Report of Proceedings, 4–18/11/43*. PRO: ADM 199/1040.

CHAPTER 13 **Escape**

1   Before Leros fell, the LRDG were provided with five escape RVs. These were Pega Island (off the south-east coast); Porto Cassio; an inlet 1,000 yards east of Angistro Point; the islet of Scrofe, and just offshore east of Assachi Point.

2   Lieutenant P. A. Mold, *The story of my adventures following the capitulation of Leros island, Aegean.* IWM: LRDG 5/4.

3   *Report by Colonel G. L. Prendergast DSO on his escape from Leros.*

4   Mold, op. cit.

5   Prendergast, op. cit.

6   Major J. M. McSwiney, DSO, MC, memoirs (IWM: 97/36/1), p. 143.

7   Clifford A. L. Clark, *Leros – From Invasion to Surrender*, published in *The Echo*, March 1998.

8   Ibid.

9   Colonel B. Tarleton, *The 2nd Battalion The Royal West Kent Regiment on the Island of Leros, November 1943.*

10 Ibid.

11 Mold, op. cit.

12 Additional report by Captain John Richard Olivey, MC, LRDG attached to his *Report on Operations in Leros*, dated 1 June 1944. IWM: LRDG 3/1. In his unofficial account written for his wife, Olivey implies that he shot only one of the two Germans, adding, 'I ... realised that I had more or less committed murder or, at least, that is what I felt at the time.' The charges he prepared may be connected with a mysterious explosion in March 1944 which left a huge crater at the site of what was presumably the main magazine.

13 McSwiney, op. cit., p. 145.

14 Prendergast, op. cit.

15 Captain John Olivey, *Long Range Desert Group in the Dodecanese Islands, Fee, Fie, Foe, Fum.* IWM: 11/3.

16 Letters to the author from Geoffrey R. Hart, June–July 2001.

17 After deducting the number of killed and the 236 escapees reported up to 17 November from the 3,282 British Empire personnel stated by the War Office to have been on Leros at the time of capitulation, one is left with less than 2,900 who became prisoners of war.

CHAPTER 14 **Aftermath**

1   The Greek Sacred Squadron (motto: 'Victory or Death') is raised only in times of national emergency. The original squadron was wiped out resisting the Spartans at Thebes in 370 BC; the second was annihilated fighting for the freedom of

Greece against the Turks in 1821, and the third was formed in September 1942 under the command of *Sintagmatarhis* Christodoulos Tsigantes with approximately 120 officers of the Greek Army who had escaped after the invasion of their homeland. In October 1943, the unit was reinforced with 230 private soldiers and non-commissioned officers. It would eventually number 1,100 officers and men. In September 1943, the Chiefs of Staff had revised their ruling concerning the use of Greek forces in island operations and General H. M. Wilson decided to dispatch a Greek force to Samos. Owing to the restricted availability of shipping, an airborne operation was undertaken by 216 Group and during the nights of 31 October – 1 November and 1–2 November some 200 personnel of the Greek Sacred Squadron were parachuted on to Samos. Many of the soldiers were middle-aged, with little experience of flying and none of parachuting. Nevertheless, the drops were successful, marred only by the loss of a Dakota due to navigational error; the crew, who baled out over Turkey, survived.

2   Uwe Wilhelm Walther, *Die guet Brandenburg alle Wege*, (number 83/Christmas 1996), p. 52.

3   Letter to the author from Uwe Wilhelm Walther, 6 April 2001.

4   As related to Sonja Stammwitz, 10 March 2002.

5   Diary of Haat Haacke.

6   PRO: DO 35/1695.

7   PRO: WO 32/11430.

8   *War Diary of the German Naval Staff, Operations Division, Part A, Volume 51*, pp. 278–9.

9   *Chiefs of Staff Committee's Note on Operations in the Aegean.* PRO: WO 106/3147.

Select Bibliography

Benyon-Tinker, W. E., *Dust upon the Sea*, Hodder & Stoughton, London, 1947.

Bevan, Pauline, *Travels with a Leros Veteran*, Pauline Bevan, 2000.

Brandt, Günther, *Der Seekrieg in der Ägäis*, Günther Brandt, 1963.

Browne, John, *Recollections of Island Warfare*, John Browne.

Butler, Lieutenant Colonel Robert, MBE, MC, *Nine Lives, Through Laughing Eyes*, Invicta Publishing, 1993.

Chaplin, Lieutenant Colonel H. D., *The Queen's Own Royal West Kent Regiment 1920–1950*, Michael Joseph, London, 1954.

Churchill, Winston S., *The Second World War, Volume V, Closing the Ring*, Cassell, London, 1952.

Cowper, Colonel J. M., TD, *The King's Own, The Story of a Royal Regiment, Volume III. 1914–1950*, Gale & Polden, 1957.

Cunliffe, Marcus, *The Royal Irish Fusiliers 1793–1950*, Oxford University Press, Oxford, 1952.

Gander, Leonard Marsland, *Long Road to Leros*, Macdonald, London, 1945.

Guard, J. S., *Improvise and Dare, War in the Aegean 1943–1945*, The Book Guild, Lewes, 1997.

Holland, Jeffrey, *The Aegean Mission, Allied Operations in the Dodecanese, 1943*, Greenwood Press, 1988.

Johnson, Edward B. W., MC, *Island Prize, Leros, 1943*, The Kemble Press, 1992.

Kay, R. L., *Long Range Desert Group in the Mediterranean*, War History Branch, Department of Internal Affairs, Wellington, New Zealand, 1950.

Knight, Colonel C. R. B., OBE, *Historical Records of The Buffs, Royal East Kent Regiment (3rd Foot) formerly designated The Holland Regiment and Prince George of Denmark's Regiment 1919–1948*, The Medici Society, London, 1951.

Levi, Aldo and Fioravanzo, Guiseppe, *Avvenimenti in Egeo dopo l'armistizio (Rodi, Lero e isole minori)*, Ufficio Storico della Marina Militare, Rome, 1972.

Lodwick, John, *The Filibusters, The Story of The Special Boat Service*, Methuen, London, 1947.

Manicone, Gino, *I Martiri dell'Egeo, L'amaro volto di una tragedia Italiana*, Casamari, 2001.

Metzsch, Friedrich-August von, *Die Geschichte der 22. I.D.*, (Bad Nauhmein), 1952.

Nesbit, Roy C., *The Armed Rovers, Beauforts & Beaufighters over the Mediterranean*, Airlife Publishing, Shrewsbury, 1995.

O'Carroll, Brendan, *Kiwi Scorpions, The Story of the New Zealanders in the Long Range Desert Group*, Token Publishing, Honiton, 2000.

Parish, Michael Woodbine, *Aegean Adventures 1940-43 and the end of Churchill's Dream*, The Book Guild, Lewes, 1993.

Pittaway, Jonathan and Fourie, Craig, *LRDG Rhodesia, Rhodesians in the Long Range Desert Group*, Dandy Agencies, Durban, 2002.

Prien, Jochen; Rodeike, Peter and Stemmer, Gerhard, *Messerschmitt Bf 109 im Einsatz bei der III. und IV./Jagdgeschwader 27, 1938–1945*, Struve Druck.

— *Messerschmitt Bf 109 im Einsatz bei Stab und I./Jagdgeschwader 27, 1939–1945*, Struve Druck.

Rissik, David, *The D.L.I. at War, The History of The Durham Light Infantry 1939–1945*, The Depot: The Durham Light Infantry.

Schenk, Peter, *Kampf um die Ägäis*, Verlag E. S. Mittler & Sohn GmbH, Hamburg, 2000.

Smith, Peter and Walker, Edwin, *War in the Aegean*, William Kimber, London, 1974.

Sutherland, David, *He Who Dares, Recollections of Service in the SAS, SBS and MI5*, Leo Cooper, London, 1998.

Thompson, Julian, *The Imperial War Museum Book of War Behind Enemy Lines*, Sidgwick & Jackson published in association with the Imperial War Museum, London, 1998.

Ward, S. G. P., *Faithful, The Story of the Durham Light Infantry*, Thomas Nelson & Sons, London, 1963.

Williams, Raymond, *The Long Road from Léros*, Raymond Williams, 1983.

Magazines and Periodicals

Drinkwater, William J., *War in the Eastern Aegean, Part 3. The Agony of Leros*, in *Volume 3, Number 5, The Military Chest*, Picton Publishing, Chippenham, 1984.

Lucas, James, *Strike on Leros*, in *Volume 3, Issue 36, The Elite*, Orbis Publishing, 1985.

Packer, Edwin, *Hard Lesson in the Aegean, Dodecanese Islands, Greece, September/November 1943*, in *Number 52, Purnell's History of the Second World War*, BPC Publishing, 1975.

Pitt, Barrie, *Into the Iron Ring*, in *Volume 10, Issue 117, The Elite*, Orbis Publishing, 1987.

Schenk, Dr Peter, *The Battle for Leros*, in *Number 90, After the Battle*, Battle of Britain Prints International, 1995.

Willis, Vice-Admiral Sir Algernon U., KCB, DSO, *Naval Operations in the Aegean between the 7th September, 1943 and 28th November, 1943*, published on 11 October 1948 as a supplement to *The London Gazette* of 8 October 1948.

Wilson, General Sir H. Maitland, GCB, GBE, DSO, ADC, *Operations in the Middle East from 16th February, 1943, to 8th January, 1944*, published on 13 November 1946 as a supplement to *The London Gazette* of 12 November 1946.

Index

All Orion/Phoenix titles are available at your local bookshop or from the following address:

Mail Order Department
Littlehampton Book Services
FREEPOST BR535
Worthing, West Sussex, BN13 3BR
telephone 01903 828503, *facsimile* 01903 828802
e-mail MailOrders@lbsltd.co.uk
(Please ensure that you include full postal address details)

Payment can be made either by credit/debit card (Visa, Mastercard, Access and Switch accepted) or by sending a £ Sterling cheque or postal order made payable to *Littlehampton Book Services*.
DO NOT SEND CASH OR CURRENCY.

Please add the following to cover postage and packing

UK and BFPO:
£1.50 for the first book, and 50p for each additional book to a maximum of £3.50

Overseas and Eire:
£2.50 for the first book plus £1.00 for the second book and 50p for each additional book ordered

---

BLOCK CAPITALS PLEASE

name of cardholder ....

address of cardholder ....

delivery address
(if different from cardholder)
....
....
....

postcode ....

postcode ....

☐ I enclose my remittance for £...........................

☐ please debit my Mastercard/Visa/Access/Switch (delete as appropriate)

card number ☐☐☐☐☐☐☐☐☐☐☐☐☐☐☐☐

expiry date ☐☐☐☐   Switch issue no. ☐☐

signature ....

prices and availability are subject to change without notice